The Black and White Media Book

Handbook for the study of Racism and Television

John Twitchin
Editor

TRENTHAM BOOKS

© J. Twitchin 1988, 1990, 1992

First published 1988 by
Trentham Books
·Westview House,
734 London Road, Oakhill
Stoke-on-Trent
Staffordshire
England ST4 5NP
Tel: (0782) 745567
Revised editions 1990, 1992

ISBN: 0 948080 09 4

Set and printed in Great Britain by:
Bemrose Shafron (Printers) Ltd, Chester

Contents

Preface

Since the first edition of this book in 1988, analysis of the media's role as 'image-maker' has been acknowledged as part of the national curriculum of schools, and the need for discussion among broadcasters of what is responsible programming in societies blighted by evidence of prejudice and discrimination has been recognised as a priority across Europe. But the need in 1992 to reprint the second edition indicates the continuing relevance of the book, not only to teachers and broadcasters, but also to the initial and in-service training of professional groups: there is a vital 'media studies' dimension to all equal opportunities policy development and implementation.

In teaching and training on multicultural approaches and on equal opportunities in education and in the public services, I have found that the *Black and White Media Shows* can serve as an excellent 'agenda-setting' and motivating way into study of the nature of stereotypical assumptions and thinking, and their damaging effects not only within a workforce but on the quality of service offered by any agency which interacts with the public as customers/clients/users.

I have noticed, too, an increasing focus in schools and colleges on drawing attention to the achievements of human civilisation, especially in agriculture and technology, in black Africa before white Europeans appeared there — such that for many tutors the book references on pp.78-79 of the 1990 revised edition have proved particularly helpful. It should perhaps be noted that the terminology of this book is 'of its time', namely the mid-80s. For reasons hinted at on p.14, at the end of the Introduction to Section 1, the talk in the early 90s is more of 'equal opportunities', 'valuing diversity' and 'anti-discrimination' than of 'anti-racism'. But while the language may be changing, the 'message' remains the same.

A final note: in 1990, a *Black and White Media Show — Part 3* was transmitted on BBC1, together with a newly edited and up-dated 30-minute programme on *Racism and Comedy*. The latter particularly has been widely used in education and in training in the public services. Separate notes on *Racism and Comedy* are available from Broadcasting Support Services, P.O. Box 7, London W3 6XJ (081-992 5522). Other teaching/training videos which relate to the themes dealt with in this book, and which have become available in 1991/2 as part of the BBC's *MOSAIC* project are listed on p.79.

For teachers, tutors, and organisers of initial and in-service training courses, free briefing papers on materials, on trainers, and on 'training trainers' seminars concerned with the related themes of stereotypes and the role of the media; cross-cultural communication; and equal opportunities policy development and implementation can be obtained by ringing 071-435 2784.

John Twitchin
1992

Acknowledgements

The outline of Section One is derived from a pioneering anti-racism workshop constructed and conducted by Brenda Thomson for Bradford LEA in 1979 (parts of which are shown in 'Teacher, examine thyself!', video available from Concord Films).

Many of the exercises and materials in Section One are described as they have been used in anti-racism workshops run by the NUT since 1982. I am very grateful to Shirley Darlington, who set them up from within the NUT's Education Depart ment, for giving me the opportunity to take part in many of these, alongside colleagues Gaynor Smith, Terry Mortimer and Joan Hafenrichter.

I want to thank the contributors to Sections Two and Three for responding so warmly to my requests for material (and for free!) and to congratulate them on providing it against a deadline of just a few weeks in the middle of the Summer term of 1987.

Although this is not a BBC book, it is to some extent a spin-off from the two *Black and White Media Shows* I produced within the Continuing Education Department of BBC T.V. in 1985/86. Whatever the weaknesses of those programmes, their strengths owe much to the support given both to the making and to the defence of the films by my Head of Department, David Hargreaves, and the then Controller of BBC1, Michael Grade.

Finally, I am indebted to Gillian Klein for commissioning this work on behalf of Trentham Books, and for her valuable editorial support.

John Twitchin

The Contributors: (at time of writing, 1987)

Angela Barry teaches English at Lister Community School, Newham.

Jim Pines was Ethnic film and TV adviser, British Film Institute, until 1987.

Dr. Bhikhu Parekh is Professor of Political Theory, University of Hull, and Deputy Chairman of the Commission for Racial Equality.

Dr. Gajendra Verma is Reader in Education, and Director of the Centre for Ethnic Studies in Education, Manchester University.

Salman Rushdie is author of *Midnight's Children, Shame,* and *The Jaguar Smile.*

Zeinab Badawi is a Reporter on *Brass Tacks,* BBC T.V. Her reflections derive from researching a documentary series on the Sudan for Yorkshire Television, shown on ITV in 1987.

Laura Sparrow is Deputy Head, Sparrow Hill Primary School, Rochdale.

Brian Thompson is an artist working on anti-racist projects in schools and colleges for Liverpool LEA.

Alec Roberts is Head of English, Bohunt School, Liphook, Hants.

Mary-Lynne Durrell teaches art/design and media education at The Beaufort School, Tuffley, Glos.

John Twitchin is a producer in the Continuing Education Dept., BBC T.V.

Racism and society: methods of group study

SECTION ONE

Racism and society: Methods of group study

Racism and Society: Methods of Group Study

by John Twitchin

INTRODUCTION

Effective teaching or training about the role of the media requires a clear understanding of the working of racism in society. Videos like *It Ain't Half Racist, Mum* [8] and *The Black and White Media Shows* [55] (Refs. pp.77-79) are best seen as aids to study of the media dimension within a wider scheme of anti-racist training and education. However, they can be used as a 'way in' to such a wider study of racism since everybody watches TV and this gives a common platform of experience on which to build. (This is how they were used in Bohunt School, for example, as Alec Roberts describes in section 3). Also, since efforts to expore white people's involvement in the working of racism often run up against initially defensive emotional barriers, it can help to start with the 'self-reflective' *Black and White Media Shows*. They act as examples of self-examination, and when used in the ways suggested in Section 4 they can soon provoke individuals and groups to reflect on how racist assumptions are affecting their own professional work. However, whether those videos about the media are deployed as a 'starter' or not, there is the need to establish a wider context of understanding of racism and society. Many heads, LEA advisers and trainers, media resources officers, college tutors and librarians, for example, feel uncertainty about how to initiate and sustain any course, staff development programme, or policy-making process on this theme: from pp.15-77, this Section suggests a content for anti-racism teaching/training together with methods and materials, for anyone for whom this may be a relatively new matter of professional concern. The material is addressed to teachers in the first instance but can easily be adapted for other professions, or for community groups.

It should, perhaps, be emphasised that Sections 1 and 4 are concerned with how white professional people within white dominated institutions see and act upon their individual and group responsibilities in a society blighted by racism in many forms. This Section makes no pretension to speak for black people, and makes no assumptions about their interests beyond an end to all forms of discrimination based on perception of skin colour. Neither does it seek to contribute anything new to theoretical debate: rather, it suggests practical ways for teachers to work together to develop their own understandings of how institutional racism functions, and of their own part in it.

5

Multicultural and anti-racist approaches: a brief overview

In the 1970s, when 'multicultural education' moved onto the agenda, many teachers assumed that it referred only what needed to be done to meet special needs of ethnic minority groups — especially in offering language support to bilingual children learning English as a second language. Some amplified this to include ways of getting to know ethnic minority pupils as individuals in terms of their different family and community cultures, both as a basis for supporting their sense of self-esteem and identity, and as a basis for bringing such cultures into what is taught in the classroom. Others took a wider view again (formally acknowledged in the title of the Swann Committee Report *Education for All,* 1985) seeing multicultural education as something for *all* children in all schools, and laying emphasis on ways of revising the curriculum in all subjects to reflect a global perspective beyond traditional Eurocentric assumptions. According to this view, it is the bulk of 'white' British children who are the most educationally deprived in an increasingly interdependent world, by the monocultural and parochial confines of many schools' curricula and the conventionally Anglocentric approach to their subject taken by many teachers. Thus the arrival of West Indian and Asian and South European workers and their families in the 1950s and 60s did much more for British society besides meeting the needs of labour-hungry industries and the transport and hospital services. It occasioned the movement towards multicultural education, so making a great contribution to a potentially richer education for all. Early concerns with ethnic minority pupils led to ideas relevant to pupils and teachers in any school, so that now multicultural education is seen not as a matter of *helping* a minority of pupils, but rather of *sharing* ideas, information and experience among all pupils. Methods and materials for multicultural approaches are described in *Multicultural Education*[1]; *Curriculum Opportunities in a Multicultural Society*[2]; *Agenda for Multicultural Teaching*[3]; *Multicultural Education — towards good practice.*[4] *(References: pp.77-79.)*

The early 80s saw political and educational developments towards anti-racist approaches — how to prepare the next generation to live together in a just and successfully multiracial society. Much more is implied by this than taking an 'anthropological' (and arguably patronising) interest in the cultural background of ethnic minority children, or even than giving an international dimension to subject teaching. The need is seen to be for teachers themselves to appreciate that racism is not just a matter of overt colour prejudice and discriminatory attitudes that they do not personally share. They need to look behind the customary assumption that racism is simply individual prejudice or misguided behaviour whose main expression is in violence and to examine the more significant concept of hidden forces of institutional racism. This is defined as a form of racism we actually reinforce by our inaction, indifference, or collusion.

Thus it is now widely appreciated that multicultural approaches, educationally valuable as they are, need to be accompanied by direct anti-racist teaching, if they are not to be open to criticism as tokenist, or as evasions of the need to study the facts of discrimination against black people and the mechanisms of institutional racism that produce those facts. Many now see multicultural education and anti-racist education as in practice two sides of a coin; or to put it another way, a key to identifying the difference between good and bad multicultural education is that the former is effectively anti-racist, while the latter is at best unwittingly patronising or tokenist, and at worst, unintentionally racist — at least by omission.

The Swann Report summarises its concept of 'education for all' in these terms:

(a) There must be a recognition that multicultural education is not simply about how to educate children of ethnic minorities, but how to educate *all* children.

(b) *Britain is a multiracial and multicultural society and all pupils must be enabled to understand what this means.*

(c) Up to now, for the most part, only those schools with experience of substantial numbers of ethnic minority pupils have attempted to tackle it, *though the issue affects all schools, all pupils, all colleges* — i.e. all students, all teachers, all LEA advisers/inspectors, all lecturers.

(d) Education has to be something more than the reinforcement of the beliefs, values and identity which each child brings to school.

(e) *It is necessary for combating racism to attack inherited myths and stereotypes, and the ways in which they are embodied in institutional practices.*

(f) *Multicultural understanding has also to permeate all aspects of an institution's work.* It is not a separate topic that can be welded on to existing practices.

(g) Only in this way can schools and colleges begin to offer anything approaching the *equality of opportunity* for all young people which it must be the aspiration of the education system to provide.

New approaches to setting up discussion of racism

Many schools and colleges are seeking to grapple with racism, perhaps as a development of concerns with multicultural approaches; perhaps because they have been asked to produce a whole school policy on the subject; or perhaps because they already have a policy, but the full meanings and implications of the word 'racism' are not spelt out — and commitment to implementation depends on making any policy 'one's own'. Certainly those schools/colleges which already have practical experience of trying to provide the Swann Committee's 'Education for All' — especially item (e) as a precondition for (g) — have found that teaching about racism in society cannot be done effectively by individual staff within specific subject areas alone. Pupils/students will be educated as much by the hidden curriculum of how the school/college is itself functioning by example as an anti-racist social organism. This is why 'developing anti-racist strategies' or 'getting an anti-racist act together' needs to happen in the staffroom as much as in the classroom. A whole staff workshop approach may be new to many schools which are used to the conventional working party approach to curriculum development. However, given that (1) statutory training provision is so restricted in terms of time and resources, and given that (2) commitment to change only comes from personal involvement in the formulation of new objectives, and given that (3) the 'new wines' of anti-racist education need 'new bottles' of training/staff development methods, this chapter offers a repertoire of 'discovery method' exercises which make up a structured framework through which groups can make their own exploration of racism on a 'D.I.Y.' basis.

These exercises should be directly useful for lecturers in institutions which provide initial and in-service teacher training; for LEA advisers and advisory teams (especially in areas where there are few specialists available, or where these are overstretched); for headteachers or other senior staff responsible for school-based staff development which may be funded through central or local in-service training programmes; or for leaders of groups of teachers, meeting perhaps in union branches or other informal groups (perhaps jointly with 3 or 4 other schools) who want to make their own examination of racism, whether as curriculum development, or as a first step to articulating an anti-racist policy, or as a boost to commitment to make an existing anti-racist policy effective in practice.

Ideally, the exercises would be used by colleagues who could continue the shared process of learning into a shared experience of implementation of whatever changes that learning suggests.

Because anti-racist strategies involve reviewing attitudes and behaviour as much as gaining information, they are not achieved by simply attending a few talks or lectures. For those who do not already have a clear understanding of how racism functions — perhaps based on direct life experience of it — it seems to require the stimulus of a sequence of meetings equivalent to an intensive three day workshop, to be followed up with a process of research and discussions with colleagues over a period of about a year to 18 months — if, that is, it is to result in significant change in practice towards an anti-racist curriculum, both overt and hidden. In a school, such a process would have to involve all teaching and non-teaching staff along with representatives of parents, governors, community spokespeople, and not least, the pupils.

Some of the exercises described below have been used in training workshops for members run since 1982 by the National Union of Teachers; they have also been used by tutors/trainers of initial and inservice courses for teachers, librarians, trade union representatives, social workers, journalists and other professional and community groups. The overall intention is indicated by the NUT's letter of invitation:

> The workshop is designed for teachers who wish to develop an awareness of the operation of racism in society in general and in the education system in particular at an institutional and personal level. It will be specifically focused around 'white' attitudes and the professional responsibilities of white teachers in a multiracial, multicultural society. It is hoped that through an exploration of the processes involved in 'unlearning' racism, and exercises aimed at strengthening participants' anti-racist understanding and techniques, teachers will be provided with information and skills which will help them to make an effective contribution to anti-racist strategies in their own schools, colleges and local associations.

(It is worth noting that the NUT is accepting here a need to examine whether its own local associations may unwittingly be colluding with institutional racism — for example, in how they decide to press for LEA anti-racist policies and action, or to support black members' interests, or to support teachers accused of forms of racism.)

To help achieve such aims, the exercises and resources outlined in this chapter offer practical ways of working through several steps, including:

— Studying the social facts of discrimination against black people, both nationally and locally.
— Establishing with colleagues a mutual understanding about the use of key terms such as racism, black, white, discrimination . . . etc.
— 'Deconstructing' or 'unlearning' prejudices we have been socially conditioned to by our language and inherited culture; or put another way, working out what genuinely equal respect for different cultures really implies.
— Analysing how institutional racism functions; identifying our own part in it; checking ways the school itself may embody forms of institutional racism.
— Drawing into conscious focus cross-cultural communication difficulties which can act as a barrier to dialogue on equal terms.
— Setting up individual and group action plans for change whose effectiveness can be monitored.

Generally speaking, study of the effects of stereotypical thinking on television in the way black people are represented would be mainly part of point three above, whilst study of why that stereotypical thinking continues on the screen would be part of point four — analysis of institutional racism.

Just as we learn most by *doing* role-play, rather than by simply watching, the group exercises in this chapter are for learning through experience rather than simply reading about. Although they are arranged in a particular structured order, they are all windows into the same house and are resources to be used and adapted in whatever order or ways the group leader can make work. Clearly, any found useful in the staffroom, or on a training course, would be shared with all pupils, adapted as appropriate for age range.

It has to acknowledged that there is no established, proven method of training in anti-racism. The 'state of the art' of anti-racism training is still in evolution and there has been little in the way of systematic evaluative survey of either the short or long-term effectiveness of different methods and materials. Much of what used to be known as 'racism awareness training' in the late 70s and early 80s has been rightly criticised for 'mere psychologism' (for failing to translate individual consciousness-raising into concerted action which effectively addresses the structural and political dimensions of sharing power over decision-making that anti-racism implies), or putting it more simply, for sheer ineffectiveness insofar as many black people could see no clear evidence of any real changes resulting from it. Indeed, it has been argued that such training simply equips 'white liberals' to be more subtly racist in their operating of our institutions, and serves to drain resources which could be better used in more black staff recruitment, or more black self-help activity.

9

This chapter assumes that realistically, black people will secure access to power, to be able to counter racism directly, only in certain areas, and only gradually over time. In the short-term, therefore, it assumes that the white people currently exercising power and discretion in operating our institutions, while seeking ways to work together with black opposition to racism and not against it, should seek to explore their responsibilities within an institutionally racist society for themselves. (Not least because it would be itself a racist assumption that the job of correcting social injustice can or should be left wholly to the victims of it.) Such an exploration would be a first step to entering direct dialogue with black people on a non-racist basis of genuine equal respect. This in turn should be part of a springboard for individual and collective anti-racist action, monitored for its effectiveness, which could range from political lobbying, through school policy making, to classroom teaching practice. The challenge of anti-racism is that it is not only complex to understand for many white people: it also requires action on many levels at the same time. The teacher acting on anti-racist approaches in his/her classroom needs also to involve the rest of the staff, since pupils are likely to write off 'Mr/Miss So-and-so' as simply pursuing a personal enthusiasm if a whole school approach has not been established. It will be all the more difficult, of course, to secure such a common anti-racist position in the staffroom, if in turn, there are no policies in the LEA and/or the union branch to legitimise and support it. However, the LEA may also be in a false position, if there is a lack of political will among the councillors and/or the communities which elect them about what policies of anti-racism or of equal opportunities really require if they are to be effectively implemented, not only in terms of staff recruitment, but in terms of the overt and hidden curriculum in schools.

It has to be admitted that among the reasons for so little apparent result in many areas is not only that anti-racism 'courses' may have under-estimated the time such training requires to be effective, and may have insufficiently analysed the institutional barriers to change, but also that senior managers, the people with most potential power to initiate or to give backing to change, have often regarded such training as something 'needed' only by junior staff. More fundamentally, however, the fact is that discrimination against black people is a social injustice requiring strong political will to secure full implementation of the law against it — particularly in its indirect forms. Such implementation in the U.S. has been achieved to a large extent by 'contract compliance', whereby central or local government places contracts only with suppliers of goods or services who can demonstrate the priority they give to positive anti-racism with figures to prove their success. In other words, government requires information not on the organisations' policies or stated intentions but on the facts of what they *do*. In the U.S., therefore, anti-racism is primarily a matter of behaviour, secondarily a matter of attitude; it is more a question of discipline than of education and training. In Britain, however, such political will is hardly in evidence; the constitutional and social traditions are very different; and black people have not got the voting power of U.S. black people (1 in 10 of the American population is black). Thus education and the media here have to tackle those prejudices that both fuel and rationalise the low priority given by many white people, and the white dominated institutional structures they work in, to positive and committed action to eradicate discrimination in all its forms against black people.

Note that while the exercises in this chapter help to focus attention on the need for white people to learn to accept responsibility for dismantling structural barriers to equality for black people, this has, of course, to be done in a way that ensures that their actions are supporting any resistance by black people to the prejudice and discrimination they experience, and are not simply 'containing' that resistance. In an area that is still 'wholly white', the exercises would be used as self-preparation by teachers not only for effective teaching against prejudices held by their pupils, but to equip the next generation — by example — to tackle the structural racism of society.

Generally speaking, if white professional people defensively avoid taking on board criticisms made by black people based on their experience of racism, or if they fail to hold black people's confidence in any genuine disagreements, this could be said to be racist conduct. However, to take such criticisms as grounds for waiting for a perfect method of anti-racist training is, in effect, a racist excuse for inaction. We all move into 'learning curves' by trying our hand, and by acknowledging mistakes. The following exercises can serve to stimulate white people into wanting to understand their responsibility for the racist features of our society as a step to action against them — whatever their political or ideological position. All the main political parties say they want good 'race relations'. All of them accept the need for a Race Relations Act in Britain. Thus this chapter is relevant to all teachers, whatever their party political affiliations, who see that the law is not in practice working as either a deterrent or a remedy to social injustice, and who accept the Swann Report's view that an educationally preventative approach is also required.

To summarise: the later exercises offer ways for teachers to work out their own answers to the question: What mechanism explains why it is that, according to the official statistics, black British people are heavily over-represented among the lowest levels according to most social indicators, and are not relatively improving their position over time — especially since racial discrimination is against the law, and since it is not the National Front that holds power in Britain? What interactive relationship is there between, on the one hand, white individuals' conscious and/or perhaps unconscious prejudices about black people — socially conditioned by our cultural inheritance — and on the other, the effect of those institutional procedures and power structures which appear to be serving to block the equality of opportunity and treatment that black British people have every right to expect?

Institutional change is, of course, a *collective* matter of re-ordering policy priorities, of revising work and decision-making procedures, of setting up new criteria of accountability. At the same time, it is *individuals* who initiate processes of collective change, who represent the institutional (otherwise the communication or reproduction of power involved in racism would be a mere abstraction) and who bring their varying levels of understanding and commitment to the implementation of policies in their area of discretion. This chapter therefore assumes (1) that there is a circle of interaction between racial prejudice as a personal attitude, and racist disadvantaging of black people as a result of the white dominant power structure of society (i.e. the former serves both to fuel and to rationalise the latter) (2) that it is the job of educators to build their own understanding of that relationship in order to be able to break that circle and (3) that the television media should be supporting that educational job, not undermining it by showing material offensive to black people; or by showing material which serves to reinforce prejudices or dismissive attitudes among the white audience; or by failing to acknowledge that they have yet fully to deal with the institutionally racist pressures that affect their own organisations and output.

The role of group leader
In a school or college where these are new issues, it can sometimes be helpful to invite an outsider to introduce the issues, leaving the staff to get on for themselves with developing their understanding and with determining their next steps of action. A suitably sensitive outside catalyst can absorb and 'take away' the defensive feelings commonly aroused in attempts to examine racism. You might seek advice on who has experience in doing this in your LEA, or who is used in other LEAs. If, however, resources do not allow for outside help, it is important to note that in her book *White Awareness*[5], Judy Katz suggests that anyone acting as group leader needs:

'A good understanding of racism. This includes both an awareness on a personal level of your own prejudices and assumptions and an ability to analyse and describe racism on an institutional and cultural level. You should be open to your own learning needs and should be a role model whose ideas, attitudes and values can be tested by individuals and the group. Your willingness to disclose your grapplings with racism and the areas that are still unresolved for you will be most helpful in the learning process of others. A climate of trust must be established in the group so that participants feel safe in exploring their attitudes and professional behaviour. It is essential to recognise how difficult it is for most white people to come to grips with racism — especially their part in it. Therefore, support and concern for the participants are critical. While dealing with the content issues — for example, those defining racism or exploring institutional racism — you must also be aware of the process issues: how people are feeling, how they respond to one another, and so on.'

The suggestions in the rest of this chapter presuppose a thoroughly prepared group leader, who can create an informal non-threatening atmosphere in which staff can together share thoughts, feelings and experiences in a process of making their own sense of how racism affects us all. The aim is not to confront people, but rather to inspire people to *confront the issue,* and through self-discovery within the group to become committed to effective action in combating racism.

It has to be acknowledged that there is no convenient consensus among white people — either of attitude, or of political views — within which to work on anti-racism: there are also wide variations within the black communities, both of politics and of forms of reactions to racism. Given these polarities, no anti-racist actions or efforts can avoid attracting criticism either of 'putting it too strongly', 'loony leftism' etc., or of 'soft liberal tokenism' etc. It is a crucial assumption here that it is racism itself, of course, which is the cause of many of these divisions. Sometimes, absorbing white participants' personal criticisms of the group leader is all part of the process: coming to terms with anti-racism is for some white people an uncomfortable experience at first, and we all have the tendency to blame or attack the messenger when we do not like the message. Trainers often remind themselves of methodological points like these, before beginning a group session:

(1) Try not to give your own opinion on things. What you as group leader think is not important, it is what the group participants are thinking that you want to draw out.
(2) Try not to use closed questioning — where one only gets a yes/no answer.
(3) Do not feel that you have to be able to answer everybody's questions. See yourself not as an expert, but as a *facilitator*. Use other people in the group to answer the question, e.g. What does anyone else in the group think? Or reformulate the question, throw it back at the person. Reformulation makes people think about what they are saying.
(4) If you are unsure of the exercise or activity you are about to do, have the instructions at hand.
(5) In the report-back sessions be aware of sexist practice. (Not only the men reporting back!)
(6) Do not be worried about SILENCE when asking questions — moments of silence can be useful at times.

In terms of preparation, this chapter assumes familiarity with the NUT policy statements *Towards a whole school policy — guidelines on anti-racism in education, Fair and Equal* and *Education for Equality;*[6] the AMMA booklet *Multicultural and Anti-Racist Education Today*[7] and the relevant sections of the Swann Report: sections (1), (2), (6) and the end of chapter 16.

It may be worth re-emphasising two points about the exercises that follow:
1. They are not about 'guilt tripping' — they are about preconditions to *empower* positive anti-racist action;
2. They require an atmosphere of mutual trust — the group leader must not let the power structures that exist get in the way of open exchange between the participants. Just as teachers seek to *value* all children equally, so the group leader needs to value all teachers equally, in what is likely to be something of a 'mixed ability' joint learning process. Such an atmosphere is made more difficult to achieve by the hierarchical authority structure of the teaching profession, together with a whole set of vested interests in the 'status quo' of that structure. Perhaps one indication of a suitable atmosphere is whether all staff can freely contribute

to an agenda of questions such as these: Why are matters of racism so rarely discussed openly and frankly in staffrooms and in departmental meetings? What is it we are afraid of? Are we inhibited by fear of possibly upsetting colleagues' sensibilities? Or of revealing our own ignorance, if not prejudices? Or of putting ourselves up for possible criticism which might harm our 'image' or presumed promotion chances? Should we not fear more the possibility that, however efficient and committed our teaching, our schooling is not giving children from ethnic minority groups the kind of self-image and the respect they need and have a right to expect, and is leaving the other children prey to social influences and attitudes based on misconception and ignorance?

Clearly, a great deal depends in a school on the attitude of the head teacher, who has potential power to enable or to block such a 'workshop' atmosphere. The informal advice of a working party at Birley High School, in Manchester, which drew up a report *Multicultural Education in the 1980s* was: 'the first thing to do, to get multicultural and anti-racist change, is to nobble the head. But if you can't do that, then get on and do it for yourselves anyway, because it's so urgent'. Some LEAs have given specific anti-racism training for head teachers and deputies, forming them into 'pyramid groups' for developing their work on a mutually supportive and continuing basis across the primary/secondary divide. In some places, teacher groups — on occasion through union branch pressure — have secured training support for their headteachers and for their advisory staff.

One final introductory note: the term 'anti-racist' has become associated with 'left-wing sentimentality', not to say 'loony left extremism', in many people's minds during the course of the 1980s. In some groups it may be helpful to quote three sources clearly not on the left wing of politics.

First, Mr. Kenneth Baker, Education Secretary in 1989, commenting on the Burnage Report:

'I want to make it absolutely clear that there is no place in our schools for racial antagonism and intolerance. This government is taking a range of measures to reduce discrimination'.

Second, Mrs. Thatcher's Government White Paper on Racial Disadvantage (HMSO, 1982) states that black people:

'represent an important source of talent in Britain but their full potential will only be realised in a society free from prejudice and discrimination'.

Third, Mr. John McGregor, Education Secretary in 1990, introducing the CRE Code of Practice for education:

'Racial discrimination has no place in the education service'.

This book is designed to help teachers in working out how they are to achieve those objectives, whatever their party allegiances.

1. WHY DO WE NEED TO TALK ABOUT COLOUR PREJUDICE?

Starting points

In a group whose members know each other already, and a general goodwill to the subject can safely be presupposed, it can be effective to start with *The Black and White Media Show — Part 1,* returning to this chapter's exercises from 'Target Groups' on, before using the *Media Show — Part 2.* However, for groups who do not know each other, and whose members are perhaps worried or defensive at the start, confidence can be built up by using the inoffensively amusing film *Fred Barker Goes to China* which is available from Concord Films.[8] This is a light comedy of what happens when Fred moves to China to take work as a hospital ancillary worker. In using comedy to sensitise people to the experience of being an immigrant worker, it raises some introductory questions of prejudice and of communication across cultures. A trainer's manual called *WorkTalk* which outlines ways of structuring information and discussion based on the Fred Barker film is available from The Runnymede Trust.[9]

Alternatively, the 'Drawbridge' exercise detailed by Katz,[5] has been often used as a 'opener', as have exercises in *Debate and Decision: Schools in a World of Change* (World Studies Project)[10] available at many teachers' centres.

Some trainers seek at the start to elicit what impressions about black people an all-white group may have arrived with. 'Who thinks there is trouble between some black people and some white people living in Britain today?' 'What do you think causes some of the problems that lead to the allegation that this society is racist?' Such open-ended questions, if there is no 'put down' of the replies, or argument with them *at this stage,* can reveal some of the group's own images and perceptions of black people (perhaps to compare with the results of a repeat of the questions at a later session/meeting).

Perhaps one of the most commonly used starting points is to invite each member to share with the group:

Where their own name comes from — and how they feel about it;

Any racist incidents they have witnessed or experienced for themselves;

Any evidence of racism or prejudice they have become aware of through talking with pupils in or out of school;

How they remember first becoming aware of how black British people feel about the way they are treated in this country;

Any steps towards anti-racist action they have already made or been associated with;

Any fears or expectations they have in being asked to join an exploration of racism as a professional concern.

That can be done as a 'listening' exercise, in pairs, with each person 'reporting' to the group what his or her neighbour has said. Apart from getting things started on an inter-personal basis, that introductory exercise often brings in direct evidence of prejudice, which helps establish why we need to talk about it.

Target Groups

Ideally the question Why do we need to talk about prejudice? would be raised by listening to black British people's experience of prejudice. Black people however have been witnessing to prejudice and racism for at least 35 years, only to meet with indifference from many ways of the white professional people with powers of discretion in the ways our institutions function. It is part of the problem of racism that many white people do not seek to hear what black people say about their experience of prejudice and racism, or if they do, tend to hear it only in 'white' terms.

So it may be wrong, at the beginning, to presuppose goodwill to the idea of hearing black experience. This does not mean that there are adequate substitutes for such face-to-face communication — it means only that white groups could often benefit from first exploring in the light of their own experience the meaning of *being white* in a multi-racial society. It is often only after such an initial step that many white people become *able* to listen properly to, and understand, what black people have to say about *being black* in such a society.

Among the mixed and defensive feelings many white people bring to group work, which can block their participation at first, is a general sense of resentment against apparently being asked to take an interest in, and accept some responsibility towards, the way black communities experience prejudice and racism. At some level of consciousness they feel that no-one has taken an interest in their own earlier or present difficulties in life, for example, as a woman, or as working class, or as someone with heavy domestic burdens, so why should they get involved in questions of social discrimination against people as black? The 'Target groups' exercise removes this blockage by giving recognition to the social experience white people have brought into the group: for many this is a vital early step in the exploration of racist oppression in society.

A. Invite participants, in pairs, to describe occasions they have personally felt put down; then ask them to say what was their role, or what grouping were they part of at the time. What was the power relationship between them and the person (or institution) that patronised or humiliated them?

B. Then pose the question: What groups in our society are 'put down'? Write up all their suggestions on a board. Usually women, disabled, black, gay, the elderly, children, working class, single parents, and many more come to mind. Ask each to select which one — if any — of these groups they have most direct experience of. Ask if some participants have not been able to identify with any group. This commonly reveals a proportion of the men, perhaps with the more senior positions, which could occasion some later discussion about how the status quo of our society most suits white middle-class professional men, such that those who still have most power in the running of our institutions are those with the least incentive to acknowledge any need for change, especially where this could imply a sharing of that power. It is not, after all, the National Front and its supporters who have power in Britain — so the question is: how is the continuing racist disadvantaging of black people, as revealed in the official statistics, to be explained?

C. The next step is to divide into 'put down' groups, with the 'spare' men invited to get together and find some common experience — perhaps as 'ex-children', or being disregarded as 'old fogies', or as 'trendy lefties', or whatever. Each group (and two can make a group) then considers and notes down in key words their answers to these questions:

1. What is good about being together with others of the same group?
2. What remarks do we never want to hear again? And why?
3. What is the media image of our group? Help or hindrance?
4. How do we wish other people/groups to behave towards us?

D. Each group's written-up replies can be displayed around the room for everyone to inspect, or you could have some report back from each group. Usually, answers to the first question draw attention to positive values of solidarity, mutually supportive and co-operative feelings, while answers to question 4 ar likely to amount to 'We simply want to be treated with equal human respect — not just in theory, but in practice — and to be consulted and heard on equal terms in any decision-making that affects us'. To this extent, white people will have found from their own experience one key element of how racism operates in oppressing its victims and why we need to examine its dehumanising effects on us and our pupils. If there is a black group, it is important to pay attention to their account of being a 'target group' and to how they want to be treated. It might also be important if the group includes black women to hear on what basis they chose whether to join the group of black people, or the group of women.

The exercise will show how black people want no more than white people want; that many black women's experience is that they are seen as black, by both white women as well as men, before they are seen as women; that 'humour' is not neutral (see p.204); that white people have often not listened to their black colleagues' experiences as black (see pp.69-70); that only by sharing power, on equal terms, can a mostly white staff avoid patronising assumptions in deciding how it is to meet the needs of a multi-racial society.

The Enemy Within
This could be a good moment, especially in an all-white group, to listen to some elements of black British experience. If this cannot be arranged on a face-to-face basis, some black perspectives of Britain as a racist society are given in the BBC documentary *Black*,[8] and the tape/film-strip or video *The Enemy Within*.[11]

Towards the end of the viewing it is valuable to stop on the picture of the N.F. group with the flags, where the commentary asks How you would feel about the N.F. marching under the Union Jack? Allow silence for thought here, for as long as possible, before asking for responses: So how *do* you feel about that. . .? It may be best simply to allow people to express their thoughts and reactions without comment or argument at this point. You could then follow on with the observation that the N.F. represents overt racism; one of the black speakers said it was the 'liberal racists' that worried him more: 'I don't know where it's coming from. . .' Do the group recognise what he is saying, what he means?

If women or men have observed, during the course of the 'Target groups' exercise, that the problem of sexism is not so much the need for consciousness raising and assertiveness among women as the need to motivate men to understand what sexism means — both individual and institutionally — then invite them to describe the analogies they see with what has been said about their needs as white people in *The Enemy Within*.

Anglo-Saxon Attitudes

A common platform of initial understanding, on educational grounds, of the need to consider racial prejudice is very effectively established by showing four short sequences from the 50 minute compilation film *Anglo-Saxon Attitudes*, which is designed specifically for this purpose.[42] The video is available at most teachers' centres,[55] or can be obtained by members direct from the NUT Education Department.[6]

As with all films in training, without proper introduction and frequent stops, it is all too likely to be watched for its curiosity value, and followed by 'discussion' at the level of desultory t.v. criticism on the lines of 'why wasn't it about what we thought it would/should be about?' This is because we mostly associate watching the screen at other times with being in a *passive entertainment* frame of mind. This is the opposite of what the group are trying to achieve, namely some *active learning*. Learning happens when the group do not simply *watch the presentation* but rather *register the content*. This can only happen if group members have already identified and noted their own gaps of information on the subject before the viewing, and if they pause on each sequence to make the content 'their own' through structured discussion and/or note-taking. The irritation felt when the video is interrupted is because the 'easy option' of watching passively, with only an illusion of learning, is being frustrated. Each sequence in the films referred to in this book requires its own response. Each pause helps group members to take responsibility for their own learning, and to share this with their colleagues. For really effective use, then, the group should start by noting down, very briefly, their individual answers to such questions as:

(1) How many people live in England? (Yes, England, not Britain.)

(2) How many of those people are black (taking this to mean, for this purpose, those of Afro-Caribbean and South Asian background)?

(3) How many are immigrants? (i.e. moved here having been born abroad)

(4) Where do most immigrant workers in Britain come from?

(5). Since 1945, how much have immigrants added to the size of the population in Britain?

(6) How many living languages — other than English — are used in England by at least 100,000 people each?

(7) What are the typical out-of-school attitudes of white school-leavers in this area towards black minority groups?

(8) Was your answer to number (7) something you feel and guess, or something you know?

(9) Do 4 year old children, both black and white, notice skin colour difference?

(10) If you've said yes to number (9) then are 4 and 5 year olds also aware of the 'social weight' attached by the adult society to being black or white?

(11) (If relevant) Do black school students in our locality experience direct discrimination in trying to find holiday jobs, or 'Saturday jobs', particularly, for example, in bakery or butchery shops, as compared to equivalently qualified white students?

(12) If your answer to number (11) is yes, then what for you are the chief ways a school should respond to that fact?

(13) How much do you know about Morocco?

Asking themselves those questions (privately and individually), whatever their answers, will make the group relate directly to the content of the video extracts. For example, the very surprise of the last question will ensure that the group will not just watch and then forget, but register by comparison and so remember and reflect on the significance of what the Moroccan girl Souad Talsi says about what she knew of Britain before coming here.

After those questions, indicate to the group that they are about to see some secondary school students in an 'all-white' suburban area on the outskirts of Leicester, a town which has a black population (of mostly Asian background) of 23%. Then start viewing a few minutes into the film with the bus shot and the commentary words 'We took our cameras . . .'

'Gus the Bus'

Stop at the end of the 'Gus the Bus' sequence on the commentary words '. . . at earlier stages of schooling.' Ask for responses to the sequence: particularly as to what challenges it poses to us. Some common first reactions are:

(1) Where are the girls?

(2) Aren't the boys just playing to the camera?

(3) Would they talk like that if there were black pupils around?

and less often said, but sometimes privately thought:

(4) The TV people have selectively got together a gang of 'non-academics' of the 'skinhead' variety and probably paid them money to say a lot of nasty things to make 'good' sensational documentary material — i.e. exploited a group of naive youngsters to advance their media careers.

These are all evasions of the point, ways of 'blocking' the challenges set up in the sequence — but they are best acknowledged as fair questions which would not arise if the film commentary had included fuller background detail:

(1) As a matter of fact, Gus normally met mixed groups of boys and girls, and he found no difference in what white girls think about black communities, whether in mixed groups or separately. Indeed, the last group he describes in the film were actually a group of young women — nurses in training.

It just happened that no girls attended on the day of the filming.
Note: The exercise 'Target groups' will have reminded everyone that racism is just one of many 'groupisms' (i.e. groups of people subject to prejudiced attitudes together with oppression deriving from exclusion from power) all of which need to be countered in education. (And the training film *Putting Women in the Picture*[55] shown on BBC1 in August 1987, is a visual aid on the evidence of sexism on television useful for both adult and school-based discussion.[54] Given the pervasiveness of sexism in our society, examples of sexism are inevitably noted in materials about racism, or in the groups' own behaviour, from time to time. Of course it is important to use anti-racist materials that are not sexist, but unfortunately even with the best intentions there are flaws in many of the resources available. This is, after all, part of the problem. Such sexism has to be acknowledged. At the same time, it is generally found not to be helpful in training to try to focus on more than one of these social injustices at a time. While it can be useful to draw parallel lessons between them, there is sometimes a temptation to evade confronting racism issues by 'sidetracking' the whole session into the more familiar (for white people) concerns of sexism and classism. Thus the sexist media presentation (in deciding to show the sequence even though it omitted any girls) should be acknowledged, but not allowed to become an evasion of the challenge of the content of the sequence: white school-leavers' prejudiced responses to other people as black.

(2) In fact, Gus Horsepool's experience is that the film shows the very least of what he hears expressed once he has got to know any group of white youngsters, whether or not there are TV cameras around.

(3) Gus says he finds that even though they may have personal black friends in class, any group of white young people reveals the same dehumanised stereotypical thinking.

(4) As a matter of fact, Groby Community School teaches on a wholly mixed-ability basis: several of the boys in the bus have 'O' levels. If this surprises teachers, that shows how prone they are to negative stereotyping in their reactions to white children — let alone to black children. As for questions of class differences, Gus has noted that he sometimes needs a bit longer to elicit that many middle-class 'academic' pupils think and feel just the same as so-called 'non-academic' working class groups: they may be more familiar with liberal disapproval of such openly expressed sentiments.

The importance of the sequence is that it poses a set of professional challenges:

(1) Are such views and attitudes typical of white school-leavers — both girls and boys — in *our* area? Do we actually know (as opposed to guess) their views and attitudes outside school? How could we check if the boys in the bus are representative? Have we or our colleagues any evidence on this? In other words — how should we seek to check if Gus Horsepool is exaggerating? What sort of attitudes survey would be needed for us to know what our white school-leavers actually think and feel outside school? The

staff at Groby considered that they needed to invite in Gus as an outside catalyst (having nothing to do with the school hierarchy, and working part-time as a rock musician, not as a teacher) to establish a true person-to-person rapport with the young people over several weeks, before raising any question of their attitudes and perceptions of black people. This was needed, if he was not simply 'to hear what teachers wants to hear', but to discover their actual out-of-school attitudes, and set up a relationship of such mutual confidence that his efforts to correct their prejudices might actually impinge on their social behaviour outside school. By implication, some staffroom agenda questions could be:

(a) Should we be pooling our experiences more often, of talking to young white people outside school?
(b) Do we need to set up new opportunities to relate to them frankly inside school?
(c) Should we co-opt a 'Gus' figure to help monitor the social awareness effects of our curriculum and methods? (Without, of course, avoiding our responsibilities by trying to delegate to that person any necessary whole school teaching response.)

(2) If it is accepted that what the boys expressed is all too typical, then can they be said to be *educated?* Should they be seen, not as 'nasty', nor as 'failures', but as pathetic victims of inadequate education? Is not the whole point of schooling to help the next generation not to be victims of gross misconceptions and ignorance? (It is not just that the boys are ill-informed about basic social facts: that ignorance is part and parcel of prejudiced attitudes towards fellow citizens which can hardly be described as civilised preparation for living in a multicultural and multiracial society.) Should it not be part of *any* school's objectives to help pupils to be able to operate independently of tendencies to seek scapegoats for social tensions in society; to be able to distinguish between people *with* problems and people *as* problems; to be able to modify their assumptions if they are revealed to be based on myth, misconception, or ignorance; and not to be prone to blaming the victim of social injustice?

(3) To discover at 16 years of age, that pupils are victims of inadequate education in these respects is patently far too late: it is no longer possible to do anything much about it. Do we agree that it should be one of our school's major aims and objectives to work out — on a whole-staff basis, and in collaboration between primary and secondary schools, as well as with parents' bodies — what kind of preventative schooling is needed against such myths and misconceptions? Are we agreed that such schooling would not simply celebrate, in both the hidden and the overt curriculum, the multicultural enrichment of Britain, but would also give high priority to equipping white children with the 'conceptual weapons' to understand, and not be victimised by, the adult, peer group, and media influences that reinforce negative images of the place of black British people in our society? (See also p.196.)

(4) What is the motive of the Groby staff in allowing the 'Gus the Bus' session to be filmed for other teachers to see? Theirs is a caring community school, with excellent examination results, and social awareness is a high priority across the curriculum. The staff there wish other teachers to share this evidence that their efforts inside school have impinged so little on their pupils' thinking and action outside school, in the hope that other staffrooms are stimulated into working out their own effective methods for relating what and how they teach directly to the pupils' social experience. Obviously, until that need is exposed and thought through, no action that is likely to be effective can be planned.

Incidentally, in terms of the questions on p.18, some facts the boys in the bus had not registered either from their schooling or from the media: (1) 47 million (Britain 57) (2) Approx. 2.9 million (3) Approx. 7% (4) Ireland and South Europe provide over 4% of that 7% (5) Less than one, since more have emigrated (6) 12 languages (See p.45).

Teachers in some schools say they hae found that pupils' attitudes can be discovered very simply (and all too often, to devastating effect) by asking them to write their impressions of (say) Canada; France; Pakistan; Jamaica; white people in S. Africa; black people in Britain. Or, indeed, the Middle East; or Morocco . . .

Souad Talsi from Morocco

Play the next short sequence from *Anglo-Saxon Attitudes* down to the shot showing the graffiti on the garage walls where the commentary asks ' . . . if teachers ignore its effects?' Souad articulates some of the pain of being at the receiving end of the ill-informed attitudes of many white teachers' blind-eye approach to those attitudes.[53] In doing so, she gives a further compelling reason why we need to examine the effects of prejudice in school. Again, there are a series of professional challenges for teachers here:

(1) Is the experience Souad describes typical? How would we find out? (Note, incidentally, her evidence that girls are no less prejudice than boys)

(2) What would we need to do, as a whole staff, to be sure that any minority group pupil leaving our school would not report similar hurts and apparent teacher indifference as Souad does, if he or she were asked to comment on their schooling by a film camera team? It is interesting that Souad had never felt able to express those points to her teachers, many of whom were astonished to find out from the film later that a girl they saw as a 'successful high achiever, with no problems' had been experiencing school life in those terms — which included a deep moral outrage on behalf of her ethnic minority classmates who did not necessarily have her powers of articulation to objectify and surmount the inner sense of hurt they were living with.

(3) Do we need a whole school policy on racist remarks (as we take for granted on other harmful and anti-social behaviour, like smoking or swearing in classrooms or corridors) so that it is not left to individual staff to decide

on their own, whether and how to deal with such incidents? Children can, of course, see it a mile off if reactions to racist terms or jokes come only from certain individual members of staff, who are likely to be disregarded as having a personal bee in their bonnet. The fact that so many teachers express uncertainty about how to handle such incidents is a symptom of their false position in the absence of a whole school policy and practice worked out with parents, pupils, and ancillary staff, as well as teachers. (See p.72.)

(4) Do we contextualise the books and films children are bound to come across outside school such as *Robinson Crusoe, Dr. Dolittle, Beau Geste, Tarzan,* so that white pupils in particular do not associate out-of-date negative imagery of black inferiority in such materials with black British people (or other ethnic minorities) in contemporary society? This general issue is raised again in much more detail in *The Black and White Media Show* — see pages 207-210 — and in the chapter of checklists pp.162-174.

(5) Looking again at the graffiti on the garage walls, what is the harm (a) to black pupils and (b) to white pupils, who pass such graffiti, especially if teachers ignore its existence and/or its effects?

Graffiti Exercise
This exercise can be very effective as a stimulus to thinking, but it requires careful handling — for example, you need to be sure that the group would not be sympathetic to the suggested 'graffiti'. If you think they might be, skip the exercise. Invite the group to imagine graffiti is found one morning painted not on school property, but in a conspicuous public spot within view of all parents and pupils arriving at the school.

(1) If it reads 'All teachers in that school are fucking racist shits', how long would the daubing remain there? (What feelings in the staffroom and what action would result? Would the Council be approached to try to remove it? Would staff themselves take direct steps to obliterate it? Or would it be ignored?)

(2) If it reads 'Wogs and Yids out' how long would it remain? (How much is it the idea and how much is it the language that is found offensive?)

(3) If it reads 'Blacks go home' how long would it remain? (Is the idea thought to be somehow less offensive if the language is less offensive?)

(4) If it reads 'Hitler was right: Britain needs Fascism' how long would it remain?

(5) If it reads 'N.F.' or 'B.N.P.' how long would it remain? (After all, curious children will wonder, at some point, what such letters stand for, or they will be told by their friends — or indeed by friends of whoever painted the letters up.) Again, what feelings and action by the staff would result? If the lettering is ignored, why is this — given that it stands for the same *ideas* as the previous three? Is it alright not to obliterate them, if teachers use children's familiarity with such symbols to teach what Fascism represents,

and how viciously dehumanising and ignorant it is to harbour anti-black — or anti-Jewish — prejudices? Anything less will leave children likely victims of peer-groups misinformation about NF ideas. By inaction, teachers will appear indifferent. If they are not demonstrably offended by such ideas, how will children realise they are offensive? Do not staff need a whole-school policy on this?

The Cumbrian Nursery

Show the next short sequence, stopping where the teacher is seen reading to the children in the mobile nursery. 4-5 yr. olds *do* know what skin colours mean: Jean Adams is acting in the light of researches documented in David Milner's *Children and Race — Ten Years On[12]* which prove that attitudes are already formed before school age. Teachers in a 'multi-ethnic' area could check with black parents (as a mutual exchange of friendship — not as a piece of professional exploitation) whether it is common to find young black children trying to scrub themselves white. If so, we need to ask what is it in the white children's words and behaviour in the nursery school or play group, that is giving the black child the idea that it would be better, growing up in Britain, to be less black. After all, does not educability depend on high self-esteem?

Many studies have confirmed the findings of a survey by Rachel Jenkins in 1963 revealing the frequency of efforts by black children to scrub themselves white; see also *The Black and White Media Show — Part 2* (p.220). What greater proof is needed of the assimilationist pressures our culture is sustaining, that young children should be seeking to deny so crucial a part of their identity? Or that Stephen, in *The Black and White Media Show — Part 1,* should be feeling inferior to white boys 'because of everything that's going on around you' (see p.207)? It is one reason why all schools need to correct the damaging and dehumanised prejudices embedded in our language and culture by boosting the idea — especially in the minds of white children — that in terms of people, 'black is beautiful'. If teachers ignore the impressions and social experience the white pre-school children arrive with, then are they not leaving them prey to all the influences outside school which currently tend to reinforce the myths and negative stereotypical thinking that Gus Horsepool finds in them as school-leavers?

This is near the heart of the matter: it calls attention to the need for primary schools to help young children 'unlearn' prejudices and negative stereotypical thinking that they have already begun to pick up from overheard parents and other adults, from impressions formed by pictures and the media, and from many socially conditioning effects of our language (explored further on pp.42-44.) Unfortunately, many teachers still convince themselves that young children, on the grounds that 'we can see them playing together, person-to-person, not black or white' are somehow impervious to the adult society around them. Perhaps such teachers choose not to notice what David Milner has documented because they are uncertain about what to do if they did take notice. Such omission by nursery and primary teachers leaves secondary teachers inheriting a false position: it may be too late at secondary stage to do much about attitudes set at 3-5 years of age and left unmodified since — especially as it is so difficult to deploy rational and factual arguments against irrationally held prejudices. Experiential methods and materials for secondary level, which do not omit the affective dimension of teaching about racism and prejudice, and which have been used at Groby School by David Selby, are listed and described by him in Chapter 9 of the book *Multicultural Education*.[1] However, such 'remedial' approaches need to be accompanied by joint committees between secondary schools and their primary feeder schools to work out 'preventative' approaches in the early years. Initial clues on ways of 'unlearning' prejudices are offered in this *Guardian* report by Yasmin Alibhai on a South London nursery (Nov. 24, 1986):

Young children are considered incapable of racial attitudes. Yet many black parents know better. Parental efforts to encourage cultural pride are eroded by overwhelming outside forces.

This was recognised in 1952 by the American anthropologist Mary Ellen Goodman who wrote 'White over brown is the most comprehensive idea to which our children are exposed. The idea pervades like a creeping fog.' Social psychologist David Milner's research shows that 'from about three and a half, children can see the differences between black and white people and know that we value them differently, that there is a pecking order, and white is higher than black.'

Racial attitudes among children are environmentally induced, and not genetically carried, and a recognition of this has led policy makers, including the DHSS, to re-think their under-fives provision.

The Aylesbury day nursery in Camberwell is unapologetically anti-sexist and anti-racist. When Norma Niccol, officer-in-charge, first arrived from Nottingham, she found a nursery 'which parents ran in and out of, totally insensitive to the needs of the mixed community it served, with all the stereotypes of black people, that they mug and steal, reinforced throughout. The parents were being hurt and the children were being damaged.'

For Norma and her deputy, Lucy, the anger they felt fuelled them into action. Norma made her office into the parents' room to give them the status of joint carers.

Next came changes to the 'totally white world': they brought in Building Blocks, a Save the Children's Fund training project to help under-fives workers give equal prominence and value to all cultural identities. Other changes were simple — paints for different skin colours, different musical instruments, foods. They are encouraged to look at themselves and talk about the way they look and feel.

'All we are doing', says Lucy, 'is giving every child, black and white, a positive self-identity. How can anyone quarrel with that?'

Avril Francis and Audrey Bobb, black workers at the nursery approve of children talking openly about race and feel it gives black children strength:

'Their defences against insults are bound to be better if they like themselves better.'

The next sequence of *Anglo-Saxon Attitudes* elaborates that approach in illustrating one London primary schoolteacher's method of 'prejudice reduction' in a multi-ethnic class — comments on this are given on pp.47-49.

2. WHY DO WE NEED TO DISCUSS RACISM?

Facing the facts of discrimination

The exercises and video extracts so far have raised the question of the need to educate against *prejudices* held by individuals and based upon misconception and ignorance. One way to raise the wider question of the need to educate about *racism* in society is to show the first opening section of *Anglo-Saxon Attitudes* after inviting the group to note their own answers to such questions as these:

(1) Is everyone here in favour of democracy — at least in theory? Then note down in a few words what it is.

(2) How much do black people experience unemployment compared with equally qualified white people?

(3) How do black school-leavers in our locality fare, given equal qualifications compared with white, in terms of finding jobs at all; in terms of finding jobs of equal status and pay; or in terms of promotion at work?

(4) If we do not know the answer to question (3), should we be asking ex-pupils to come back to the school to share their experience in this locality with us?

(5) What did Lord Scarman's Report on the 1981 disturbances in Brixton and Toxteth have to say about why they happened only in areas with large black communities?

In viewing the first section of *Anglo-Saxon Attitudes* you could usefully stop on Lord Scarman's words '. . . lack of job opportunities', to ask the group: Are not his observations, so far, almost insultingly obvious? It should hardly need a top judge to tell us that when you have a mass of people smashing property in their own community there must be something wrong with the social conditions there. The important question (never apparently put by news journalists to Lord Scarman) is surely, if he is right that black communities are living in particularly disadvantaged conditions, then why is that? What is the fundamental cause of those social facts? *Anglo-Saxon Attitudes* went to the Lords to ask him his personal view.(His answer is given in print at the bottom of p.216.)

Now play the rest of Lord Scarman's contribution and stop on his last words.

Lord Scarman, of course, was no black, 'Left-wing', extremist — as a Law Lord, he was a pillar of the white dominant Establishment of Britain. So what did he mean, and is he right? This chapter is an aid to working that out for ourselves.

Now play on the film to the station porter shot and the commentary words '. . . ill-equipped for the job market'. Generally speaking, attempts to discuss racism are likely to be no more than emotional moralising if not founded on the facts about the social position of black people in Britain. It is vital that the group should establish these clearly, and on an agreed basis, for themselves. You could use the book *Black and White Britain, the Third Policy Studies Institute Survey*[13,] or the summary of it in the Runnymede Trust Bulletin No.169.[9] That book is an essential source of factual information partly because it includes the official figures from 1984. One of the blockages in the mind of some teachers is an impressionistic view that British history demonstrates how after a generation or two, all immigrant groups have 'mixed in' alright, so that black immigrants' children will do the same if the process is just left well alone. The Policy Study Institute figures are significant for establishing that the black British children of those who came here in the 50s and 60s are not relatively improving their social position, unlike previous groups such as the Jews, the Huguenots, etc. This, of course, is because they are identified as black, and remain discriminated against as such in Britain. Only active anti-racist measures will change this. Further sources for the official figures are: *Ethnic Minorities in Britain — Home Office Research Study No.68* (HMSO) and *Racial Disadvantage,* the white paper reply to the Home Affairs Committee, made by the Conservative Government under Mrs. Thatcher in 1982 (HMSO). These documents demonstrate what governments of all parties have known about what is happening to black people such that they accept the need for a Race Relations Act, outlawing direct and indirect indiscrimination. The findings of the 1980 Report *Half a Chance?*[14] gave proof of the nature and extent of outright discrimination faced by black school-leavers when seeking jobs, despite the equal opportunity legislation.

Test surveys carried out in London, Manchester and Birmingham in 1984/85 confirmed that the level of illegal discrimination in job recruitment is not improving over time — see P.S.I. report *Racial Discrimination: 17 years after the Act,* Colin Brown and Pat Gay, available through C.R.E.[14]

According to the 1985 Labour Force Survey (published in the Department of Employment's *Employment Gazette* on 7th January 1987) black people in Britain are twice as likely to be unemployed as whites, and the jobless rate among those of Pakistani or Bangladeshi origin is three times that of whites. In terms specifically of youth unemployment, while 16% of white youngsters aged 16-24 were out of work, 24% of youngsters of Indian, 34% of West Indian, and 48% of Pakistani and Bangladesi background were unemployed.

In that context it is significant to note that the minority groups tended to have better qualifications than white people. While 13.4% of white men had high qualifications for work, the equivalent figure for the others was 18.3%.

Other research in 1986 showed that of a group of 5th formers, 44% of white youths found apprenticeships, compared with only 14% of equivalently qualified black youths. Such national statistics will have much more meaning, of course, if supplemented by the figures for the group's own locality.

The local Community Relations Council will be able to furnish evidence of discrimination; or secondary teachers could do the same as the 5th year tutor and the careers teacher at an Ipswich High School, who made a simple check among their own school-leavers. They found that one month before leaving school none of the black students (12% of the school's population) had jobs to go to, compared with nearly a quarter of the white students. The next year, the Ipswich Association of the NUT did a larger scale survey for all secondary schools. Again young people from ethnic minorities were shown to have much less success in finding employment — little over 10%, compared with over 50% of white school-

27

leavers. And they were careful to check that neither lack of effort in their job-search, nor lower qualifications, could be identified as significant factors to explain this. (See *Job opportunities in Ipswich for black school-leavers,* NUT Ipswich Association).

The findings of the Ipswich teachers are confirmed by other surveys in Bristol, Leicester, Bradford and London. In Lewisham, for example, a careful and detailed study found that black school-leavers were three times more likely to be unemployed than their white peers. And those who did get jobs had made more applications, attended more interviews, and had taken longer to find work than their white contemporaries, even when they had comparable qualifications. Despite this extra effort, fewer black school-leavers had found the kind of work they wanted, so that they were less satisfied with their jobs. (This report *Looking for Work* is available from the CRE,[14] which can also supply *Half a Chance?* the disturbing report of a study of 100 firms in Nottingham, which proves the extent and nature of the discrimination black youngsters still face in finding work.)

This difficulty of discrimination is added, of course, to the educational disadvantage many black pupils share with working class white children. (Further references can be found on pages 30 and 31 of the Swann Committee Report.)

While of course there are individuals and small groups who are exceptions to the general rule, the evidence is that those black youngsters who *do* get jobs are more often working below their level of ability, and face discrimination in promotion. (Chapter 11 of the book *Multicultural Education*[1] called 'From school to work' indicates steps for teachers to help prepare youngsters for these realities.) *Passports to Benefits?*[9] documents racism in social security; *Living in Terror*[50] documents racist attacks and harrassment; while for evidence about forms of direct and indirect discrimination in housing, the group could refer to the CRE document *Hackney Housing Investigated,* a formal investigation on how such discrimination occurs, the gorup could refer to the paper *Race and the Inner City* by Professor John Rex, one of the public talks reproduced in the booklet *Five Views of Multi-racial Britain* which is available from the Commission of Racial Equality.[14] One way to keep up-to-date about the facts and figures of discrimination is to subscribe to the *Runnymede Trust Bulletin.*[9] The Trust's pamphlet *Different Worlds: racism and discrimination in Britain*[9] gives a summary of facts used by many teachers with school students.

Once the national and local facts have been laid down and acknowledged you might ask whether the group agree that democracy, at least in theory, is the settling of social priorities by the will of the majority (whatever the mechanism for measuring this) *subject to* the full protection of the rights and interests of minorities. Without this latter condition we could have a form of tyranny by the majority over any permanent minority. In other words, the acid test of whether a democratic system is working properly is to check whether the rights and interests of minority groups are being fully protected in practice, as well as in theory, within that system. Since the figures demonstrate forms of systematic and unchanging disadvantaging of black people, additional to any disadvantage they suffer as working class and/or as women, then democrats must be concerned about this basic injustice in our community, and will need to reflect whether many black people, *as black,* are somehow being excluded from the power and decision-making which determine life chances in our society. If teachers agree that their job includes equipping young people to take their part in helping our democracy function well in practice, then they have given themselves another reason for needing to deal with racism in schools. (A fuller exposition of this point is given in the section on political education in The Swann Committee Report, pp.334-340; there is detailed discussion in *Prejudice Reduction and the Schools,* by James Lynch.[44] The BBCs *MOSAIC* project presents the evidence of discrimination in the 1990s in video form.[55] Further discussion questions could be:

Why are the documents outlined above, and the facts in them, not widely known?

Is this because the media have not drawn full and proper attention to them?

Could that in turn be related to the fact that the media institutions have so few black reporters and producers?

Why is the Home Office document titled *Ethnic Minorities in Britain,* given the fact that it is about the evidence of discrimination against people perceived as black?

3. WHAT IS RACISM?

Meanings Exercise

This exercise is designed to help the group to start to build its own understanding of the interactive relationship between prejudices held as personal attitudes (and conditioned by cultural inheritance) and racist disadvantaging of black people as a result of white dominant power structures in society. Words like 'racism' are used as loose umbrella terms, and mean very different things to different people. Little of use can emerge from discussion if some initial effort is not made by the participants to establish at least some mutual understanding, or working definition, of terms such as prejudice, racism, black, white, discrimination, etc.

The word 'black', for example, is used by some on an assumption that it refers to some so-called 'racial' group; by some as signifying a particular culture; by some as a 'political' term — those excluded as a group from a white dominant power structure; and by some as a way of distinguishing people of African and Caribbean descent from those of Asian background. This chapter is generally meaning 'black' in the 'political' sense, to refer to British people of Afro-Carbibbean and South Asian background — i.e. those shown by the statistics to experience the most discrimination on grounds of skin colour. Patently, in any cultural sense, it would be vital to recognise the differences between the Asian and west Indian cultural backgorunds, and indeed between different Asian countries and regions, and between different west Indian islands. the cultural differences must not be overlooked just because of the common experience of colour discrimination within British society.

The word 'racist' is commonly used as a term of abuse, and is often muddled with personal attitudes which should be more properly described as 'prejudiced', so it has been found helpful in the following exercise always to start with the meaning of 'prejudice', before moving onto the key word 'racism'. It is a real problem that the term 'racism' carries so heavy a pejorative load: this deters many white 'liberal-minded' people from tracing the ways its institutional forms affect the results of what we do, however well intentioned. Our self-esteem is dented if we find that we are associated with elements of racist thinking or attitudes in the way our institutions are run, however unwittingly. Thus, in introducing the exercise you may draw attention to the fact that 'racist', as a noun, is sometimes used to mean 'racially prejudiced person', and sometimes (especially by some black people) to refer to 'whites in a racist system'. (Some people underline the distinction by saying 'racialist' for the first meaning.) It is for the working of a system that 'racist', either as a noun, or as an adjective for racism, is mostly used in this chapter. If the distinction is not clear, many in the group are likely to assume that they are in some sense personally under attack and may simply defensively resist the exercises, rather than seeing them as an interesting and professionally important opportunity to explore previously unconsidered ideas in trying to improve the quality of our service/schooling in the interests of all. This issue is addressed in the light of the Swann Report's discussion of definitions of 'prejudice' and 'racism', in the AMMA booklet *Multi-Cultural and Anti-Racist Education Today*,[7] and NUT's *Towards a whole-school policy*.[6]

Procedure for meanings exercise

Ideally, break up into groups of not more than ten with up to 30 minutes for PREJUDICE and 45 minutes for RACISM. If there is not time, then do (C) below for 'prejudice', quickly in 15 minutes, before doing at least (C) for 'racism' over 45 minutes.

(A) **Brainstorm**
  (i) Ask the group individually to scribble down in keywords, what sorts of things they mean, and understand others to mean, when using the word 'prejudice' (and then later 'racism', 'black', 'white' . . .)
  (ii) Ask each member in turn to declare his/her ideas, building up a list of all the overlapping concepts that emerge.

(B) **Discussion**
  Ask the group to review the list:
  (i) is anyone unclear about any of the ideas?
  (ii) does anyone disagree with any of them?
  (iii) is there any agreement on which are essential and which inessential?

(C) **Stimulus**
  As an aid to discussion, circulate copies of the 'What do we mean by' list. Ask each member, over 5 minutes,
  (i) to underline which to them are the most important words or ideas
  (ii) to add anything significant they think has been left out.

Then ask each in turn to declare what they have marked and added, and why. Some common ideas are deliberately not included on the definition sheets (prejudice as 'fear of the unfamiliar', or 'that great time-saver that allows us to be hold strong opinions without checking our facts'; or racism as 'prejudice plus power') to see if the group choose to formulate them for themselves.

(D) **Definition**
    If there is time, it can help to focus the discussion to ask each small group to try to agree some 'working definition', however long or short, that could be reported back and compared with what other groups have come up with, although it is not essential to reach a consensus.

What do we mean by the word 'prejudice'?

1) Any preconceived opinions or feeling, either favourable or unfavourable (*praejudicium* = before judgment);

2) Holding to an attitude despite contrary available evidence, information or experience;

3) An unfavourable opinion or feeling formed beforehand or without knowledge, thought or reason;

4) Unreasonable feelings, opinions, or attitudes, especially of a hostile nature, directed against a racial, religious, or national group, identifiably different from our own;

5) Negative personal perceptions that discriminate against individuals seen only in terms of being representative of such a group;

6) Personal attitudes towards other people, usually based on negative group stereotypes, which are not inborn but learned as children from adults and reinforced by the media and peer-group talk;

7) A partial rejection of a person on the basis of his or her real or supposed specifiable characteristics;

8) A tendency towards biased judgements, normally perceived in others rather than ourselves;

9) An inability to move beyond an initial response of seeing someone in terms of a projected generalised label in one's mind rather than as a person.

What do we mean by the word 'racism'?

1) Perpetuation of a belief that human races have distinctive characteristics that determine their respective cultures, usually involving the idea that one race is superior and has the right to dominate others; together with a policy of enforcing such asserted right and a system of government and society based upon such a policy;

2) Assertion of rights and interests of a particular racial group, who assume superiority, however unwittingly, and have power to enforce this, to the detriment of other racial groups;

3) The treatment of a minority, identified by racial background, as scapegoats for social stresses, injustices, or conflicts of interests affecting the whole society;

4) An inadequately acknowledged residue of the colonial encounter between white and black, in which personal attitudes and behaviour come second, and institutional power and pressures come first;

5) The conduct generated by the belief that some races, however identified, are inferior, not in this or that respect, but *as people*, and that, therefore, their interests and feelings do not deserve to be regarded as equally important or worthy of respect as those of any so-called superior race;

6) Action that, regardless of the intentions involved, defends the advantages that whites have because of the subordinated position of black minorities, and based on, or fuelled by, culturally sanctioned beliefs, involving dehumanising stereotypes, and/or paternalism, and/or ethnocentrism;

7) A combination of prejudiced attitudes against black people and the power to implement action based on these, which leads, however unintentionally, to disproportionate under-privilege and disadvantage for black people in a white dominant society;

8) Justifying the relative disadvantaging of a group, through an attempt to 'biologise' social structures;

9) A way of rationalising a fear that the privileged position of one's own ethnic group in society might be eroded;

10) Racism, whether individual, cultural or institutional, is no less racism for being unintentional or unwitting: racism is defined by effects, not motives.

Comments on the Meanings Exercise

None of the 'meanings' on the lists above are necessarily 'right' or 'correct' — the point is that the group should review together the variety of overlapping ideas as a beginning of a process of reflection on racism which will be further developed as a result of later exercises.

It may help some groups to narrow the focus to 'colour prejudice'. Discussion can profitably turn on the significance of the word 'learned' in No.6 on 'Prejudice'. Only if it is accepted that we are not born with our prejudices — that they are socially conditioned — can teachers seek to 'unlearn' their own and their pupils' prejudices based on misconceptions and ignorance. (A propensity to being prejudiced may be a universal, psychologically 'endemic', feature of human beings — but the actual prejudices we have are different according to which society we are brought up in: they can therefore be unlearned.)

Most of us recognise prejudice as attitudes built on negative stereotypes which are hardened, and wide open to reinforcement, by the media. A definitive analysis of research and ideas on prejudice is *The Nature of Prejudice* by Gordon W. Allport.[15] Stuart Hall, in the booklet *Five views of multiracial Britain*[16] documents the process by which social stresses in Britain have been channelled into a concern with 'race' since the 60s and 70s. The apparent need for scapegoats in a society with growing social tensions, is of course all too depressingly familiar. A comprehensive treatment of the nature of prejudice, of its acquisition, and of educational approaches for dealing with it, is set out in *Prejudice Reduction and the Schools,* by James Lynch.[44]

It is to be hoped that in discussion of racism, it will have become clear that the common use of 'racial', as in 'racial disadvantage' is, strictly speaking, a misnomer for 'black'. Also clearer should be distinctions between 'scientific' and 'popular' concepts of race; between 'colour' and 'race'; between 'black people' and 'ethnic minorities'. Discussion could focus on the terms 'assumed superiority' and 'unwitting', and particularly on the recurrence of the word 'power'. The question might be put: while both black and white people can be deeply *prejudiced* as individuals, can black communities be *racist* in Britain? The group might consider the view that while black people can of course be racially prejudiced, to the extent that 'racism' has a power element (i.e., that racial prejudice becomes 'racism' when it is the basis for operating institutions with the effect, in practice if not in theory, of perpetuating forms of black disadvantage or 'blocking of life-chances') then on the whole, black people can only be victims of racism in Britain, as they lack the power to affect white people's 'life chances', however prejudiced they may be. After discussion, clarification of terms can be helped by viewing the first 40 slides of *Recognising Racism,*[17] or by study of the Swann Committee's formulations (Report pages 12/13 and pages 28/29).

This chapter uses 'racism' chiefly in the sense of number 7 on the list; and it assumes 'anti-racist' teaching or policies to be concerned not simply with personal prejudice or overt behaviour against black children in school, but also with the education of all children to live in a society characterised by 'racial' (i.e. black) disadvantage and widespread (illegal) discrimination. In other words, this chapter uses 'anti-racist' as an adjective to refer to education directed towards combating structural injustice in society — a society characterised by two facts needing resolute action: many white people have stereotypes of black people which involve assumptions of white superiority, and are based on misconception and ignorance; and such attitudes underlie, or are (perhaps unwittingly) used to rationalise the ways the structures of power work to perpetuate forms of black (called 'racial' in the official documents) disadvantage.

One of the difficulties with using the terms 'racism' or 'racial' is that they legitimate and perpetuate an outmoded pseudo-scientific concept of discrete 'races' with specifiable characteristics. Modern biology acknowledges that there is only one 'race': Homo sapiens.

As Steven Rose, Professor of Biology at the Open University, observes in the pamphlet *Race, Education and Intelligence,* NUT, 1978:[6] The concept of race has no meaning for a biologist — it is a sociological construct.[54]

Bhikhu Parekh notes in *The experience of black minorities in Britain:*[18]

> It is pertinent to ask if race is even a useful concept. Essentially it is a biological term and rests on the assumption that mankind can be divided into different groups on the basis of specific biological properties. It is generally recognised that all such biologically based modes of classification run into difficulties. It is also admitted that, as a result of racial intermingling over the centuries, no pure races can be found. Further, biological properties such as colour of skin, texture of hair and shape of nose or cheek bones obviously do not *cause* the behaviour of the people these properties belong to. Therefore race cannot be a basis for explaining or inferring human conduct. In the light of these and other difficulties do we need the concept of race at all? It has no explanatory value and only creates confusion and muddle.
>
> It is, of course, true that while rejecting the concept of race we may nevertheless retain the concept of racism. It is not inconsistent to say that although mankind cannot be objectively divided into races, some people *think* that it can be so divided.

Bhikhu Parekh expands on this point, and offers further observations on words like 'prejudice' and 'racism' on pp.111-116.

'Racism' is still the most widely used term for referring to the social facts of discrimination based on a perception of skin colour as 'black' in Britain, and so it is being used in the context of this chapter. Some people use 'racism' to include the treatment of 'white' ethnic minority groups as well as black people, since they too experience prejudiced attitudes (see, for example, the last of the Swann Report). Note also that this chapter uses 'anti-racist' throu. (rather than terms like 'non-racist' or 'racial equality') on the assumption ᴸ while black groups remain under-represented in the seats of power — nationally, locally and in institutional decision-making — only active anti-racist steps *in the short-term* to counter the injustice of the status quo can produce what most people claim to want — that is, no racism, no discrimination, and racial equality — in the long-term.

To recap: The first aim of the exercise is to help think out what is the difference between the concepts 'prejudice' and 'racism'. Generally speaking, whatever else it is, prejudice is something individuals have — a matter of personal attitude — while racism is a structured feature of a society — a matter of power relations. The tendency of common parlance to reduce racism to simply individual prejudice results in forms of Assumption One, on pp.57 and 61.

The second aim is to establish the groups' own working definitions of each term. The exercise will show how no two people share exactly the same assumptions — all have different points of emphasis in what they think they mean. Many people find their organisation's anti-racist policy statements acceptable enough; but nothing actually happens, partly because staff are each interpreting the key terms in their own way. There is no universally accepted 'right' definition, so any group must decide its own understanding of words and concepts it is using, and must make its 'nearest consensus' meaning explicit in any policy statement, especially if anyone else (like parents and governors) is going to understand it.

In a third step, the group needs to go on to make its own sense of the *interaction* summarised on pp.11-12. This is something to return to after the following exercises.

Mapping different views and perspectives

All professional practice, whether consciously or not, implies a rationale. While individuals in any staffroom will differ in opinions about, and commitment towards, anti-racism, there will be an 'average' or 'lowest common denominator' of assumptions that make up the hidden curriculum of any school or organisation. This exercise helps a staff make its 'group ideology' conscious and explicit — an essential step towards effective group action.

1. Hand out copies of p.45, giving groups of 3 or 4 five minutes to decide what they think would be most appropriate headings, or descriptive labels, for the three vertical lists. Each small group announces its ideas in turn. Seek agreement that by and large the lists *do* represent three different ways of thinking, and check whether all can understand how the author Robin Richardson intended them in general terms to illustrate assimilationism, multiculturalism and anti-racism.

2. If the group have seen Souad, the Moroccan student on the video, you could ask each group to *guess* where she would be most likely to 'place' the operation of their staffroom — i.e. the average group assumptions — as between A B or C (if she were to work there, say, for a year). Many will report back A or B or between A and B. Now ask Would she be right — at least generally speaking? And after necessary discussion move to 4.

3. If they have not seen Souad, ask where they see themselves as a staff group currently operating as between A, B or C.

4. Where would each group *wish* the whole staff to be seen operating as between A, B or C?

C, or between B and C, they have probably set up a key item for
nda: What are we going to have to do differently, in the way we
nning our department or organisation, to be seen delivering the
alues C or B/C, rather than A or B? Do our joint policies and,
r practices, make clear to any student, parent or governor, that
acist territory' (not an establishment that actually colludes with
......om or merely tokenist multiculturalism)?

A map of Tensions and Controversies

A	B	C
Immigrants came to Britain in the 1950s and 1960s because the laws on immigration were not strict enough.	Ethnic minorities came to Britain because they had a right to and because they wanted a better life.	Black people came to Britain, as to other countries, because their labour was required by the economy.
Immigrants should integrate as quickly as possible with the British way of life.	Ethnic minorities should be able to maintain their language and cultural heritage.	Black people have to defend themselves against racist laws and practices, and to struggle for racial justice.
There is some racial prejudice in Britain, but it's only human nature, and Britain is a much more tolerant place than most other countries.	There are some misguided individuals and extremist groups in Britain, but basically our society is just and democratic, and provides equality.	Britain is a racist society and has been for several centuries. Racism is to do with power structures more than with the attitudes of individuals.
It is counter-productive to try to remove prejudice. You can't force people to like each other by bringing in laws and regulations.	Prejudice is based on ignorance and misunderstanding. It can be removed by personal contacts and the provision of information.	'Prejudice' is caused by, it is not the cause of, unjust structures and procedures. It can be removed only by dismantling these.
There should be provision of English as a second language in schools, but otherwise 'children are all children, we should treat all children exactly the same' — it is wrong to notice or emphasise cultural or racial differences.	Schools should recognise and affirm ethnic minority children's background, culture and language . . . celebrate festivals, organise international evenings, use and teach mother tongues and community languages, teach about ethnic minority history, art, music, religion, literature.	Priorities in education are for there to be more black people in positions of power and influence — as heads, senior teachers, governors, education officers, elected members; and to remove discrimination in the curriculum, classroom methods and school organisation; and to teach directly about equality and justice and against racism.

4. WHAT IS CULTURAL RACISM — CAN IT BE UNLEARNT?

Individual racial prejudice is obvious enough, ranging from bigotry that consciously refuses to accept some individuals or groups as entitled to the full respect due to a fellow human being (that might come out in the staffroom through remarks like 'I don't like teaching *them*') through to well intentioned paternalism (expressed in remarks like 'Don't speak *that* language here, you must practise your English'). Less obvious is *cultural racism*: the tendency of a group to feel that their way of doing things is the 'right' way. This may be simply because they are conditioned by upbringing to think so, and think that what is familiar to them is the best. (It is often said that 'those who live in our country should learn our ways' but even on a narrow and ethnocentric interpretation, what *are* British ways? Scottish, Irish, Welsh, English, Protestant/Catholic, Southern/Northern . . .?).

Some critics use terms like 'Anglo-centrism' or 'cultural imperialism' in this context, to describe any failure to see the English language and heritage as making up 'just another culture' which is itself enriched by dialogue on terms of mutual respect with the other cultural backgrounds that British society now includes — be they Welsh, Irish, French-Canadian, Bengali, Greek Cypriot, Caribbean, East European Jewish, Estonian or Black American . . . It is perhaps worth remarking that in referring to 'cultural backgrounds', it is important to reflect not only the historical traditions and customs of different groups, but the modern changing realities that different communities experience. In other words, no less important than the history are the dynamic and evolving forms of such cultural values as children from different groups experience them in interaction with their peers.

'Cultural racism' is a vast subject: this section offers some brief and introductory points on just two aspects of it: history, and language.

Cultural Racism in History
Picking up the idea of assumed superiority as an element in racially prejudiced attitudes, a revealing exercise is simply to review alternative interpretations of Britain's imperial past, and of world history in general. These throw into relief the impressions most people will have gained from traditional history books. (The book *Multicultural Education,*[1] sets out two school history syllabuses being used to help pupils appreciate the past as an interplay of culturally autonomous interpretations, i.e. of interestingly different, and equally valid, points of view; also Bhikhu Parekh discusses in Chapter 8 how study of history calls for imaginative and open-minded powers of empathy with different social cultures.)

Many teachers are using the two booklets *Roots of Racism* and *Patterns of Racism,* available from the Institute of Race Relations,[19] along with the set of history posters *Whose world is the World?* now available in most Teachers' Centres. Ask the group in pairs to examine one of these posters for five minutes; then to report the content back to the whole group in sequence. Next, seek reactions to the view of history presented. If some are critical of 'simplistic views', or 'bad graphic design', then invite them to work with the Teachers' Centre to make a better set of posters! The point the posters effectively raise for discussion is whether children and adults carry into their image of Britain today an inadequate and 'ethnocentric' view of history with overtones of black inferiority.

Many people have found that they were acting on unexamined and out-of-date assumptions, through reading accounts of African history like J.D. Fage's *A History of Africa*[20]; Walter Rodney's *How Europe underdeveloped Africa*[21]; Basil Davidson's account of the slave trade *Black Mother*[22]; books and articles on universal history by Geoffrey Barraclough; and most particularly, *Black Settlers in Britain* by File and Power.[23] (See also p.113) and references 48-58) Peter Fryer.[51])

Martin Bernal's *Black Athena*[24] uses linguistic evidence to demonstrate that European culture as a whole was itself derived from black African roots through ancient Egypt and the Phoenicians. The archaeological and anthropological evidence for the black origins of Egyptian civilisation (the first that written history records) is set out in *The African Origin of Civilisation — Myth or Reality?* by Chekh Anta Diop.[25] Recent discoveries are described in *Blacks in Science.*[48]

It is important to correct misimpressions about the nature of the slave trade. Many teachers and others have inherited a simplistic view that it was ended solely by British moral leadership inspired by Wilberforce and backed up by the British Navy, and have underestimated the forces of economic change at the time and *most particularly the forces of black resistance.*[50-53] Key books here Walter Rodney's *West Africa and the Atlantic Slave Trade,*[21] C.L.R. James's *History of Black Revolt,*[26] and *Slaves who abolished Slavery,* 2 vols by Richard Hart[27] (one of the foundation members of Jamaica's nationalist movement, whose detailed research in Britain's Public Records Office pulls the veil from the history of slave revolts). His preface to Vol.2 begins:

> The Slave Rebellions and Maroon Wars of Jamaica began to interest me in or about the year 1940. These were the years in which the militancy of the workers, which had come to the boil in all the widely scattered colonies of the British West Indies in the late 1930s, and the new nationalistic upsurge, were taking organisational form.
>
> One of the problems confronting the pioneers of the new popular movements was the formidable historical legacy of a widespread lack of racial self respect. Garvey's oratory in the late 1920s and early 1930s, had struck a responsive chord and the experience of participation in his movement had provided many thousands of people with a foundation for self assurance. But even so, the task of inspiring national self confidence was a formidable one.
>
> This historical legacy of self denigration was only partly attributable to the objective circumstances of generations of enslavement and cruel exploitation. It was also the contrived effect of a system of education and indoctrination deliberately designed to promote a loyalty to the prevailing imperialism and an acceptance of the domination of whites over blacks.
>
> Many peoples who have been subjected to alien domination have been able to draw strength and inspiration from their own legends and history. The Jamaican people were at a disadvantage. The imperial power had largely succeeded in erasing from

their memory their African cultural heritage. Jamaica had no legends, but it did have a history. And here were aspects of that history which, if brought to the people's attention, could provide abundant inspiration for future struggles against oppression.

Jamaica, the largest and most populous of the British islands, was one of the arenas in which large numbers of slaves struggled for their freedom with unflagging determination. Their successes, initially partial, were finally crowned by the achievement of the abolition of slavery at a considerably earlier date than would have been possible without their intervention.

Jamaica was not the only sugar colony outside of Saint Domingue in which the slaves fought for their freedom. There were few islands or mainland colonies in the Caribbean area which did not produce their counterparts of the Jamaicans Cudjoe, Tacky and Sam Sharpe, their embryonic Toussaint Louverture.

Revelling in Britain's liberal image earned by the abolition of the slave trade and slavery, most historians have paid little or no attention to the frequent and formidable rebellions and conspiracies of the slaves, or the extent to which these events influenced the British decision. The suspicion is unavoidable that this is only partly to be explained by ignorance of the facts. The reluctance to investigate and assess the role of the blacks suggests a desire, perhaps sub-conscious, to erase the record of their decisive participation in the anti-slavery struggle.

The focal point around which the political history of the West Indies revolved for upwards of two centuries was the refusal of large numbers of the involuntary migrants from Africa passively to accept their enslavement. European opposition to slavery was aroused and grew over the years not only in response to the class interests of the rising bourgeoisie (discussed in Volume One, Chapter 7) but also because the slaves in the sugar colonies were continually offering and conspiring to offer violent resistance. The idea, sedulously disseminated, that the enslavement of Africans was part of the natural order of things, was challenged again and again, as much by the casualties among the whites engaged in the trade and employed on the plantations as by the disclosure of the sufferings endured by the blacks.

From *Slaves who abolished slavery,* Richard Hart

This and other quotations could be used as handouts for group discussion or information exchange. One patent implication of Richard Hart's work is the need in our schools and libraries for popular and vivid presentations of African history (social technical and cultural achievements, linguistic and religious development, etc.) *before* the period of European exploitation. This has been done with South American Indian cultures — for example with the Incas of Peru, or with the Aztecs in Mexico. How else can teachers displace images of 'blackness' based on negative stereotypes reflecting only caricaturing constructs of Western European culture? Is it enough to teach a view of 'black' as equal to 'white', if that equality is still only on 'white' terms? Without a sense of positive distinct identity how can true equal respect be established? The need is for school resources drawn from the work of present-day African and Caribbean scholars and historians, who present their own history in terms of its relationship with the present (post-colonial) African and Caribbean nations. Examples would be *The African Heritage,* a 2-part history for junior secondary schools from Zimbabwe,[28] and *Africa's Peoples in the Past,* from Kenya.[53] (A strong hint here for etc. teachers keen to contribute to materials in Teachers' Centres as well as in their own classes!) Further sources appear on p.78.[48-58]

Catalogues of such resources are issued by Afro-Caribbean Education Resources (ACER) Wyvil School, Wyvil Road, London SW8 2TJ; Raddle Bookshop[25]; Bogle L'Ouverture/Walter Rodney Bookshop[21]; and local Afro-Caribbean Resource Centres like that at Mundella Centre, Green Street, Nottingham NG2 2LA; as well as The Africa Centre, 38 King Street, London WC2E 8JT.

Vital additional documents for discussion here are David Hicks' *Images of the World* and *Bias in Geography Textbooks,*[29] supplemented perhaps by his resource book *Minorities*[30]; the handbook *World Studies* 8-13[31]; and *Censoring Reality* by Beverley Naidoo[32] (which reviews critically how the history of South Africa has been told), Basil Davidson's *Africa — History and Achievement,*[33] and the texts listed on p.79.[48-58]

The BBC documentary *Black*[8] illustrates very graphically some of the historical sources of the intellectual justifications for black Africans' supposed 'inferiority'. (And Richard Hart[27] includes revealing extracts from the influential speeches of the 18thC. planter-historian, Edward Long.)

A wider perspective on 'culturally racist' attitudes of superiority inherited as a 'residue of history' is offered by Ivan Illich.[34] The extract reminds us that rationalisations of the slave trade and of colonialism were themselves part of a broader, and continuing, set of white Eurocentric assumptions:

> The West exported a dichotomy between 'us' and 'them' unique to industrial society. This peculiar attitude toward self and others is now worldwide, constituting the victory of a universalist mission initiated in Europe.
>
> In Rome, *barbarians* could become members of the city, but to bring them into it was never the intent or mission of Rome. Only during late antiquity, with the Western European Church, did the alien become someone in need, someone to be brought in. This view of the alien as a burden has become constitutive for Western society; without this universal mission to the world outside, what we call the West would not have come to be.
>
> The perception of the outsider as someone who must be helped has taken on successive forms. In late antiquity, the barbarian mutated into *the pagan* — the second stage toward development had begun. The pagan was defined as the unbaptized, but ordained by nature to become Christian. It was the duty of those within the Church to incorporate him by baptism into the body of Christendom. In the early Middle Ages, most people in Europe were baptized, even though they might not yet be converted. Then the Muslim appeared. Unlike Goths and Saxons, Muslims were monotheists, and obviously prayerful believers; they resisted conversion. Therefore, besides baptism, the further needs to be subjected and instructed had to be imputed. The pagan mutated into *the infidel,* our third stage. By the late Middle Ages, the image of the alien mutated again. The Moors had been driven from Granada, Columbus had sailed across the ocean, and the Spanish Crown had assumed many functions of the Church. The image of *the wild man* who threatens the civilizing function of the humanist replaced the image of the infidel who threatens the faith. At this time also, the alien was first described in economy-related terms. From many studies on monsters, apes and wild men, we learn that the Europeans of this period

saw the wild man as having no needs. This independence made him noble, but a threat to the designs of colonialism and mercantilism. To impute needs to the wild man, one had to make him over into *the native,* the fifth stage. Spanish courts, after long deliberation, decided that at least the native of the New World had a soul and was, therefore, human. In opposition to the wild man, the native has needs, but needs unlike those of civilized man. His needs are fixed by climate, race, religion and providence. Adam Smith still reflects on the elasticity of native needs. As Gunnar Myrdal has observed, the construct of distinctly native needs was necessary both to justify colonialism and to administer colonies. The provision of government, education and commerce for the native was for four hundred years the white man's assumed burden.

Each time the West put a new mask on the alien, the old one was discarded because it was now recognized as a caricature of an abandoned self-image. The pagan with his naturally Christian soul had to give way to the stubborn infidel to allow Christendom to launch the Crusades. The wild man became necessary to justify the need for secular humanist education. The native was the crucial concept to promote self-righteous colonial rule. But by the time of the Marshall Plan (after World War II), when multinational conglomerates were expanding and the ambitions of transnational pedagogues, therapists and planners knew no bounds, the natives' limited needs for goods and services thwarted growth and progress. They had to metamorphose into *underdeveloped* people, the sixth and present stage of the West's view of the outsider. Thus decolonization was also a process of conversion: the worldwide acceptance of the Western self-image of *homo economicus* in his most extreme form as *homo industrialis,* with all needs commodity-defined. Scarcely twenty years were enough to make two billion people define themselves as 'underdeveloped'.

From *Shadow Work,* Ivan Illich

A lavishly illustrated documentation of how similar ideas and images were developed towards the Irish is available in *Nothing but the same old story — the roots of anti-Irish racism.*[35] Together with the videos *The Irish in England*[8] that booklet shows how cartoons, 'jokes' and news coverage still reflect denigratory, prejudiced stereotypes embedded in English culture since the Middle Ages. It relates the history of English attitudes towards the Irish to the history of attitudes towards native Americans, Africans and Indians. (A media studies analysis of how Ireland's history has been told on television is given in *Television on History — Representations of Ireland,* a monograph by Bob Ferguson.[29]; see also *The Irish Dimension* in *Multicultural Education Review* No.8, 1988, from Brimingham MDU.[17]

Revealing aspects of the cultural legacy of British colonialism are set out by Bhikhu Parekh in his reflections on pp.116-119. Teachers and trainers will find important information and insights in his *Asians in Britain* — available both as a video public talk[8] and in print in *Five Views of Multiracial Britain*[16] — and in his Open University paper *The experience of black minorities in Britain.*[18] Also relevant here are Salman Rushdie's comments on the 'cultural fashion' of nostalgia for the Raj (pp.130-133) together with Jim Pines' account of reappraisals of their experience being made by black film makers (pp.103-111).

A further powerful way of reinforcing insight into how cultural assumptions lingering from the days of Empire still animate white reactions to black British people today, is to view Salman Rushdie's Channel 4 talk *The New Empire in*

Britain, available from Albany Video,[11] or from Concord Films,[8] or available on an off-print from New Society, 9.12.82.[36] Important insights into cultural racism past and present, are given in other books on p.79.[56-58] The checklists offered on pages 162-174, should also be directly useful here.

All these materials will indicate to teachers and others the need to work together to prise into consciousness the ways that their assumptions have been conditioned by ideas from our cultural past; and then in turn to teach the historical contextualisation — and its consequences — to the children, a job all the more important while so much of the media (papers, films, comics, books and television) are still simply transmitting, and therefore legitimating and reinforcing, dehumanised 'traditional' images and ideas of black people.

The two *Black and White Media Shows*[55] described in Section 4 are largely contributions to the study of 'cultural racism' as it manifests itself at various levels of subtlety on the TV screen. They illustrate how disparaging stereotypes of black people, drawn from the days of slavery and colonialism, are still an accepted part of some television comedy and of some drama; and how unconsciously dismissive attitudes and stereotypical assumptions about black people still inform much coverage of sport, news and current affairs, and other factual programmes. Part 1, in particular, examines how gross images from the Deep South of white stereotypical constructs of black people — such as the 'rolling eyes simpleton', Uncle Tom, Aunt Jemima, the golliwog — live on in the culture we have inherited alongside Victorian ideas of black inferiority in terms of 'primitive', 'jungle', 'native', 'white man's burden', etc. A training scheme following the general structure of this chapter could well build in the use of *The Black and White Media Shows* at this stage.

English Language

One commonly used way of illustrating how assumptions are embedded in our language, as well as in our image of history, is the 'Black' and 'White' exercise. List on the board all phrases and uses that the group can think of, first of the word 'black' and then of 'white'. Then work through them, deciding by general consensus if each use carries negative, positive or neutral associations. Adding up the totals is a way of discovering just how heavily usage of the word black is laden with negative associations. What is the effect when such words are applied to people? In particular, what is the effect on white children's self-image if they feel white represents positive/good and black represents negative/bad? And what is the effect on black children's self-image when they find that they are described as 'black' in a culture which generally associates the term with things negative/bad? ('White' is self-idealization of course: we are mostly shades of purply puce, just as most 'black' people are actually shades of bronze or brown. See p.112.)

The American black actor Ossie Davis made a study of the synonyms for 'whiteness' and 'blackness' in Roget's Thesaurus. He found that 'whiteness' had many synonyms that are 'favourable and pleasing to contemplate' and only 10 with negative connotations, and then only in the mildest sense. 'Blackness' turned out to have no less than 60 synonyms which are distinctly unfavourable; and in addition to those, it has 20 directly related to race.

'The English language is my enemy . . . Any creature, good or bad, white or black, Jew or Gentile, who uses the English language for purposes of communication is willing to force the Negro child into 60 ways to despise himself, and the white child 60 ways to aid and abet him in the crime'.

Richard Hart makes a similar point[27]:

The Spanish word 'negro', meaning 'black', had been derived from the Latin 'niger' with no derogatory connotations. But it had become an English word expressing the concept of primitiveness, savagery, servility and blackness all rolled into one. Its contemptuous derivative 'nigger' was popularised in numerous scurrilous limericks and ditties.

Throughout the greater part of the two centuries of slavery in the British West Indies there were individuals in Britain and the colonies who condemned the cruelty with which the slaves were treated. These well meaning humanitarians nevertheless tended to weaken their case by the acceptance, perhaps unconscious, which most of them gave to the premise of Negro inferiority.

No doubt they thought of the slaves as 'God's creatures', but even that concept allowed for a great deal of latitude. With few exceptions their advocacy had little to distinguish them from members of the Society for the Prevention of Cruelty to Animals. Their arguments were, in consequence, comparatively ineffective and so remained until changes in the structure of Britain's economy following the Industrial Revolution brought them powerful and practical new allies.

So deeply was the concept of black inferiority implanted in the Anglo-Saxon mind during the period of slavery that, in Britain and the U.S.., it not only outlasted the abolition of that institution, but survives into the 20th century perpetuating prejudices, creating tensions and providing contemporary rationalisations for racial discrimination.

It was as a positive rejection of this that the US Civil Rights Movement adopted the slogan 'Black is beautiful', as a result of which 'Black' has now acquired a 'political' meaning in some contexts, symbolising pride in cultural background and self-assertion against unjust treatment.

Other examples of the way we can be victimised by our very language in trying to be anti-racist, would be the unconscious use of the word 'people' (this is discussed as assumption No.21 in the later Assumptions exercise pp.58,63 and 220); the way most of us accepted the media's exclusive use of the word 'riots' in relation to the street disturbances of 1981 (see *Black and White Media Show Part 2*, pages 215-217); or indeed the use of the word 'racial' when we simply mean British people of Afro-Caribbean or Asian background (see pages 29-34). The term 'minority' means 'numerically fewer than' a majority, but is often taken to imply 'something less than'. The group might think through the implications of 'host community' as a way of referring to a majority white group; of 'racial disadvantage' as an official euphemism for the facts of discrimination against black people; of 'second generation immigrants' as a term frequently used to refer to young black British people — but rarely to young white children whose parents have come from overseas. Bhikhu Parekh's comments on language on pp.111-116 should be referred to here.

Attitudes to Community Languages

This is another crucial aspect of 'cultural racism': the attitudes, and therefore the behaviour, of teachers and other professionals towards the multilingual nature of British society. This is a touchstone for whether we are in practice treating others' cultural values with the respect that we would normally expect to be shown towards our own. It is not possible to respect the culture of any community without recognising the significance of that community's own language, or indeed, the characteristic ways in which people in that community may speak English. More even than religious traditions, or social or domestic customs, it is language — the way people communicate and share their thoughts — which symbolises and embodies a culture and its values. (This will become clear from the 'Fred Barker' exercise on pp.46-47.)

No teacher would deny that good education depends on respect for the child and for the knowledge and abilities the child already possesses. Equally no-one would deny that a bilingual person has more resources and can communicate with a wider range of people than someone with only one language; someone conversant with two languages and cultures can be enriched by both. This means that a child's competence in a mother-tongue is an accomplishment, rather than a 'problem'. Unfortunately, mono-lingualism has long been the norm in most parts of Britain, with the exception of Wales and parts of Scotland and N. Ireland. Those who speak only English, with perhaps a smattering of French or German, find it hard to understand how schooling in two or more languages is taken for granted by people in many parts of Europe, Asia and Africa.

It would be a form of cultural racism, if teachers see no need to equip themselves to develop all the language skills of potentially bilingual pupils, or if examiners were to expect higher standards in Asian languages on some assumption that only pupils with a mother tongue 'advantage' would be candidates. Given the D.E.S.-backed researches which demonstrate that children with mother tongues other than English learn both standard English and their community language better, as well as develop their all-round cognitive flexibility more, if taught bilingually in the early years of primary schooling, then schools not equipped to do this are relatively disadvantaging such children. At the same time, such schools will be missing the opportunity to give second language skills to English mother tongue speakers — language skills which are now not merely culturally enriching, but directly useful in any public service work in all the multilingual areas of Britain. Racist disadvantaging can occur also if schools fail to accept that a qualification in a modern Asian language can be at least as useful for their pupils as one in French or a second 'foreign' language. Most FE colleges and universities now accept any subject taken at GCSE or 'A' level among qualifications for admission (except for a few specific courses). So this is another sense in which there is educational waste, if not actually an imposed disadvantage on pupils, if their grounding in speaking languages other than French and German is not built on in school. Apart from that, the UK now has at least 100,000 Arabic and Panjabi speakers, and as many Urdu speakers; Britain also has many commercial and other links with Middle Eastern and Asian countries. Ability to communicate in a language spoken locally would have obvious advantages for people who meet the public in their work — in the national health service, industry, education, law and, indeed, almost every sector of British life.

A more general 'hidden curriculum' cultural racism arises where teachers fail to inspire interest in bi- or tri-lingualism as a positive model for both educational achievement and cultural enrichment. For example, a teacher who is overheard saying 'They don't speak English' may be speaking truthfully of some pupils, but is demonstrating negatively stereotypical thinking which the other young children will take to suggest that there is something wrong with 'them'. If instead, 'potential bilinguals' were spoken of with pride, this will tempt children who speak only English to ask 'Please Miss/Sir — what's a bilingual?' and once it is explained, 'Can we/I be bilingual, too?' Attitudes which will be unconsciously emulated are displayed by the terms we choose to use. Dismissive attitudes towards others' cultures are also conveyed if schools put community language classes in lunch hours — indicating that such language do not warrant the same status as European languages; or if it is assumed that no 'English' children would be attending them; or indeed, if classes are timetabled to clash with other essential subjects like physics or maths. (Questions of language are discussed by NUT[6] and AMMA.[7])

A multilingual society: but where is television?

Put the question to the group: how many living languages other than English are being used in England by at least 100,000 people each? (The answer is 12: Chinese, Arabic, Panjabi, Urdu, Bengali, Gujerati, Hindi, Polish, Italian, Turkish, Greek, Spanish.) In the ILEA alone, 57,000 pupils, one fifth of those enrolled, speak a language other than English at home. To that extent, we live in a multilingual society: a cultural enrichment all teachers will of course need to draw to attention of all pupils as a basic fact of social awareness. Unfortunately, even though television sometimes claims to be 'reflecting society', such teaching will receive scant support from the pupils' television viewing at home. No-one would know England to be multilingual from watching television. Indeed, you could ask the group if they have ever seen any other language than English on television in England, and if so what language was it? Usually few white people in England can think of any programmes which are not exclusively in English, with the possible exceptions of the language courses (which seek to motivate adult learning of European languages) and perhaps the BBC Sunday morning offering *Asian Magazine* (which ceased in early 1987, to be replaced by *Network East*). A high proportion of *Asian Magazine* was in fact in English; the billing in Radio Times was exclusively in English;

the parts not in English were conducted in a form of Hindi. Critics have observed that not only are the rights to information, entertainment and education of those licence payers who do not speak English hardly being acknowledged and met, but that the linguistic realities of Britain are generally not being demonstrated across the whole output — even in the factual news and features output, let alone the more popular fictional shows. The community languages are almost wholly confined to local radio.

The BBC's *Tele-Journal* has been an honourable exception to the general pattern of failure to reflect, let alone to encourage, models of bilingualism: though that too, has again featured (so far) only the European languages. English television thus broadcasts a permanently dismissive hidden curriculum message to pupils, both black and white, about Britain's languages other than English, and it is crucial that teachers show genuine interest in, and encouragement of, community languages to counter this cultural racism. There are white teachers learning Urdu in places like Peterborough and Manchester (as shown in *Languages for Life,*[8] the film which puts the case for mother-tongue and community language teaching); unfortunately, their good example to pupils is hardly realistic for all teachers to follow. Nevertheless, if all teachers were at least to learn 100 words of at least *one* of the community languages in their area, that would communicate both to parents and to pupils something of an intention to treat other cultures with the respect they deserve. Teachers will be helped to do this by the beginners' language series in Urdu show on BBC TV in 1989;[55] or by following the twenty 10-minute episodes of a course in spoken Urdu offered by BBC Schools Radio from Feb.1988 (teacher's notes from Brighton Polytechnic). The Linguistic Minorities Project reports (Inst. of Education, London University[29]) give detailed facts on Britain as a multilingual society.

Fred Barker — the sequel

One tactical stimulus to discussion of the concept of 'cultural racism' is to continue the imaginary saga introduced by the film *Fred Barker goes to China*[8], inviting teachers to embroider the details and develop new episodes in the story from where you leave off. (It is a narrative replete with stereotypical terms and thinking, and so operates at two levels (a) by identification with Mr. & Mrs. Barker and (b) by identification with a 'Chinese' viewpoint.)

After being unemployed for two years, Fred Barker's family life is suffering badly. His friend Jim receives a postcard from their old workmate (before the factory closed) Charlie, postmarked 'Peking'. It gives an impression that no-one is out of work there, and jobs are available running the buses and cleaning the hospitals. Fred and Jim write to Charlie to fix them up with such jobs, and duly emigrate. When he gets there, Fred is disconcerted to find how long it will take him to earn enough to be able to bring his family over to join him (though fortunately, there are no divisive immigration laws to prevent this). He learns some Chinese, he works hard for long hours, and takes great pains to adapt himself — though never enough, it seems, for some of the Chinese. When the rest of the family come over, he is astonished at how quickly his son picks up the language, while his daughter, born a year later, becomes totally bilingual, it appears, almost from the start. (There are bilingual teachers at her nursery school.) On some occasions, both the daughter and the son (who conscientiously learned 'The Thoughts of Chairman Mao' by heart before leaving England and practises his ping-pong for hours each day) come home upset. None of the Chinese in the class want to join his team in the table tennis tournament and they laughed when his bat and shorts were thrown into the water showers; she has overheard some parents of her friends telling them in a hostile manner 'not to play with round-eyes'. The children seem to be turning off their schoolwork, so Fred and his wife go to consult the form teacher and the deputy head. The teachers — in a conversation held entirely in Chinese — are most concerned, especially as they have recently been away on an in-service course in multicultural education, and the school has had a working party charged with drawing up an anti-racist policy in line with local education ministry directives for the last 18 months. 'Rest assured, Mr. & Mrs. Barker, we now want to encourage the Chinese children into an attitude of respect for cultural differences'. 'That sounds good' say the Barkers, 'How are you going to achieve that?' 'Well, we're starting voluntary English classes in the lunch hours, Morris dancing classes after school, and we're planning to ask all the English mothers to make fish and chips with bacon and eggs for a cultural evening once a term; and to get the English children to present Assembly on Guy Fawkes Day and on Christmas Day. After all we can relate to fireworks alright — we invented them. We've ordered a consignment of bowler hats for dressing up and as a specially broad-minded initiative we'll be teaching about your Western primitive and cannibalistic religious rituals'. 'Just a minute' interrupts Mrs. Barker, 'I've never liked fish and chips, and I've never met anyone with a bowler hat; and although we're not religious I can assure you you've misunderstood the doctrine of transubstantiation — perhaps if you talked with the priest down at the church . . .' 'No need, Mrs. Barker — I've read it all up from books by the best Neo-Marxist/Leninist experts on Western reactionary superstitions that we have . . .' 'But' says Fred, 'how can you respect or understand Englishness in your school when neither of you speaks one word of English? That's surely why you've missed what it's all really about'. 'Oh no, Mr. Barker, as teachers we're able to teach respect for another culture through teaching some of the social customs, the arts and the crafts, the history and the religion; you don't have to be able to speak the language . . .'

'HEALTH WARNING'. This story has used gross stereotypes to stimulate self-reflection about stereotypical thinking. (Anyone who feels that this should not be done, even as an initial way of 'starting where people are at' could replace 'China' by some artificial place name.) In extending the story and reflecting on its implications you will see if the group raise this issue for themselves. If they do not, then this shows how hard it is to 'see' stereotyping, and how far the group has yet to go. Ask how they would feel about the story if they were Chinese.

Teaching against prejudice at primary school
Some practical clues about teaching against cultural racism are offered in the next two sequences of the *Anglo-Saxon Attitudes* film. At Ecclesbourne Primary

School in North London Barbara Roberts is seen in effect helping to 'inoculate' the primary school children against the kinds of prejudiced attitudes they will be imbibing from their cultural surroundings or, to put it another way, helping them to 'unlearn' some of the forms of cultural racism they have already been affected by. When you stop at the end of the sequence you may care to note that if Barbara appears to some members of the group rather stiff or even patronising in her manner towards the children, this is a wrong impression — the media people have failed to capture her approach adequately on film. You should get the group to discuss these points about the *way* she was teaching:

(a) How Barbara was ready frankly to review her own personal attitudes (such a readiness is not all that common among professional people with qualifications);

(b) How she is very far from ignoring skin colour differences, and how in her project 'Ourselves' she risks no split between the skills she wants to teach and the children's social experience;

(c) How she 'legitimates' the idea of moving to find work, and of speaking in other ways than in standard English alone, by putting herself up front as a person, before asking any children about their family background (thus avoiding patronising or exploitative approaches, or insensitivity to children's self-consciousness);

(d) How she makes the point that to reject non-standard English accents or dialects is partly to reject the person;

(e) How she teaches against stereotyping, by the simple device of putting hands on black and white paper;

(f) How she supports mother tongue skills in the classroom as much for the respect it wins in the eyes of other children, as for the cultural support it gives to mother tongue speakers (on this last point, the issues and information for schools on mother tongues or community languages are set out in Chapter 12 of the book *Multicultural Education*[1] and presented graphically in the film *Languages for Life*.[8])

Especially important is to note:.

(g) How Barbara Roberts first sets up *a context of similarity,* before referring to any differences. It is not clear from the film that she first asks the children to outline their fingers in pencil and to identify all the ways our hands are the same. Only then does she ask them to colour them in, so that colour differences are seen as marginal, not the main thing about hands. In the same way, the children have read and discussed *Aesop's Fables* before Barbara asks the Turkish boys to share (bilingually) one of them in their mother tongue. This prevents any assumption that an initially strange sounding language must reflect 'strange' ideas or people. Barbara wants children to regard differences of language or skin colour as positive and interesting, not in a negative way as strange, exotic, or simply because different, threatening.

The next sequence of *Anglo-Saxon Attitudes* shows similar principles operating in the context of an all-white primary school. Given the special value of 'people contact', some 'all-white' primary schools have now engaged in joint activities over time with so-called 'multi-ethnic' schools. It is vital to note that these are not visits, but joint activities over a considerable period of time, and that they need very well prepared teachers to help correct the wrong or misleading information that the children are likely to pass on if left entirely to themselves in the course of such activities. The headteacher shown, David Houlton, describes the scheme and its results in detail in *Multicultural Education.*[1] What is impressive in his account is how quite young children, on the bases of the mutual respect and friendships they build up, can confidently 'put right' their own parents' prejudices or misinformation. Conditions for successful 'exchanges' are elaborated in the section on 'Inter-ethnic Contact' (pp.121-2) of James Lynch's *Prejudice Reduction and the Schools.*[44] See also David Houlton's *Cultural Diversity*[48].

5. WHAT IS INSTITUTIONAL RACISM AND HOW DOES IT OPERATE?

This is the form of racism most white people find hardest to bring into conscious focus, partly because we are so much participants in it: we are involuntarily the beneficiaries and the agents of it. Individual racial prejudice and forms of cultural racism come together in institutional pressures which work in effect to the benefit of some more than others. As defined by David Wellman, it is action 'based on culturally sanctioned beliefs, that regardless of the intentions involved, defend the advantages that whites have because of the subordinated position of racial minorities'. (See also Swann Report, pages 28-31).

This is the aspect of racism which moves beyond the emotive, psychological context of 'prejudiced attitudes' into the context of matters of political power, hierarchy and status. It is the form in which we are all involved in racism whether racially prejudiced or not in our personal relationships and which perhaps most clearly shows why for anti-racism, good intentions are not enough. But it is also the form which can make us most uncomfortable as we become aware of it. It often causes feelings of guilt or anger, born of the frustration that we were not ourselves responsible for events of the past, and yet cannot escape the fact that we live on the benefits of past and present exploitation, rationalised by assumptions of black inferiority. Neither can we escape the cultural trap of our language, in which so many of those past rationalisations and attitudes remain embedded. As a result, many white people feel defensive or seek to evade recognising that it remains part of the black experience of British society to feel oppression and low status, which is expressed in many overt ways, but also in many subtle and indefinable ways. However, as the primary headmistress says later in the film *Anglo-Saxon Attitudes,* such mixed emotions have to be experienced and lived through as part of the learning process. After her feelings of anger and of being threatened subsided, she felt more confident about adopting a strategy of anti-racist multicultural education based on full equality of respect and opportunity, and without risk of tokenism, patronising assumptions, or confused conceptions.

Exercise in designing a subtly racist school

The concept of institutional racism is a new idea to many people. This exercise helps move the group's thinking beyond questions simply of individual teachers' attitudes, and questions simply of multicultural exchange in schools, to thinking about institutional pressures, particularly in the exercise of power over decision-making in the school system. The exercise provides a 'scaffolding' for the group to bring into consideration, and to build its own meaning for the idea mentioned earlier, that even perhaps without conscious prejudice, 'white dominant' power and influence is wielded through institutions whose working unintentionally excludes black people from power, and whose procedures function in ways which represent barriers to black people being able to affect their own 'life chances'.

The aim

The aim is to allow participants to think out some of the elements of what is called 'institutional' racism and how this functions in the school system. Better understanding of the mechanisms which perpetuate disadvantage is a vital first step towards determining what action is needed (a) to combat them in the school and L.E.A. itself, and (b) to equip the next generation to dismantle them in the wider society. And the exercise should help teachers discover how it is often an entirely unwitting combination of habitual assumptions, 'normal' behaviour and traditional procedures that support black disadvantage, rather than conscious and overt anti-black prejudice.

The procedure

It is important to point out that each small (8/10) group is to design a subtly racist school system, rather than an obviously racist system on the apartheid model. The idea is to work out what kind of schooling would in practice preserve white majority advantage over a black minority in some imaginary society, where teachers are not personally colour prejudiced, racial discrimination is against the law, and L.E.A. policies formally favour equal opportunities for all. Ask one rapporteur in each group to set out the features of such a system in notes, perhaps on a large flip chart, as a visual aid for report-back. On a separate sheet another rapporteur could make notes of the explanations for why and how each feature of the invented system would *in effect* work to maintain black disadvantage. (Essentially the group will be thinking of 'apparently reasonable' practical barriers to the implementation of well intentioned, but still largely theoretical, anti-racist policies.) It is usual, but not necessary, to assume that the school includes a proportion of children of Afro-Caribbean and/or Asian background; groups can decide to invent either a primary or a secondary school. Emphasise that it is to be an exercise of *imagination*. It is normal for groups to find it a bit hard to get started: but after the first 5-10 minutes ideas will begin to flow. The following questions, as a handout, would help. The more time given to groups, the more 'subtle' the insight they gain.

Designing a subtly racist school — stimulus questions

1) What *curriculum* would be taught? In what ways, if at all, would it be appropriate for education in a multicultural society?

2) What would be the school *language policy* on (a) bilingualism, (b) community languages, (c) mother-tongue teaching for English-second language speakers, (d) E2L support? How much, if at all, would parents be directly asked to help in mother-tongue teaching, and under what conditions?

3) What would be the *staffing* policy, e.g. Would there be ethnic minority staff? What would be their roles? What posts of special responsibility would there be? Who would get them and on what criteria?

4) What would be the *catering policy* for school meals, etc?

5) What kind of *assessment tests* would be used?

6) What would be the content and methods of *RE teaching?*

7) In *assemblies,* what festivals etc. would be recognised, and how would they be handled?

8) What 'pastoral' care would there be, and what means of *communication to parents?*

9) *Cultural evenings* — would there be any? If so, what would they involve?

10) How much, and what kind of *games, swimming and PE?* What would be the arrangements for these?

11) What priority would the school give, if any at all, to *in-service staff training and development* in (a) multicultural approaches in the curriculum; (b) teaching anti-racism; (c) improving cross-cultural communication skills in parent-teacher dialogue? What would be the arrangements for covering to send staff on L.E.A. courses, or in organising school-based DIY staff meetings and workshops?

12) How would the school decide on *use of resources* from the L.E.A., e.g. staff allocated under Section II LGA; capitation; etc.

13) How would the school handle, if at all (a) racist incidents in the locality; (b) racist jokes or remarks among pupils in school; (c) racially prejudiced statements or argument expressed by parents; (d) racist observations made in the staffroom? Would such matters be left to individual responses, or would there be a whole-school policy? If the latter, what would it be?

14) How much encouragement and support would be given to English-speaking teachers to *learn languages,* such as Urdu, Panjabi, Bengali?

15) Would *checklists* on racism and sexism be used in relation to books and materials? If so, how?

16) *School uniform* policy? *Name* of school? Does it have a *motto?* Describe the *headteacher!*

17) Would the fact be recognised that there remains a great deal of unconscious racism — ranging from fairly obvious to very subtle — *in the television that pupils* — and parents — *are watching*? If so, what priority would be given to teaching about it, and how would such teaching be done?

18) What emphasis on *authority v. democracy*; and on purely academic achievement in the running of the school?

19) What emphasis would be given to *the arts* in the curriculum and/or in after-school activities, and what kinds of music-making, drama, dance, painting and drawing would be resourced and encouraged?

The two essential questions:

20) In each of the above (or however far the group get) *how would the issues be decided and by whom?* In particular, would there be direct involvement of parents and community in the policy making — and, if so, how would this be organised and articulated?

21) In each of the above, *if little or nothing is actually to happen, what reasoning or factors would be used to explain why?*

Stimulus questions for designing a subtly racist union branch (See also the union/association checklist on pp.72-74)

Structure
Officers?
Executive committee?
Rules — any co-options?
Sub-committee?

Meetings
Subject-Agenda — how decided?
Information about — how communicated?
Priorities for meetings?

Ethnic minority members
Do we monitor membership?
Have we surveyed members and asked if any particular concerns?
How would we react if they asked for a special section?
Have we taken equal opportunity (in employment) issues up with the management?

Union policy on combating racism
Special meetings held to discuss?
What follow-up action decided?
Relations with local authority on these issues?
Deputation?

Casework
Do we know of any particular issues affecting black members?
Any special measures to assist black members?
If members have difficulty in implementing policy in own schools, how can we assist?
In all the above items, it is important to consider who takes decisions and sets priorities, and to give reasons for action or inaction.

Stimulus questions for designing a subtly racist library

(1) What is the acquisitions policy
   (a) on books? (Would importance be placed on black authors?)
   (b) on music/records? (Would the music be wider than European classical?)

(2) How do the staff find out local community needs?
   (What resources are given to this task? And when done, who decides which needs get priority?)

(3) What is the staffing profile and policy?
   (What minority groups are represented on the staff — and in what roles?)

(4) What is the languages policy?
   (Not only on books and periodicals but on joining forms and information posters.)

(5) How are the library services communicated to the local community?

(6) What is the policy concerning which local organisations are allowed/encouraged to use rooms and/or display areas?

(7) Are racist books/materials labelled or contextualised as such?

(8) How are staff training needs identified and met?

(9) What kind of security staff? Do they have any training? If so, how is it done?

(10) What advice would be given to schools?

(11) What media education, if any, would be offered?

(12) How would staff respond — if at all — to racist incidents in the library? Is there a defined strategy known to staff and borrowers? If so, who would do the defining?

The most important questions:

(13) Who is consulted on 1-12? Who decides on 1-12?

(14) In each case, if little or nothing is to be done, how is that justified?

Similar questions can be devised for designing a subtly racist college; housing dept.; arts centre; social work dept.; local newspaper or radio station; national broadcasting organisation. . .

Once your groups have described their invented school in report-back, two crucial questions for discussion would be 'What are the differences between such an imagined school, and the school system we ourselves are currently operating?' and 'What did it *feel like* to be designing an institution with deliberately racist effects?'

Concepts to bring into conscious focus, in discussion of what that exercise has revealed about how subtle racism operates, would include:

(1) Ways of *marginalising* the interests of ethnic minorities;

(2) Making *tokenist* gestures towards minority interests and cultures, i.e. 'paying lip service' (see important comment on statement 20, page 63);

(3) Acting on the basis of *stereotypes* in general, i.e. 'they all . . .' and negative stereotypes in particular — especially, perhaps, in terms of lower expectations of some groups of ethnic minority children;

(4) The effects of *omission* to modify, adapt, or change ways of thinking and doing things in school, despite the changing multicultural, multilingual, multi-faith, and multi-racial character of the community the school is serving.

(5) Making decisions on *patronising,* paternalist assumptions about others' cultural values — or, as some critics put it, 'white cultural imperialism'. (The women in the group are usually well able to explain how this patronising element operates, and how it feels. Truly equal respect for other cultures requires great sensitivity and imagination, and a real willingness to listen and learn. For example, can one genuinely respect a culture for its arts and social customs, while wholly ignoring its language? see pp.44-48);

(6) Hidden *assimilationist* assumptions in decisions about the use of resources in school, i.e. 'incorporation' — in effect treating black ethnic minority children and/or staff only insofar as they are the same as white;

(7) *Excluding minority groups from power* by using majority voting without special safeguards for minority interests, and the deployment of black staff on a basis of *responsibility without power;*

(8) *Building in failure,* i.e. sending only individuals away on anti-racism training courses, with no report-back at school (see p.10); overlooking the need for monitoring arrangements of the effects of policies; leaving whole-school issues only to small working party groups (see p.69) — in other words, unthinkingly adopting customary procedures which serve to sabotage in advance any *effectively practical outcome* of well-intentioned moves;

(9) *The rationalising* of failure to review attitudes and to modify procedures on a shared power basis, through the *'doing nothing'* syndrome, i.e. such 'recipes for paralysis' as consideration of lack of resources, difficulties in spending time on working out priorities and where race issues come in them, 'not rocking the boat', or 'it's too difficult', etc. The 'challenge of the need to tackle resource implications' becomes 'realistic problems we can't do much about', i.e. excuses for avoiding giving priority to effective anti-racism. Such

rationalisings usually imply a failure to see that it is *all* children's needs that are at stake in tackling racism in classrooms, staffrooms and L.E.A. administration, together with defensiveness about vested interests and power structure.

Many people find some of these concepts unfamiliar and difficult clearly to understand in abstract terms. This is partly because in a strongly 'white dominant' culture, white people have not needed personally to think about how black disadvantage is maintained, not being direct victims of it themselves. Thus the group leader's job is to encourage each member to contribute to thinking of practical features for an invented subtly racist school system and in the proceess of reviewing these, to tease out the concepts (1) — (9) and any more the group can think of. There is more description of some of the elements of institutional racism in schools in *The Realization of Anti-racist Teaching,* by Godfrey Brandt,[37] on p.158 of *Cultural Diversity* by David Houlton[48], and in the NUT's *Education for Equality.*[6] Once the concepts have been thoroughly discussed, it can be important to ask any black colleagues or participants if they consider the practices the white groups have invented and described to be *really* subtle. (Further points on institutional racism at local level: p.72-73.)

The sort of hidden assumptions that can lead individual 'well intentioned' teachers and educational administrators unwittingly to go along with institutional racism can be explored through the next 'Assumptions' exercise.

6. WHAT ARE THE UNCONSCIOUS ASSUMPTIONS THAT FUEL THE WORKING OF INSTITUTIONAL RACISM?

Some teachers' inaction, if not indifference, in regard to racism and the harm it is creating for pupils, both black and white, is rationalised by a range of 'arguments', whose dependence on assumptions which hide factual ignorance, paternalist or assimilationist attitudes, harmful stereotypes, cultural ethnocentrism, and 'blaming the victim' of social injustice, may not be obvious at first. Indeed, it is a feature of institutionalised racism that although individuals operating the institutions may have 'liberal' views, they justify no change by what appear on the surface to be reasonable and practical observations. The following statements are not fictional — they have been reported as those still most commonly said or thought by teachers. Many are not in themselves necessarily racist; but all are remarks whose meaning needs to be checked, as they could be symptomatic of the unconsidered assumptions that explain why teachers, and others with discretionary power within our institutions, seek to evade the need for action and change to counteract the present 'status quo' of injustice to black people, evidenced in the facts of black disadvantage and the prevalence of varying degrees of colour prejudice in our society.

The exercise consists simply of handing out copies of the 57 statements to the group and inviting them to comment on the hidden assumptions. (Where a group wish to talk at length about the substantive issues raised in some of the statements, you might suggest that you go back to those issues after working through the rest of the list.) In effect, this exercise not only brings hidden assumptions into conscious focus — the pre-condition for anti-racist action — but it also gives practice in thinking through their own replies as confidence-building preparation for those occasions when teachers meet objections to multicultural and anti-racist approaches.

Clearly, in any one group session you will use only a selection of those most relevant to your situation; however, it is a list members of the group could take away to peruse for themselves, or to talk through more informally later. You might find it useful to distribute the list of statements for some personal reflection in advance of the group discussion. A much better way of using the list would be as the basis for role-play exercises in which teachers practise discussing the school's objectives with sceptical parents, governors, senior or junior staff colleagues, union/association members or representatives, even LEA advisers and inspectors. In a 'mixed ability' group, the exercise can puncture complacency among 'sophisticates' as much as develop insights and self-reflection among 'beginners'. The point of it, either as discussion or as role-play, is to stimulate a sharing of ideas on an aspect of racism described in the editorial of *Multiracial Education* (Summer 1981) in these terms:

> In the paper 'The Whites of their Eyes'* Stuart Hall, when considering racism as ideology, has made the distinction between *overt* and *inferential* racism — the inferential differing from the overt in that statements are being made which have racist premises and propositions inscribed within them as a set of *unquestioned assumptions.* Thus statements can be made without the racist predicates upon which they are based ever becoming visible — and so this more insidious kind of racism tends 'to disappear from view into the taken-for-granted naturalised world of commonsense'. Invisible even to those who formulate the statements, we can see that racist discourse does not rest on their conscious intentions.

> * Stuart Hall 'The Whites of their Eyes' in *Silver Linings, Some Strategies for the Eighties.* Lawrence and Wishart 1981.

Assumptions Exercise: 57 Varieties

Can you identify (a) inadequate or wrong information, and (b) possible hidden assumptions which are racist in effect, behind these statements? What points would you make in replying to them?

1) 'I'm not colour prejudiced, so there's no need for me to study the facts of black disadvantage.'

2) 'I treat all the children the same — in our school we make no difference between children, black or white.'

3) 'Our black pupils are a problem in this school — because they are very different, you know.'

4) 'They don't speak English.' *or* 'They haven't got any language, you know'.

5) 'I can't talk about attitudes towards racism with my colleagues — some of them would find it personally offensive, and raising such topics directly can be counter-productive.'

6) 'Multicultural education is all about black children or, as we say now, ethnic minorities, isn't it?'

7) 'Many immigrant children just can't perform so well — and that's not prejudice: our assessment tests, well tried since the '40s and '50s, prove it.'

8) End of term general essay exam question: Describe an English village.

9) 'If the Asian children don't eat the curries we provide as an option at lunch, then it's their own fault if they are tired in the afternoons.'

10) 'Some black groups, usually the Afro-Caribbeans, don't seem to have much opportunity or encouragement from their parents to get homework done on time.'

11) 'Different social customs are all very interesting, but they are irrelevant to my curriculum.'

12) 'More mother-tongue in school time would be fine — but while the Authority has such tight limits on resources it simply isn't practical.'

13) 'Positive discrimination either means lowering standards or giving unfairly preferential treatment, or both.'

14) 'We have to treat them as slow learners, at least while their English is so inadequate.'

15) 'It simply makes sense to use extra resources offered because we have minority children in our school, on a school bus driver or an extra teacher of English or maths, or a swimming pool, or a new piano, or replacement slide projectors, etc., because not only the ethnic minority children benefit from such things, but everyone else does, too.'

16) 'I favour black equal rights — I've made several suggestions of ways we can help them.'

17) 'Little positive comes of ethnic minority community meetings because it is obvious they don't properly understand how our system works.'

18) 'You can't expect teachers to adopt a multi-cultural approach until the Authority provides enough of the right materials.'

19) 'The LEA's policy is really admirable — but it's only what I've been doing all the time.'

20) 'We're very keen on multicultural approaches: for some years we have let them have Asian evenings at school, and we celebrate Diwali and Eid in assembly. Although there are only three children of Hong Kong parents, we had a special display on Chinese New Year.'

21) 'People often find it hard to know whether black people want to be called 'black' or not.'

22) 'You can't start being heavy about nationality jokes the kids make in the playground — after all, there have always been Irish and Taffy jokes, and all humour depends on stereotypes.'

23) 'If there's an NF or BM meeting in the town, then to refer to it in school would be bringing politics into the classroom and children must be left to make up their own political opinions.'

24) 'I find it hard to talk about racism freely and frankly when there are black people in the room.'

25) 'We do now offer Asian languages in the secondary school — there are lunch-time lessons available for both Urdu and Panjabi speakers.'

26) 'We give Asian languages full equal respect in our secondary school curriculum — Urdu and Bengali are taught up to 'O' level standard.'

27) 'If Muslim, Sikh or Rastafarian parents send children to a Church of England primary school, then they must accept that their children should join in the Christian forms of worship followed in assembly.'

28) 'I can't teach Muslim ways, because I can't sympathise with the way they regard and treat their women.'

29) 'The Afro-Caribbean boys have so much natural ebullience compared to the Asians — that's why they're so difficult.'

30) 'Many parents don't speak English well — but our school notes can be translated for them by their children, or by their friends and neighbours.'

31) 'Our school is very democratic — the Head really does accept a majority vote. And we are continually disappointed that so few parents, especially the Asian parents, actually turn up to PTA meetings.'

32) 'Multiculturalism is all very well in theory — but there's little point in it while só many white parents really don't want their children to be eating Asian food, or doing projects about Africa, or discussing racial discrimination. They tell us that's not what they send their children to school for. It's not our job to try to change their minds; and even if it were, there's simply no way you could persuade a lot of them anyway.'

33) 'So our working party report says some of our schooling is racist: but they would say that, wouldn't they — it's the trendy lefty group who are on it.'

34) 'We don't do multi-cultural education in our school because we have none of them.'

35) 'We've done one thing properly — we used a racism checklist to get rid of all the old-fashioned racist books in school so that teachers can't use them unwittingly, and the children won't be exposed to stereotyped pictures and stories.'

36) 'In our school we respect other cultures by looking at their social and artistic customs, and at their history and religion. You don't need to learn the language.'

37) 'But the Asian parents tell us they don't want their children to be taught any language other than English. So isn't it patronising if we say they should want mother tongue teaching?'

38) 'However desirable mother tongue, bilingual teaching might be, it is ridiculously impractical — we obviously couldn't learn all the 12 or 13 languages spoken by children in this school.'

39) 'But there just aren't enough bilingual Asians qualifying to become nursery and primary school teachers. Muslim girls won't go away to college, for example.'

40) 'I agree with equal rights — our job is simply to help black youngsters achieve better qualifications at school.'

41) 'Racism is purely a class problem — white working class youngsters have all the same problem as black youngsters.'

42) 'Racism is a capitalist tool — only when exploitative economic relations are overthrown will there be no racist oppression of black people.'

43) 'The real problem is the racism in and between the black communities — what do we do about *that*?

44) 'You can't talk to their communities — who represents them? They're either split into too many factions, or they reject their official representatives as 'Uncle Toms', or both.'

45) 'You seem to be saying we must listen ot the blacks and do everything they say.'

46) 'When in Rome, do as the Romans do.' Doesn't this mean that it's *they* who have to adapt?'

47) 'This is just another educational fashion or fad. Like primary school French, it'll have its day and then disappear.'

48) 'Schools can't change society.'

49) 'Racial attitudes come from parents — it would be unfair to set children against their own parents.'

50) 'It's wrong to draw attention to skin colour differences — young children play together person to person, not black and white.'

51) 'All immigrant groups expect a rough time at first — by the third generation they integrate and the problems disappear.'

52) 'Aren't you chasing an impossible dream? Name me one successfully harmonious multi-racial society anywhere in the world.'

53) 'There is a colour problem in this country — that's why I think we must help the blacks to help themselves more.'

54) 'Isn't there a danger of over-emphasising the minorities' cultures?'

55) 'Attacks on Asian British homes are appalling — but wouldn't the police be able to protect them better if they weren't all living together in a community of their own?'

56) 'Most children's image of blacks comes from the media, so whatever we do in school is undermined by the 'problem-oriented' negative image of blacks on TV — that's where the problem lies.'

57) 'We don't need anti-racism training because
  i) we have no problems in our school. Pupils and staff all get on together well.' or ii) we have no/few black children.'

A useful leaflet, *Prejudice Plus Power — Challenging Racist Assumptions,* was issued by the N.U.T.[6] in 1985. In 1984, black teachers in Hounslow were invited to advise the Director of their perceptions of the LEA policies and practices. Their report 41 (see p.69), reveals a wide range of common assumptions made by white teachers in a 'multi-ethnic' area. Both documents amplify the 57 above.

Another method of recognising — in order to counter — the assumptions behind commonly used statements has been used effectively in many schools: in small groups, each person takes several blank cards, writing on each card any remarks they have heard, which they would think of as racially prejudiced. The cards are collected up, shuffled and handed back round the group. Each person selects just two they think worth discussing, then reads them out to the rest of their group, saying why they selected them. Next, each small group decides which two cards they want to discuss — establishing why they are the most important and making notes to report back on their selection in turn to the large group.

The notes would summarise for each statement:
(1) What assumptions does it embody?
(2) Why is it racist?
(3) What should be done, as on-the-spot response?
(4) What should be done in the longer term about their wider social implications and their curriculum/policy implications?
The 57 statements could be used to supplement that method.

Comments on the 57 statements

These are not 'correct answers': they are only some comments that a group leader may find useful to feed into discussion, or into role-play exchanges, to stimulate the group to work out their own reply in each case.

(1) This fails to distinguish between prejudice and racism — a distinction which should have become clear as a result of the earlier meanings exercise. The assumption that because we are not personally colour prejudiced there is no need to study the black experience of discrimination in our society, nor to take any positive anti-racist actions, is in effect to go along with the status quo, to be party to the racial discrimination evidenced in the official figures. To take no action is to collude with institutional racism.

(2) If this means all children are equally *valuable,* then that is fine (though why not say so?). Unfortunately it could mean that a teacher is seeing children at best only for what they have in common, or at worst, according to some self-reflecting 'ideal pupil' model. Either way, it is a failure to respect the blackness of black British children, and to recognise that their self-respect depends on a positive image of their differences. In fact, children are not all the same, nor are they simply individuals to be treated as such. They are individuals with various different group identifications — girl/boy, working class/middle class, black/white. Messages informing these group identifications are being beamed in to each child constantly from 'the hidden curriculum' of their social lives. Because our society has inherited a culture which wrongly associates blackness with inferiority and negative images, schools need positively to support awareness and pride that 'Black is beautiful' — and that black children are part of the Black Consciousness — as much as they are already in effect making white children feel it is good to be white.

(3) Differences, such as they are, are not a problem — they are an enrichment. If any challenges or difficulties arise, a school does not have a 'pupil problem' because 'they are different'; if anything, it has a teacher problem — because of staff inability to adapt their approaches to take account of such differences.

(4) The way we put things demonstrates our attitudes: any remarks starting with 'They' is all too likely to signal a dehumanised stereotype, but this also indicates a negative and dismissive attitude towards other languages than English which children overhearing will pick up as a hidden curriculum message. The fact that some children are learning English as a second language could be put positively: 'we are proud of our potential bi- (or tri-) lingual children, i.e. they know, or are learning several languages.' (see page 45)

61

(5) This is often an evasion of responsibility. Initial apparent 'hardening of attitudes' does not necessarily mean that there will not be some positive long-term effects, even from a direct 'confronting' of racist views and attitudes. But part of 'fear of being offensive', or of producing 'counter-productive' results is often uncertainty, and a need for more information on the subject, and about ways to raise the issues effectively, which could be positively sought. This chapter, and the book as a whole, are aids towards this.

(6) Multicultural education is actually for and about *all* children (as Swann confirms); and 'ethnic minority' does not always equal 'black'.

(7) You cannot draw cross-cultural comparisons from out-of-date assessment tests evolved in one culture, about culturally different groups of children. And why are children born in this country still often referred to as 'immigrant children'? What are the assumptions that lead to black British children more often being described as 'second generation immigrants' than are such 'white' children? (See pp.112-3.)

(8) Why only English? Could this not disadvantage any child with little experience of English rural life, and lose the wealth of different experience children with family backgrounds from overseas might bring?

(9) This could be 'blaming the victim' for our failure to consult ethnic minority parents or community spokespeople about catering methods that will ensure their children can and do eat something nutritious at school dinner.

(10) This could be to see some ethnic minority children in terms of a stereotype of a group too socially disadvantaged to be expected to do well at school. The assumption that some children 'don't get parental support' or 'don't have opportunity to do homework', may be simply wrong (especially given the number of black 'Saturday' or 'supplementary' schools set up and run by Afro-Caribbean parents' groups) or be masking the fact that the syllabus is irrelevant, or that parents have not been invited to discuss the teachers' methods and how they may help.

(11) This would be an excuse for not wanting to bother about bringing our teaching up to date in and for a multi -cultural, -lingual, -racial, and -faith society.

(12) As many schools have found, there is both expertise and willingness among the communities to give free help in doing this (see pages 13-15, 32-34, 131-142 of the BBC book *Multicultural Education,*[1]) — at least as a short-term measure until funding priorities are re-set.

(13) Positive discrimination, in the sense of 'positive action', as opposed to 'reverse discrimination', is designed simply to correct previous imbalance and injustice in equal opportunities. In a status quo of negative discrimination, a period of positive discrimination, at least in the short term, is needed if equality, or no discrimination, is to be established in the long term. Discussion should also turn on: Who decides what qualities and criteria are appropriate for a job? How is it decided what premium in multi-ethnic schools should be placed on 'role models' in the staff, and in all schools on the value of a black perspective? Even if it were true that some black candidates are relatively inexperienced or have some particular difficulties, perhaps in communication skills, then is this not more a reason for arranging for appropriate training to equip candidates to do the job well, rather than an excuse for not appointing them?

(14) Failure to distinguish between 'inadequate English' and 'slow learning'.

(15) Leaving use of resources allocated by L.E.A.s for particular children's special needs to the discretion of each headteacher or head of department can in effect mean that the resources are used towards assimilation (treating black children only in so far as they are the same as white) rather than to support particular learning needs and developments towards a pluralist curriculum.

(16) Wanting to assist the achievement of black ethnic minority communities' equal rights in practice, but not wanting first to find out what such communities feel they need in their own terms, is, however charitable, a form of racist paternalism.

(17) *'They* do not understand how *our* system works'!! Whose system? It is supposed to be a system for everyone and not something only a white person could explain. If anything, should not No.17 say 'We have made a bad job of working out a system'?

(18) The assumption that multicultural education cannot be adopted because we lack the right resources and materials, or the right training, is a failure to see that it is actually only 'good teaching': it is the way available materials are used, and the attitudes brought to this, that are the crucial point. (The community itself can be the text book, and the home and social experience of the class itself the best 'audio visual aids' for understanding that this is a multicultural and multi-racial country in which we live.) It is a dimension in all subjects and teaching practice, not a separate subject.

(19) This might mask agreement only in theory with an LEA or school policy, without commitment to operate the policy in practice. This will be a major danger where teachers have not been personally involved in the research and decisions that go to the making of such policy.

(20) This, of course, is tokenism; paternalism is also revealed in the words 'let them have'. It is vital in discussion of tokenism to distinguish between good and essential 'first steps', as the beginning of a process of change, and 'tokenist moves', seen as sufficient, as an excuse for not moving further in the direction of change.

(21) Since 'black' people know whether they want to be called black or not, then who are the 'People' at the start of the statement? If teachers — or the media — are daily using the word 'people' to mean only white people — or even if they are unintentionally taken to mean only white people — then what is the hidden curriculum message (a) to black people and black pupils, and (b) to white pupils? Clearly, to speak habitually on the assumption that whites are 'just people', while blacks are 'black people', is in effect to imply that black people are 'not proper people'. (See p.220)

(22) As children from Welsh and Irish backgrounds will confirm, such jokes can be hurtful. This also indicates tendencies in the teacher to a lack of sensitivity and to stereotypical thinking, which are inimical to the aim of education. By laughing at, or ignoring, racist jokes, we are supporting our own prejudices as well as legitimating those of others. (It could be useful here to listen again to the Moroccan girl, Souad, in the film *Anglo-Saxon Attitudes*, and refer to points on humour made on pp.204.)

(23) It is unprofessional naivety to ignore the 'political' influences on children outside school — sometimes even directly by NF or BM supporters. 'Politics' are already in the classroom: so it is actually a 'political' act to ignore racism — in effect, to pretend that everything is fine when, as the children themselves have already realised, it is not. Teaching against racism is within the official policy of all the major political parties. It would be useful for discussion here to refer to the Swann Report (pp.334-340) on political education.

(24) The inhibition of some white people if questions of racism arise when there are black people in the room could be a symptom of the dis-ease of white racism — failure open-mindedly and frankly to learn about ourselves in terms of attitudes to blackness of skin and to the injustice of discrimination against black people, with and through the contributions of others.

(25) Perhaps justifiable as a 'first step', but the hidden curriculum message to children not in such classes is that such languages are less 'important' or 'valuable' — a reflection of 'cultural imperialist' assumptions (see page 45) — as confirmed by the Sikh schoolboy, Dilbagh, in the film *Anglo-Saxon Attitudes.*

(26) It would be racist disadvantaging of those with Asian mother tongues, if 'A' levels are only available in European languages.

(27) Would Jewish or Roman Catholic children be required to join in Protestant Christian worship?

(28) This is thinking only about how Muslim men behave: apparently ignoring the culture of the Muslim women. It also fails to distinguish between different forms of Islam in different countries. But the main point is that you do not have to agree personally with something to be able to teach about it, and to teach in a way that is both respectful and 'sympathetic' in reflecting the differences within other cultures (including the fact that there are many forms of women's movements within the Islamic world, as within the heavily male-dominated and patriarchal traditions of both Judaism and Christianity). Important reading here would be *The Hidden Face of Eve — Women in the Arab World* by Nawal El Saadawi[38]; *Beyond the Veil* by Fatima Mernissi.[39] and *Belief in a mixed society,* by Christopher Lamb.[47] (As a Sudanese Muslim woman, Zeinab Badawi makes some comments on pp.137-138.) Comparative cultural studies becomes a disguise for racism if reduced to 'awarding points' to some cultures rather than others, of if 'ugly' practices in so-called 'Third World' countries are not accompanied by appreciation of their 'good' practices and by pointing out some of the 'ugly' practices of the British as well.

(29) Stereotypical assumptions about black children's behaviour can be seen in the view, for example, that they are most likely to be to blame for, or must have been the first to start, any quarrel; or, more subtly, in the belief that some ethnic groups are less deferential because of 'natural ebullience'.

(30) This is a failure to see that when parents speak another language, notes and messages sent out from school only in English could act comparatively to disadvantage them.

(31) So who sets the PTA meeting agenda? Does information to parents indicate that decision-making on how the school is to serve the children's needs depends on their advice and votes? Assumptions about 'majority rule' either in the staffroom or PTA, can sometimes mask the importance of safeguarding the interests and needs of particular ethnic minority children.

(32) It is part of being an anti-racist, multicultural school to involve white parents in developing the school's policies — to be prepared to explain convincingly to parents the school's educational objectives and what their children gain from a multicultural approach in preparation for living in a multiracial society. (See also comment 49: staff could usefully practise such discussion in role-play). And parents — themselves the victims of mis-education in the past — can learn from their children (see comment on p.49 about David Houlton's report in *Multicultural Education*[1] on the primary school exchange shown in *Anglo-Saxon Attitudes).*

(33) Would not the group agree that it is simply prejudice to dismiss *what* a group says because of *who* they are? And that it is racist to seek excuses for continuing with school practices whose racist dimension has been brought to the staff's attention?

(34) On this, see the Swann Report, Chapter 1 and Chapter 6, and comments 6, 46 and 57.

(35) The point is to teach the checklist to the children, and to use the racist books to teach *why* they are racist, since pupils are bound to come across racist books like *Robinson Crusoe* and *Dr. Dolittle* outside school. (See checklists section, pages 162ff).

(36) This is 'cultural imperialism' especially as 'we' expect those with 'other' cultures and languages to learn English as the essence of 'our' culture. (See pp.44-47.)

(37) Not if those parents are not aware of the DES-backed research findings, which demonstrate that standard English is learned better when taught bilingually with the mother tongue (see p.44 and pp.131-139 of *Multicultural Education*[1]).

(38) At least some attempt to learn some of even one language spoken as a mother tongue, other than English, would demonstrate respect for other languages — the vital 'hidden curriculum' message to all the class (see pp.44-46, and (f) on p.48).

(39) All the more reason for teachers to learn at least one of the languages of their school communities!

(40) No — our job is to re-educate attitudes of whites, whether now or for the future running of our institutions. The job is not to 'help blacks to achieve equal opportunities', it is to help whites — or preferably blacks and whites together — to remove the barriers currently operating against equal opportunities.

(41) This demonstrates ignorance of the evidence of the additional disadvantage experienced by black youngsters, on top of disadvantages they may share with their white peers as working class, as women, as handicapped, etc. Some local research into job take-ups is likely to give confirmation of this (see pages 27-28).

(42) While they work for a revolution, which could prove a medium or long-term task, left-wingers (no more than right-wingers) should not ignore injustice to black people in the immediate short-term, within the present economic system. And given the strength of anti-black attitudes within the 'working class' how can left-wingers be sure that forms of racism would not survive any 'anti-capitalist' transformation if efforts against cultural racism have not been part of the effort for political change? Racism cannot be wholly 'reduced' to classism. It appears, for example, that the non-capitalist Soviet Union has continued to oppress its Jewish minorities. As Bhikhu Parekh has commented[18]:

> Some scholars argue that racism is a product of capitalism. The explanation highlights an important point, but remains inadequate. Racism preceded capitalism, as is evident in the history of Greece and Rome, and it survives in Communist societies. Further, racism is not always in the interest of capitalism, as is evident in the opposition expressed to it by some South African and American capitalists; nor do the racially motivated immigration controls in Britain or the massacre of the Jews in Nazi Germany seem to have an over-riding economic logic. An economic explanation cannot account for the different types of racism developed in different capitalist societies.

(43) If racism is prejudice plus power, then can there be racism — as opposed to prejudice — between black minorities in Britain? To the extent there is such prejudice,

then that is for those communities to sort out. White people have no business to criticise it until they have dismantled prejudice and racism against black people. In other words, even if these statements were true, it is not a reason for evading our responsibility to tackle the racism of the white community.

(44) This suggests that talking to black communities can happen only if they arrange themselves in ways and terms convenient to white people. White British society is split into many different ideological, social and interest groupings — why is it assumed that the black British communities should be any less so?

(45) No — white people must be concerned to hold black people's respect, in any disagreement, for the reasons their ideas or proposals are turned down. The aim is for a dialogue of genuine equal respect, i.e. the aim should not be for equality of dialogue or treatment on white terms, but on equal terms. This is an essential condition of any attempt to run the school system in an anti-racist manner, and an essential objective of this chapter and the book as a whole.

(46) What a cultural impoverishment for the Romans! No wonder their Empire fell apart: they were too narrow-minded and culturally imperialist to be able to adapt and change! In any case, how much have Britons abroad 'done as the Romans do'? Why expect others to do what we do not do, or find difficult to do? And, of course, we are not 'them' and 'us', we are all a multicultural and multiracial 'us' in Britain.

(47) Multicultural and indeed anti-racist teaching is not a new method or subject or educational theory. It is an updating, in response to major social transformations, of good teaching practice.

(48) Perhaps not. But this is not a reason to evade our responsibility at least to try and run our school as an anti-racist institution. In other words, whilst schools cannot alone rectify major inequalities in society at large, it is a form of racist attitude to use that fact as an excuse for not examining whether the school is unwittingly reflecting within itself the racist discrimination operating in the wider society, or is failing to do what it can, both as a social organism and through its curriculum, to avoid reinforcing the attitudinal and institutional factors which cause those facts of racial discrimination. And, as a matter of fact, schools *are* partly responsible for the attitudes of the future generation of adults, and so do contribute to what happens in society.

(49) This is why parental involvement is so important. Many are victims of mis-education in an earlier generation. After all, some parents smoke and swear, and some are illiterate. This does not mean that we allow smoking or swearing in school, or that we omit to try to teach their children to read and write. On these aspects, we take trouble to equip ourselves with educational and social reasons for our school practice and policy, so as to be convincing to such parents. (And note top of p.49.)

(50) This displays ignorance about how perceptions and attitudes are formed, by social conditioning, even before school age. (See *Children and Race — 10 years on* by David Milner,[12] and p.24.)

(51) Leaving aside whether it has ever been right for immigrant groups to 'get a rough time', so-called second and third generation black people are different from previous children of immigrant parents, in that their blackness of skin remains an identifying feature whether or not they seek to 'integrate' or 'assimilate' themselves. This is why the evidence in the P.S.I. Report (see pp.26-7) of unchanging 'disadvantage' for black British young people is so significant.

(52) Again, this should not be an excuse for inaction towards a more just multiracial society: indeed, all the more reason for determination.

(53) There is no such thing as a 'colour problem of blacks'; there is a problem of white racism and of dismantling the barriers to equal treatment and to mutual respect.

(54) This is to see multicultural education as only cultural enrichment. In any case, it could be useful to ask — how much would be left in a school, if everything of so-called 'English' culture was taken out? This could put the question of 'over-emphasis' into perspective.

(55) This demonstrates ignorance of the facts of discrimination in housing (see p.28). It may also imply that the trouble arises because the British Asians are there in the first place, rather than because of white racism; or that the trouble is because of 'young hooligans', rather than because of schools' failure effectively to educate against 'mindless prejudice'. Either way is a case of blaming the victim: an evasion of one's own responsibilities.

(56) All very true; but the media are only there because we let them be — so have we complained to the producers and editors in charge? And while doing that, are we teaching youngsters in what ways the media has not yet 'got its act together' in reflecting a multicultured and multiracial society with due sensitivity? (That's what the rest of this book is for.)

(57) (i) Even if it were wholly true, we cannot be blind to reality in society 'outside school'. (ii) Anti-racism is about those white attitudes in both children and adults, that, whether a school has black children or not, lie behind the facts of discrimination. As Peter Newsam commented in the T.E.S. (June '86): 'To dodge the issue of racial injustice in all-white schools may be racist because it disproportionately disadvantages black youths when some of those untaught white youngsters later become employers, football fans, union officials or join the police.'

7. ADDITIONAL TEACHING/TRAINING FILM RESOURCES

At this stage, the rest of the film *Anglo-Saxon Attitudes* can serve as a valuable reinforcement of the thinking and experience developed in the exercises and materials so far. It includes, for example, some glimpses of a subtly racist school design by a group of white teachers in training in Bradford. This is particularly interesting for a group which has just completed the exercise for themselves.

Another sequence illustrates the purple armband exercise at Groby School. This is one of a series of anti-racist experiential teaching exercises for use in secondary schools — especially in all-white areas — which are described by Dr. David Selby (when Head of Humanities at Groby) in *Multicultural Education*.[1]

Other experiential methods at Groby School can be seen in the film *Education versus Prejudice* from the series *Multicultural Education*.[8] Another way of developing the issues among 5th and 6th formers is to use *Why prejudice?*[8] from the BBC series *Scene*.

Moving to the primary level, the BBC documentary *Black*[8] includes extracts from *The Eye of the Storm*[8] which shows experiential techniques being used in an all-white school in Iowa (the brown/blue eyes experiment). Some teachers have felt that the method shown in *The Eye of the Storm* is verging on the unethical — they have not been happy that the end justifies the means. *Black* shows British schoolchildrens' reactions to watching that film; and *A Class Divided*[8] is a remarkable followup film made 20 years later, in which the Iowa pupils, now parents themselves, reflect back on their youthful experience and its value for their education. Even more remarkably, the Iowa teacher is seen using the same exercise effectively with an adult group of prison officers.

A class divided

After a viewing of *A Class Divided* discussion could usefully turn on questions like these:

(1) Why does Jane Elliot emphasise that the blue/brown eyes exercise is something all teachers — even more than pupils — should experience? (And by doing it, not watching others on film.)

(2) What general points does the exercise demonstrate about pupils' self-esteem and learning; and about teacher expectations and learning?

(3) Is it sufficient for such an exercise to be 'good for the children's education' in the sense of learning about prejudice, if this is not supplemented by also equipping the children to be effectively supportive of the political and social changes needed to counter racism (especially supportive of active resistance by black people)?

(4) Why did Jane Elliot first try the exercise on hearing of the death of Martin Luther King?

(5) What did Jane Elliot observe about the assumptions and 'hidden curriculum' effects on the white audience of the way white journalists conducted news interviews at that time?

(6) Is the silence of the brown eyed group in the prison officers training session even more significant than what Jane Elliot says?

(7) Is the inability of the blue eyed group to articulate their sense of resistance, as significant as the silence of the brown eyes group?

(8) Are white teachers who object to the apparent abuse of her teacher-role power (albeit in a form of role play for an educational aim) actually avoiding recognising that the world is not fair to some groups?

(9) What would be alternative methods of teaching this same lesson effectively?

In the widely used ALTARF film *Racism: the Fourth R*[40] black and white pupils, teachers and parents relate their experience of racism and the way schools have either ignored it or fought it. Among examples of anti-racist teaching, we see how young children can identify unreal racist stereotypes perfectly clearly for themselves — and point them out to the teacher. This is a useful model for primary school teachers wondering how they can 'teach the checklist' to young children (see pp.162-164). ALTARF have also published a book, *Challenging Racism* which outlines strategies to implement anti-racist teaching and policies at all age levels. Topics include the Irish in Britain, languages and mother tongue teaching, social studies, police in schools, the position of black teachers and anti-racist policies.

Alec Roberts describes further video resources on pp.179-184 and Laura Sparrow lists practical materials on p.152-153. Resources and materials are comprehensively listed in *Teaching for Equality — Educational resources on race and gender,* from The Runnymede Trust.[9] A selective list of practical resources is given in Appendix 1 of Chris Gaine's *No Problem Here.*[45] Teachers of lower secondary pupils can use the BBC Schools TV series *Getting to grips with racism,* while the *MOSAIC* project offers a new range of training videos.[55]

8. HOW WELL DO WHITE PEOPLE LISTEN TO BLACK PEOPLE?

In a society blighted by white racism, black people cannot enter a dialogue on equal terms with white people about working jointly towards improving 'race relations' unless those white people can show evidence both of their willingness to learn about the mechanisms of black disadvantaging and of their active determination to combat them — to 'dismantle structural racism'. As noted on p.60, in May 1984, the Director of Education in Hounslow wrote to black teachers and their heads:

'As part of our strategy for tackling the educational issues arising in our diverse society, I am now proposing to seek the views of teachers from minority groups on these issues . . . I shall be asking this group of teachers to advise me on their perceptions of both the issues involved and of the Borough's plans and developments to date. I am conscious of the fact that, for whatever reasons, the policy makers in the Education Department are all from the majority culture.' (Report, *The Great Divide,* 1985[41])

How many LEAs, colleges, schools or union local associations have taken such an initiative as part of their identification of needs, or as part of a monitoring exercise on the implementation of policies? Even when this is done, however, little change will result if white advisers, teachers or union representatives hear the black staff colleagues only in defensively 'white' terms.

Hearing on white terms
One way of raising the question of white people's difficulty in 'hearing' black people's experience *on equal terms* is to view the film sequence in *Anglo-Saxon Attitudes* illustrating some debate in the Manchester school working party. A year after their report was completed, the working party are clearly concerned to find that despite three years of research, it is not leading to swift or far-reaching changes in teaching practice throughout the school. They are left with a fear that change is too slow 'to counter the tide of racism in society'. Since, as they say, it took the group three years to 'raise their consciousness', the logic is that working parties may not be the most effective way of seeking multicultural and anti-racist change in a school: it ideally should be organised as a whole staff involvement from the start.

It is interesting that many teacher groups do not see this point at first. In workshops, many have acknowledged that they simply regarded Corinne, the young black teacher, as 'too emotional', 'strident', 'unreasonable in her demands', 'not arguing effectively her own case', even as displaying an 'all too familiar chip on shoulder' attitude. However, other teachers see her as making clear points with commitment, which are (albeit unwittingly) patronisingly and systematically ignored. In discussing their own impressions of the sequence, members of your group might consider:

What points can they remember (a) the black teacher making? (b) the white teachers making? Do they recall more of (b) than (a)? If so, why?

What were Corinne's first words?

What was the response to that, for her, fundamental point?

Why was it completely ignored?

Why do the teachers repeat *three times* the argument 'if it has taken us three years, we can't blame the rest of the staff . . .'?

Do they think she hasn't heard it or understood it?

Does it serve as a way of not responding to the new points she has raised?

Is one effect to make her *seem* 'unreasonable' to many white viewers?

What happens when she starts to explain that 'white liberalism is to her more dangerous than . . .'

Why was she not asked what she meant?

On reflection, would they see her 'manner' (a) partly as a symptom of being placed in a false position as 'token' (b) partly as frustration that there is little acknowledgement to the points she makes (c) partly as expressive of the fact that there is an emotional dimension to the subject of black children's achievements — and she knows, living amongst them, that many black parents expect her to represent their passionate concern about this — but it is a dimension that white people in a 'professional' and institutional setting are embarrassed by, or at any rate, ill-prepared to recognise or acknowledge?

Another video example is outlined in Section 4, pp.210-211.

Cross-cultural communication

As will have become clear, one indication for a school in a 'multi-ethnic' area of its effort to be anti-racist is the extent, both in quantity and quality, of its sharing of power over decision-making with all sections of the community it serves. It has to be admitted that 'cross-cultural' communication difficulties can act as a block or disincentive to the dialogue this implies. White teachers often report that they are uncertain whether they are fully understood by some black parents, or community spokespeople who were born abroad and whose English, though fluent, was not their first language. Training videos made in 1990-92, which analyse unconscious cross-cultural communication difficulties which lead to failure of mutual understanding, in particular when white teachers and college staff meet Asian-born parents, are listed on p.79.

The *Crosstalk* booklet[43] offers information, analysis and training suggestions. It begins:

> The film *Crosstalk* and this booklet examine some of the ways in which people jump to the wrong conclusions and explore how cumulative misunderstandings can create and reinforce negative group stereotypes. In other words, we examine the process whereby differences in ways of speaking can lead to a form of indirect racial discrimination. This process is central to an understanding of why members of minority groups are not treated fairly or adequately, even where there is goodwill on both sides and apparently fair procedures are operating.
>
> There has been little recognition of how cross-cultural communication difficulties can result from culturally specific uses of language and how these difficulties can, wrongly, identify minority ethnic groups as less competent, educated or co-operative in the eyes of the majority group.
>
> The film examines examples of communication difficulties in terms of the analysis of cross-cultural communication on three levels:
>
> (1) *Different cultural assumptions* about the situation and about appropriate behaviour and intentions within it.
>
> (2) *Different ways of structuring information or an argument* in a conversation.
>
> (3) *Different ways of speaking:* the use of a different set of unconscious linguistic conventions (such as tone of voice) to emphasise, to signal connections and logic, and to imply the significance of what is being said in terms of overall meaning and attitudes.

9. SO WHAT SHALL WE DO TO COMBAT RACISM?

The aim of these materials and exercises is not simply to bring unwitting forms of racism into conscious awareness as a self-indulgent exercise for its own sake, nor simply to make more sense of what LEA policies on anti-racist multicultural education and on equal opportunities mean. They can be justified only as a preparation for a better informed and effective active contribution to combating racism. Many schools have found that such action has to be a whole staff commitment, which in turn depends on each individual accepting responsibility for their own learning in this area of professional development; on a common understanding of the words used in policies; and on full involvement of all in the research, consultations, and decision-making on policy and how it is to be implemented. Any emotion engendered (e.g. defensiveness, guilt, depression) needs to be channelled into energy for action towards change in the social conditions affecting black people, and towards reversing any collusion with institutional racism. Such action will need to be collective (creating allies) as well as individual. So how to set about it?

Anti-racist strategies

(a) One might ask the group what areas they feel need practical follow-up; write these on the board, seek a consensus on groupings and priorities of these ideas, and then invite them to make up small groups to determine action. There would then be a report back from each group outlining its plans.

(b) Another way could be to distribute copies of a suitably-spaced page headed 'During the next two weeks; month; term; six months . . .'
At LEA level we should . . .
As a school we should . . .
In my dept. we should . . .
As teachers in class we should . . .
In union or association branches we should . . .
As an individual I shall . . .
Organisation of action could then be built on the result of that questionnaire.

(c) Tables One and Two (pages 75-76) are another useful basis for establishing action that is both committed and realistically effective. They give a checklist of factors which need to be present at school level. The tables are simply a collection of statements of the obvious, made by headteachers; but it can help to codify what we already know into a checklist.

They usefully emphasise the need for a many-pronged, multi-faceted strategy, and can assist with reflection and evaluation (have we done this?) (are we doing that?) as well as with preliminary planning. (The tables were compiled in this form by Robin Richardson, to contribute to in-service activities in Berkshire.) You could (a) ask your group, in 2's or 3's, to work through copies of the tables, sharing anecdotally their own experiences of successes (when the right hand column was operating) and of failures (when the left hand column was operating). Or (b) you could cut copies up, giving small groups the jumbled statements (without the headings) and a large piece of paper with glue. They then arrange or piece together the statements under headings they work out for themselves (e.g. one group might describe them as 'the DO's and DONT's of curriculum development; another group might reveal the interactive, or mutually reinforcing, effects of the factors by arranging them into benign, or vicious, circles). Or (c) you could simply ask groups to improve the lists — what would they add or change?

If this exercise, together with the exercise in designing a subtly racist school/library/union branch, etc. (pp.49-55) have been done thoroughly , the group should be able to draw up plans of action for countering institutional barriers to anti-racist change. Such plans would need to be timetabled, with arrangements built in for regular monitoring whether effective progress is being made. A systematic series of checklists for whole-school policy development and implementation is available in James Lynch's *Prejudice Reduction and the Schools*.[44] The process of establishing a school policy is discussed in Chris Gaine's *No Problem Here*,[45] and in David Houlton's *Your Multicultural School*.[46]

Many groups find it alarmingly easy to invent a subtly racist organisation, and to rationalise its features in 'liberal' terms. Even more disconcerting is the difficulty groups find when they go on to think out in detail how an *anti-racist* organisation would be structured and run. As an indication of one set of starting points, a teacher union group asking itself 'So what do we need to do to operate in an anti-racist way?' might arrive at a checklist for action which included questions such as these, considered at a course for NUT divisional secretaries in 1983:

1) Has your Division/Association discussed and disseminated among members the Union's policy statements on combating racism and on multicultural education?

2) Have the subjects of combating racism, multicultural education, and how to implement Union policies locally, been on the agendas of your meetings?

3) Have you a working group or sub-committee on anti-racism/multicultural education in your Division/Association, reporting to the main Executive Committee?

4) Has your LEA a policy on combating racism, on equal opportunity and on a curriculum appropriate for a multicultural society? Has your Division been involved in consultation with the authority on these issues?

5) If your LEA is entitled to claim Section 11 grant for additional staff for schools with substantial ethnic minority populations, does it do so? Is the authority able to identify the Staff it employs under Section 11 and to describe their duties in meeting 'special needs', as required under the new Section 11 regulations? Are their posts additional to the staffing complement of the school?

6) Do you know whether you have any black/ethnic minority members in your Division/Association? Where are they? What scale posts do they hold? Do these adequately represent their experience/responsibilities?
If you have none, should the reasons for this be examined?

7) Do black/ethnic minority members come to Union meetings and participate in Union affairs? Have efforts been made to involve them? Have they been encouraged to stand for office, or has co-option to committees been considered? Who determines the agenda at meetings, especially what priority is given to black members' concerns? Have you surveyed black members' grievances (particularly, perhaps, on questions of promotion)? Have you reviewed why black members sometimes ask for a separate section within a branch/division?

8) Is your Division/Association aware of the attitudes of ethnic minority/other *parents* towards the education their children receive in schools locally, with particular reference to combating racism, the incidence of racial attacks, education for a multicultural society, language policy, the curriculum, difficulties concerning the British Nationality Act and school trips abroad, passports etc. Do ethnic minority parents attend parents meetings at school? What steps are taken to encourage them to do so?

9) Have you considered joint meetings with the local Community Relations Council/CRE/NAME groups to discuss these issues as they affect teachers, pupils and parents?

10) Have you a *local* NUT policy on racism, equal opportunities and multicultural education? Have you consulted members on issues such as the collection of statistics on

an ethnic basis (pupils and teachers)? Has your Division/Association issued a local policy statement, pamphlet, discussion document or questionnaire for members?

11) Have you sent any representative on NUT anti-racist training courses? Would you like to see the union run more of these — nationally and regionally? Have you any plans to organise local conferences, courses or anti-racist training workshops?

12) Have you invited outside speakers on race/multicultural issues to address meetings/discussions in your Division/Association?

13) Have you ensured that your school reps and members know of the addition to the Professional Conduct Code which makes racist remarks or behaviour an offence under the Code? Would your school representative know what to do if such a case was brought to their attention?
Have you circulated the 'Guidelines on Racist Incidents' leaflet to members?

14) Are you monitoring the effects of your LEA policy?
(a) Does your Division/Association support the provision of ethnic minority language teaching in the curriculum of local schools? Have you urged your LEA to make such provision, with adequate staffing, resources and in-service training for teachers?
(b) Is adequate English as a Second Language teaching provided for those pupils who require it? Are their needs adequately catered for in secondary schools well as at primary level?
(c) Do you call on your LEA to provide in-service courses on education for a multicultural society for its teachers? Or to sponsor teachers financially and with supply cover to attend such courses elsewhere?
(d) Does your LEA have an Adviser for Multicultural Education? If not, have you asked that one should be appointed? And have you checked that the other Advisers have both commitment and competence to help teachers establish an anti-racist approach across their subject area?
(e) How clear are LEA procedures on racist remarks or comments — by teachers and by pupils?

15) Have members been involved in examination of textbooks, curriculum materials and print and broadcasting media for racist stereotypical imagery and thinking?

16) Has your Division/Association kept a record of racial harassment or the spread of racialist literature and propaganda in schools?

17) Can you identify 'institutionalised racism' operating within your Division/Association of the Union? What steps would you take to identify and then deal with it?

18) Has your Division/Association appointed an 'anti-racist' officer to supervise the implementation of the above measures and to assist with local casework?

19) What support would you like from Union headquarters to assist your Division/Association with implementation of Union policy on anti-racism/multicultural education?

THE MANAGEMENT OF CHANGES AND IMPROVEMENTS IN SCHOOLS

Table One: Factors within a school affecting failure and success

A project is likely to fail if:

1) The head and senior staff are perceived to be lukewarm or opposed — their views being evident in what they don't say or do as well as in actual remarks or actions.

2) The staff most involved in the project:
— do not feel that it is their own, but that it has been foisted on them from outside;

— have not been involved in diagnosis, deliberation and decisions from the very earliest stages;

— do not adequately understand the project's aims;
— seldom or never talk about points of disagreement or uncertainty amongst themselves.

3) The staff responsible for the project do not have adequate knowledge, professional skills and personal qualities.

4) The staff most affected feel that their personal and professional identity is threatened, and that the project is merely giving them more work, anxieties and frustrations.

5) Other staff are ignorant, suspicious or anxious about the project, or are critical and hostile. The project is creating or uncovering discord, dispute, disharmony in the staffroom.

6) There are meagre material resources — space and time, and books, audio-visual aids, funds for visits etc.

7) The project has low prestige and status amongst pupils — it is not closely linked to whatever material success which they seek, e.g. in academic progress, tests, exams.

8) The project has low prestige and status amongst teachers — it is not linked closely to whatever material success which they seek, e.g. promotion, extra responsibility, more involvement in decision-making; it may on the contrary actually damage their career prospects.

A project is likely to succeed if:

1) The head and senior staff are clearly seen to be in favour — both formally, e.g. in meetings and statements, and also informally, in everyday conversations.

2) The staff involved in the project:
— feel that the project belongs to themselves, that it is home-grown;

— were involved from the start in diagnosing the problem to be solved, and in pondering and deciding what should be done;

— have an excellent grasp of aims and principles;
— clarify doubts, uncertainties and disagreements in discussion with each other.

3) The staff responsible are very well informed, and have considerable teaching skills and relevant personal qualities.

4) The staff most affected find that their identity and values are enhanced, and that the project is bringing new satisfactions and challenges.

5) Other staff are well-informed about the project, and take a friendly and sympathetic interest. The project is contributing to debate, but also to a sense of unity.

6) There is adequate or generous provision of time and space, and of teaching materials.

7) The project has high status in the eyes of pupils because it is linked to various rewards and achievements which they value, e.g. examination success.

8) The project has high status in the eyes of teachers because involvement in it involves, or may lead to, promotion, better career prospects, more seniority, more participation in decisions.

THE MANAGEMENT OF CHANGES AND IMPROVEMENTS IN SCHOOLS

Table Two: Factors <u>outside</u> a school affecting failure and success

A project is likely to fail if:	A project will probably succeed if:
1) Senior members of the LEA (elected members and education officers) are lukewarm or opposed — their views being implicit in non-decisions and non-statements as well as explicit.	1) Senior members of the LEA are clearly seen to be in favour, e.g. through their presence on platforms and through formal statements and speeches, and also informally.
2) There is little or no inservice training available for staff, and what does exist is (a) demoralising and (b) at inconvenient times.	2) There is intensive inservice training available, which builds teachers' confidence as well as their skills. It is in school-time with supply cover.
3) Professional associations, networks and unions are lukewarm or opposed.	3) Associations, networks and unions, both locally and nationally, are in favour.
4) Parents and other local people are anxious, critical or opposed. There is perhaps adverse publicity in local press, both reflecting their anxiety and arousing it.	4) Parents and others take a well informed interest in the project, and encourage it. There is favourable coverage in local media.
5) There are no extra resources — staffing, money, materials etc.	5) Extra resources are provided.
6) There are no rewards for pupils in taking part in the project — e.g. it does not help them to get better qualifications for a job or further/higher education.	6) For pupils, involvement in the project is linked to, and perhaps contributes to, good qualifications with regard to a job or further/higher education.
7) There are no rewards for teachers for taking part in the project — e.g. regarding career prospects, and recognition; and there is no enhancement in the reputation of the school.	7) Teachers who take part receive recognition, and have improved career prospects; the school as a whole has an improved image and reputation.
8) There are no penalties for not taking part in the project — the school continues to receive pupils, resources, parental support, and teachers continue to receive recognition and promotion.	8) Non-involvement in the project means that the school will lose crucial resources which it needs to remain viable; and individual teachers' careers may be damaged.

Evaluation and Monitoring

It might be worth noting that immediate reactions are not necessarily the best guide in evaluating anti-racism training/discussion sessions. Many participants need some time and personal reflection to 'digest' the ideas. A better test of effectiveness is whether the staff/group wish themselves to reconvene to monitor progress and to share experiences or difficulties, or what they have learned in talking with black and white parents, pupils, and community spokespeople, as a basis for determining their further individual and collective steps of action.

Monitoring would need to cover not just black representation (in the staffroom, in the LEA, in the union or association, in the PTA) and black pupils' achievement, but questions like: Should we find someone like Gus Horsepool to check whether our schooling is impinging on pupils' out-of-school attitudes and behaviour? Do our black pupils now have full confidence, both as individuals and through self help or political organisations, about ways of handling the forms of discrimination they are likely to run into? Do our white pupils, both as individuals and as future employers or future members of unions or political organisations, now have full confidence about tackling the discrimination they are likely to be party to (i.e. are they equipped to identify and expose institutional racism around them)? Have we found effective ways of 'deconstructing', or analysing, the media as a source of pupils' images of a multiracial society? Perhaps the most crucial test, in 'multi-ethnic' areas, must be whether black parents, along with white parents, have confidence in the staff, can sense the effects of transformation of the school into an anti-racist 'organism', and are fully involved in all decision-making.

Afterword

This Section has set out ways to establish the need for identifying and *recognising* forms of racism in the curriculum and in the institutions of education. There are many books and resources on what anti-racist thinking, once established, might mean in terms of classroom practice: as a visit to a local Multicultural Resource Centre, or the catalogue from ACER (see p.40) will show. The exercises and materials described in this Section One could all, of course, be used in class — adapted for age level; Section Four indicates ways of raising issues about the specific role of the television media in racism.

Note: This Section expands upon Chapter 15 of 'Multicultural Education'[1].

References

1. *Multicultural Education,* ed. Twitchin and Demuth, 2nd edition 1985, BBC Publications, P.O. Box 234, London SE1 3TH.
2. *Curriculum Opportunities in a Multicultural Society,* ed. A. Craft and G. Bardell, Harper & Row, 1984.
3. *Agenda for Multicultural Teaching,* A. Craft and G. Klein, Longman Resources Unit, 62 Hallfield Road, Layerthorpe, York YO3 7XQ.
4. *Multicultural Education — towards good practice,* ed. Arora and Duncan, Routledge, 1986.
5. *White awareness: handbook for anti-racist training,* Judy Katz, Univ. of Oklahoma Press, 1979. Available from Housmans Bookshop, 5 Caledonian Road, London N1.

6. *Combating racism in schools* and *Education for Equality* and *Towards a whole school policy (1989)*, NUT, Hamilton House, Mabeldon Place, London WC1H 9BD. *(01-388 6191)*.

7. *Multi-Cultural and Anti-Racist Education Today*, AMMA, 7, Northumberland St, London WC2N 5DA (01-930 6441).

8. Concord Films, 201 Felixstowe Road, Ipswich, Suffolk IP3 9BJ. (0473 76012).

9. The Runnymede Trust, 11, Princelet Street, London E1 6HQ (071 375 1496).

10. World Studies Project, 24 Palace Chambers, 9 Bridge Street, London SW1A 2JT.

11. *The Enemy Within*: tape/film-strip, British Council of Churches 35-41,Lower Marsh, London SE24 7RL; or video from Albany Video Distribution, The Albany, Douglas Way, London SE8 4AG.

12. *Children and Race — Ten Years On*, David Milner, Ward Lock Educational, 1982.

13. *Black and White Britain — the third PSI Survey*, Colin Brown, Heinemann, 1984.

14. Commission for Racial Equality, 10-12 Allington Street, London SW1E 5EH.

15. *The nature of prejudice*, Gordon Allport, Addison-Wesley, 1979.

16. *Five Views of Multi-Racial Britain*, C.R.E., 10-12 Allington Street, London SW1.

17. *Recognising Racism*, a filmstrip/slide and cassette presentation, setting out the concept of institutional racism, by Dr. David Ruddell, available from MDU, The Bordesley Centre, Stratford Road, Birmingham B11 1AR. This is a 'British' version by a Birmingham teacher, of the filmstrip and cassette 'From Racism to Pluralism' by Patricia Bidol, available from Racism/Sexism Resource Center for Educators, 1841 Broadway, New York, NY10023.

18. *The Experience of Black Minorities in Britain*, Bhikhu Parekh, Open University Educational Enterprises, 12 Cofferidge Close, Stony Stratford, Milton Keynes. MK11 1BY.

19. Institute of Race Relations, 2-6 Leeke Street, Kings Cross, London WC1X 9HS.

20. *A History of Africa*, J.D. Fage, Hutchinson, 1978.

21. *How Europe underdeveloped Africa* and *West Africa and the Atlantic Slave Trade*, Walter Rodney, Bogle-L'Ouverture, 1972, 141 Coldershaw Road, London W13.

22. *Black Mother*, Basil Davidson, Penguin, 1980.

23. *Black Settlers in Britain*, Nigel File and Chris Power, Heinemann, 1981.

24. *Black Athena — the Afro-asiatic Roots of Classical Civilisation*, Martin Bernal, 1986, Free Association Books, 26 Freegrove Road, London N7 9RQ.

25. *The African Origin of Civilisation*, Chekh Anta Diop, Lawrence Hill & Co., obtainable from Raddle Bookshop, 70 Berners Street, Leicester.

26. *History of Black Revolt*, C.L.R. James, Race Today Publications, 165 Railton Road, London SE24 OLU.

27. *Slaves who abolished slavery: Vol.1 Blacks in Bondage (1980); Vol.2 Blacks in Rebellion (1985)*, Richard Hart, Institute of Social and Economic Research, University of the West Indies, Kingston 7, Jamaica.

28. *The African Heritage*, Gumbo, Sibanda, Moyana; Z.E.B., P.O. Box BW-350, Harare, Zimbabwe.

29. Available from Centre for Multicultural Education, Institute of Education, 20 Bedford Way, London WC1H OAL.

30. *Minorities*, David Hicks, Heinemann.

31. *World Studies 8-13*, Oliver and Boyd.

32. *Censoring Reality*, Beverley Naidoo, British Defence and Aid Fund for Southern Africa (BDAFSA), Unit 22, The Ivories, Northampton St., London N1.

33. *Africa — History and Achievement*, Basil Davidson, Commonwealth Institute, Kensington High Street, London W8 6NQ.

34. *The three dimensions of public choice* from *Shadow Work*, Ivan Illich, Marion Boyars, 1980.

35. Available from Information on Ireland, Box 189, 32 Ivor Place, London NW1 6DA.

36. *New Statesman and Society*, 38, Kingsland Rd., London E2 8DQ.

37. *The Realization of Anti-racist Teaching*, Godfrey Brandt, Falmer Press, 1986.

38. *The Hidden Face of Eve,* Nawal El Saadawi, 1980; Zed Books, 57 Caledonian Road, London N1 9BU.
39. *Beyond the Veil,* Fatima Mernissi, Al Saqi Books, 26 Westbourne Grove, London W2.
40. *Racism the 4th R:* a BBC 'Open Door' programme available as video from ALTARF, 38 Mount Pleasant, London WC1X OAP.
41. *The Great Divide: unconscious or deliberate?* Minority teachers advisory group Report, Education Dept., London Borough of Hounslow, Lampton Road, Hounslow, Middlesex.
42. Details from John Twitchin, 071-435 2784.
43. *Crosstalk* booklet: £5 from BSS, P.O. Box 7, London W3 6XJ.
44. *Prejudice Reduction and the Schools,* James Lynch, Cassell Educational, 1987.
45. *No problem here,* Chris Gaine, Hutchinson Educational, 1987.
46. *Your Multicultural School,* David Houlton, New Education Press, 1987.
47. *Belief in a mixed society,* Christopher Lamb, Lion Paperback, 1985.
48. *Blacks in Science,* ed. Ivan van Sertima, Transaction Books, 1988.
49. *Staying Power — the history of Black People in Britain,* Peter Fryer, Pluto Press, 1984.
50. *Black People in the British Empire: an introduction,* Peter Fryer, Pluto Press, 1988.
51. Jagdish Gundara on Black Resistance in *Race, Migration and Schooling,* ed. John Tierney, Holt Education, 1982.
52. *In resistance,* ed Gary Okihiro, University of Massachusetts Press, 1986.
53. *Africa's Peoples in the Past,* John Osogo and Atieno Odlianbo (junior school history textbook for Kenya), Longman Kenya Ltd., 1978.
54. *Not in our genes,* Rose, Lewonkin, and Kamin, Pelican Books, 1986.
55. For information on repeats for off-air recording, and on current output and training notes relating to anti-racism, write to BBC Education, London W12 7TS. In particular the *MOSAIC* series, begun in 1989, includes a wide range of training videos about discrimination and about the historical roots of white attitudes towards black people — as well as *The Black and White Media Show* — part 3. (1990). For information by phone, call 081-746 1111.
56. *White over Black: American attitudes toward the negro,* Winthrop Jordan, Pelican, 1969.
57. *Civil Rights and the American Negro — a documentary history,* ed. Blanstein and Zangrando, Simon and Schuster, NY, 1969.
58. *The African Trilogy,* China Achebe, Picador, 1988.
Beloved, Toni Morrison, Chatto and Windus, 1987.
Creation, Gore Vidal, Grafton Books, 1982.

MOSAIC teaching/training videos available with notes from BBC Education (081-746 1111)
Equal opportunities at work: Race
Recognising racial discrimination at work
Equal before the Law?
Evidence Unseen

Training Videos from BBC Enterprises on cross-cultural communication (Ring 081-576 2361 for free briefing paper)
Crosstalk
Crosstalk at Work (Performance Appraising across cultures)
Recruitment Interviewing across cultures
Counselling and Advice across cultures

Training manuals for the above available separately from B.S.S., P.O. Box 7, London W3 6XJ. 081-992 5522.

For further information about training on these themes, contact John Twitchin, 071-435 2784.

Perspectives on 'cultural racism' and the media

Black Mythologies: The Representation of Black People on British Television

by Angela Barry

Preface

When I first began my dissertation on black images in British television early in 1986, (from which this chapter has been extracted) I realised that I could trace my involvement with the subject back to a precise moment — twenty years before. As a teenager recently árrived from Bermuda, I had sat watching *Till Death Us Do Part* and heard Alf Garnett calling people like me 'wogs' and 'coons'. I had shed a few silent tears. It was not that I was naive in matters of racism. At that moment, Bermuda was in the painful process of desegregation and on our T.V. screens the faces of Civil Rights marchers were just beginning to replace those of the bug-eyed black man-servant and the fat black mammy. But Alf Garnett had struck a nerve untouched by the others. Perhaps it was because the American icons were familiar to me; perhaps it was because I was unused to British social realism. Perhaps I had not expected 'this sort of thing' in the Mother Country. For whatever reason, my first encounter with Alf Garnett stayed with me, but tucked well away because I could not have shared my experience of hurt with my school-mates. After all, *Till Death Us Do Part* was universally acclaimed as one of the funniest things on television.

Years later, I found myself in a London classroom listening in (as teachers do) on a conversation of some of my pupils. These pupils were mainly, but not exclusively, black, and all dwellers of the inner city. They were discussing the previous evening's edition of *Black on Black*. Their discourse was eclectic, their level of analysis somewhat superficial, but what was striking was the confidence with which the black pupils articulated their views. It occurred to me how many changes had taken place, not only within television, but within British society itself.

It was not until I had been awarded a year's secondment, that I had enough time quietly to reflect on the factors and events which separated my early experience from that of my pupils. These reflections eventually took shape and became 'Black Mythologies'. Now that I am back in the classroom once more, it is clear to me that there is no room for complacency. Although some advances have been made, the battle against racism — on television, in the classroom and beyond — is far from being won.

Note that I have chosen to define 'black' not as 'all who are not white', but as Afro-Caribbean. This is not to say that parallel issues of representation do not affect people from the Indian subcontinent.

Introduction

The black presence on British television is as old as British television itself. The 1936 issue of the Radio Times heralds the inauguration of the new television service and the very first programme on the bill is a variety show featuring the 'coloured pair' known as 'Buck and Bubbles', described as 'versatile comedians who dance, play the piano, sing and cross chat'. Against this duo, let us juxtapose a contemporary black television personality. My choice here is Darcus Howe, who, despite earlier press branding as a militant, was to be found in the early summer of 1986 not only presenting and co-editing Channel Four's current affairs programme *Bandung File* but also acting as anchor-man to BBC2's *Caribbean Nights*, a celebration of Caribbean culture, which ran for seven consecutive nights. What could possibly have happened in the intervening years to supplant fleet-footed 'coloured' comedians with black poets discussing black poetry? The whole world of change implicit in the 1936 and 1986 black personas is the subject of this essay. I intend to show that the changes occurred painfully, unevenly, often reluctantly; that the changes came about through pressures from outside the medium as well as within it; and that there are many changes yet to be made. The 'evidence' is drawn from the handbooks of BBC and ITV; though not an adequate susbstitute for viewing of programmes they are indices of the two organisations in terms of their priorities and preoccupations.

My title takes its inspiration from Roland Barthes' *Mythologies*. By analysing a wide range of elements of mass culture, Barthes sought to put into sharp focus those things determined by History which were in fact masquerading as manifestations of Nature. In his own words, 'I resented seeing Nature and History confused at every turn, and wanted to track down, in the decorative display of *what-goes-without-saying,* the ideological abuse which, in my view, is hidden there.'[1]

In the series of short essays which form the first part of the book, his conception of myth was the traditional one, incorporating Levi-Strauss's idea of myth as a means of classifying and organising reality. In the long essay at the end of the book, entitled 'Myth Today', he attempted to redefine the term. Barthes, the linguist and sociologist, saw myth as a means of communication, but deprived of its political and historical context — 'depoliticised speech'. The nature of the relationship between meaning and form was peculiarly kinetic, a kind of cat-and-mouse game with the form distancing itself from aspects of the meaning; appearing innocent and natural, while at the same time distorting signification and shedding context. For the myth consumer, myth had the comforting feel of reality. It seemed to be a system of facts when, as a semiological system, it was only a system of values. Barthes argued that myth operated as the faithful servant of a given society by transforming History into Nature, by bridging the gap between semiology and ideology. When looking at the images of black people on British television, I will use Barthes' definition of myth.

A second major philosophical idea threads through this essay, that of ideological hegemony as articulated by Antonio Gramsci. When Barthes saw myth as being flooded through with ideological information, Gramsci envisaged a similar process on a grander scale. He maintained that in Western society the dominant class ensured that their ideology not only seeped down to the masses but also won them over and gave at least the appearance of representing them. Here Gramsci made a significant departure from other Marxist philosophers and their vision of the two-tiered system of economic base and superstructure which revolution would overturn. For Gramsci, a transformation of society would be much more complex than this because an 'ensemble of relations' existed — between politics, the law, religion, culture — which enabled a certain world view to be disseminated and made acceptable to a broad spectrum within that society, even if it was not in their interest. Hegemony worked, in the words of Carl Boggs, 'to induce the oppressed to accept or 'consent' to their own exploitation and daily misery.'[2] Echoing a point made by Barthes, the power of ideological hegemony lay in its ability to give value-ridden concepts the feeling of being 'natural' or 'common sense'. History has many examples which show that physical coercion alone cannot maintain indefinite control. But a system which combined physical coercion (or the threat of it) with a sense of 'belonging' to that system — this was infinitely more subtle, complex and difficult to replace. The media, and television in particular, have a vital role to play in the dialectic between force and persuasion and in this essay, I will attempt to show that television was an excellent indicator of the consensus view of black people; that it exerted pressure on and was responsive to that 'ensemble of relations' described by Gramsci.

Yesterday's Myths (1953-1971)

A wide-angled shot shows the crowded gangplank connecting the S.S. Ascania to the firm Portsmouth dock. The camera zooms in for a close-up shot of the faces of the new arrivals. Although they come from all over the Caribbean, the narrator's voice identifies them as 'Jamaicans'. A slightly military air plays as the camera lingers over the black faces — clean-shaven, well-groomed, smiling — while the Received Pronounciation of the narrator tells the viewer that these 'Jamaicans' have come 'with good intentions to serve the Mother Country'.

The year was 1953 and the importance of this account of the landing of 'Our Commonwealth friends' was two-fold. To begin with, the early Fifties witnessed an opening up of television to a mass audience, with the post-war resurrection and expansion of BBC television and the brash entrance of its rival ITV. It was probably clear even then that the new supremo of mass entertainment and information was going to be television, with its singular ability to bring new worlds of image and sound within the intimacy of the living room. There must have been many for whom the sight of those 'Jamaicans' arriving in Britain was the nearest that they had ever come to a real black person. The text of the BBC newsreel was clear enough. Those were undoubtedly strangers — their black skins bore eloquent witness to that — but there was a connection and that connection was the relationship between the Mother Country and the Commonwealth.

This was the period during which notions of Empire were giving way to notions of Commonwealth. Britannia might not rule the waves as before but she still maintained the pivotal position in relations between its territories. Informing all of this was a sense of family, with Britain the benevolent parent-figure. This attitude was reflected in both Parliamentary parties. Mr. Henry Hopkinson, on the traditional Right of the Tory Party, put it thus: 'We still take pride in the fact that a man can say 'Civis Britannicus Sum' whatever his colour may be and we may take pride in the fact that he wants and can come to the Mother Country.'[3] These sentiments were later echoed by Labour's Hugh Gaitskell, along with what appears to be mild surprise at the realization that the ideology of Empire also moved powerfully within those benefitting least from it. 'We are responsible for them and they think of themselves, as anybody who has been there knows, as British people. Oh yes they do. It is rather moving. I found when I was there that they look on us as the Mother Country in a very real sense. . .'.[3] So when British viewers saw the smiling 'Jamaicans' on their screens, the potential menace of their 'otherness' was overridden by the comforting aura of Commonwealth with its roots in the glorious imperial past. Amidst the austere realities of post-war Britain, the dream of Commonwealth enabled Britain to lay legitimate hold onto a somewhat weary sense of national greatness.

Greatness was not an easily-found commodity in the Fifties. Anti-climax hung heavily in the air. Having put 'Gerry' to rout, Britain was now faced with building up the national economy. The Conservative government looked to its colonies for manpower to help with the service industries of public health and transport. They answered the call and by 1955, thirteen ships were arriving full of people hopeful of work. It was during this decade also that television learned its craft and became a credible arm of mass communications.

Large-scale black immigration coincided historically with the post-war expansion of television. So television can be seen as a barometer of the opinions of the 'host' population vis-a-vis the black communities. However the barometer comparison is inadequate as it assumes a relationship whereby television responds neutrally to social and political pressures of the outside world, whereas television, as well as responding to stimuli, is actively engaged in constructing reality with images taken — sometimes refined, sometimes exaggerated — from the prevailing, consensual world view.

The Fifties, then, saw television and Twentieth-century black settlement of Britain still at an early developmental stage. Both were sorting themselves out. 'Race' had not yet substantially impinged upon the national consciousness. After the initial enthusiastic welcome for 'our Commonwealth friends', few television programmes alluded to anything whatsoever to do with the growing numbers of blacks in Britain. Black issues were articulated with nothing but a deafening silence. But there is an interesting rider to this.

At this time, a programme started whose success carried it almost into the 1980's and earned it the 1961 Montreux Golden Rose Award. It was called the *Black and White Minstrels Show* and what a fascinating programme it was! An evolution from the radio tradition of 'Swannee River' type minstrel shows, its success seemed asured from the start, with its popular melodies and slick choreography.

The visual text was devastatingly simple — a Deep South fantasy transplanted in Britain, with beautiful pale Southern belles being courted by black-faced crooning beaux, possible in the fantasy because of the knowledge that behind the black paint, the man touching the white woman was as white as she. Here we have the spectacle of the white man pretending to be black, rather like Marie Antoinette playing at being a peasant girl in the gardens at Versailles. This nostalgic evocation of the Old South — with its happy slaves who knew their place — was a true American icon, which struck a chord with the British people too. Perhaps it was a hankering after earlier, trouble-free times. Were there imperial resonances in the Dixie melodies? Whatever the reason, the fact of the success of this pure caricature of blackness is indisputable as is the fact that this was the only consistent image of blacks on television from the late Fifties — until Nottingham and Notting Hill exploded.

The 'race riots' in Nottingham and Notting Hill in the summer of 1958 put the official goodwill between Britain and its new black immigrants under severe strain. By the next summer, anti-black disturbances flared up in Notting Hill again and a black carpenter Kelso Cochrane was murdered in the street. The main casualty was the reputation of the new black immigrants. Let us be clear about this — the black community suffered the race attacks; Teddy Boys 'bashed' black workers for sport but by some tortuous logic, the blacks themselves were to blame. In the hands of Fleet Street and the television newsrooms, these events became the hottest news around. The blandly smiling face of the new immigrant gained definition, acquired real features which clearly spelled out menace. The reassuring penumbra of 'Commonwealth' evaporated, leaving the stark 'otherness' of the black intruder. The potent myth of the black as trouble-maker was born.

In *Mythologies,* Barthes used as a recurring illustration the photograph of the Negro saluting the French flag. On the surface, the black soldier appeared to be paying homage to 'La France Metropolitaine' — innocently, patriotically — one individual, who happened to be black, showing his love for his country. But in the very innocence of the image, Barthes wrote, 'it becomes the accomplice of a concept which comes to it fully armed, French imperiality.'[1] The image or myth of the black person as trouble-maker was in contrast to this. The awe-struck African soldier was replaced with the image of he who brings leprosy into our country; he who frightens our women; he who, by his very presence, causes riots to break out around him. But like Barthes' soldier, that image was used as a justification for something else — in the case of the trouble-maker, he was made an accomplice of the measures used to contain and restrict black people.

In 1962, the Conservative Government passed the first of the Commonwealth Immigration Bills, placing restrictions for the first time on the right of entry of people from the Commonwealth. The 'theory of numbers' had gained credibility and was put into practice. 'Commonwealth' was beginning to have a sinister alter ego. As the country prepared for the General Election in 1964, in at least one constituency 'race' was high on the agenda. Peter Griffiths and Conservative Party in Smethwick fought an overtly racist campaign and strode into Parliament with the slogan, 'If you want a nigger for your neighbour, vote Labour.' What was television doing with all this? Certainly the corridors of power were ringing with the debate about 'coloured immigration' and in towns and cities all over the country, the real-life dramas of settlement were being lived out by both black and white communities. Here is where the mirror theory of television breaks down because nowhere in the television agendas of the early Sixties (as evidenced in the handbooks) was this reflected. Television stepped back from the fray and although the Notting Hill effect echoed quietly into the mid-Sixties, scheduled programming as a whole did little to reinforce the trouble-maker image.

Instead a second myth took root. The seed did not actually have to be planted — it was already there, dormant. So it was that the Sixties witnessed the flowering of the myth of the black as entertainer. Alongside the mimesis of the *Black and White Minstrels Show* came a small army of real black artists, marching regularly across the television screens, proving for all time their special facility for song, their special connection with rhythm and dance. Different musical traditions were on offer. Black American music featured prominently, from Twisting Chubby Checker, to Duke Ellington and opera singer Mattiwilda Dobbs. The Caribbean was also represented by singers like Harry Belafonte and, interestingly, calypsonian Cy Grant on his own slot on the *Tonight* programme, making authentic use of calypso as a vehicle for social comment. The Negro Dance Theatre of Rio de Janeiro appeared on the BBC in 1961 as did, a few days later, Sierra Leone's National Dancers. Then there was home-grown Shirley Bassey, the girl from Tiger Bay, winner of a devoted television audience from as early as 1966. The black diaspora achieved a reasonable degree of visibility during this period and without a doubt the appeal of these singers and dancers was wide-ranging.

I would be the last person to challenge the centrality of music and dance in black cultures across the world. However the cumulative effect of those singers and dancers, at a time when black people had no other voice, was to decontextualise them, stripping them down to the bare bones of the song and the dance. So that even Paul Robeson who used song to celebrate black values as well as to expose racist white America, even he, under the persuasive imagery of the black entertainer, would be remembered as 'that marvellous singer'. He was indeed a marvellous singer but he was also a lawyer and much more. It is arguable that the mythology of the black entertainer existed before the introduction of television, but certainly by the mid-Sixties the image was fixed set and still in the Eighties maintains a steady grip on general perception of what black people are.

One feature of Barthes' concept of myth was that it was hermetically sealed so that myths about the same thing but of very different natures could coexist quite comfortably. This was the case in the mid-Sixties when the black entertainer evolved coterminously with the revitalised trouble-maker myth. The symbols embodied in these two myths were diametrically opposed — between the pleasure-giving entertainer and hell-raising trouble-maker, there was a world of difference. But it is in the nature of television that these two conflicting images could live naturally together with the minimum of difficulty. One reason for this was that the hell-raiser in question was American. The 1965 BBC Handbook had a photograph of James Farmer, head of CORE (esteemed at the time to be at the radical end of the civil rights movement) being interviewed on the *Encounter* programme. In 1966, Rediffusion did a documentary called *Marked for failure,* a study of the 'the Negroes of Harlem'. In that same year, according to the BBC Handbook, the Watts riots 'produced some of the most spectacular action film coverage in recent years'. Despite the fact that immigration and 'race' carried on being important issues in Parliament, the media sought to keep British problems at arm's length. Racial strife was an American phenomenon and it seemed inconceivable that British cities could ever ring to the chant, 'Burn, Baby, burn'.

While all of this defining of images was going on, the black people themselves were involved in the scramble for decent jobs and housing. The *Age of Aquarius* was simply a song, not a social reality. A paramount difficulty was making sense of the now Labour government's contradictory attitude towards them. Labour's reversal of policy on Immigration, in their White Paper of 1965, was seen as the first betrayal. This was swiftly followed by the counterbalance of the Race Relations Bill which, though lacking any political muscle, was supposed to show that the legal system had at last recognised the existence of racial discrimination. Three years later the pendulum swung again with the 1968 Commonwealth Immigrants Bill which, with its 'grandfather' clause, dropped all pretence of being non-racial. Black people's feeling of rejection was exacerbated by the appearance at about this time of *Till Death Us Do Part.* Johnny Speight devised this comedy to highlight and ridicule the bigotry expressed in Alf Garnett's views. Unfortunately, the overall effect of the programme was the opposite. The public airing of Alf Garnett's prejudices gave them a real legitimacy. And the black viewers heard themselves being called 'wog' and 'coon', without even having a black character in the programme to make them something other than an invisible threat, skulking beyond the television screen.

To complete the picture of the Sixties, overlapping with the opposing figures of the happy-go-lucky entertainer and the rioting malefactor there was a third image — the starving Biafran child. By the outbreak of the Biafran war in 1967, Europe was starting to get over the worst traumas of African decolonisation. France's Algerian adventure had come to a bloody close and country after country in Anglophone Africa was hoisting its new national flag. Here in Britain, a deep sense of ambivalence remained and television coverage of African affairs, though limited, demonstrated this. The erstwhile terrorist and Mau-Mau leader, Jomo Kenyatta, appeared on *Face to Face* in 1962, now in the mantle of reconciler and statesman. In 1965, Independent Television told the story of the slave trade, concentrating on the fight for abolition, rather than the consequences for Africa. In 1967, the year when Biafra seceded from Nigeria, ATV presented a programme called *Lost Shangri-La,* a look at contemporary problems in Africa. The choice of title *Lost Shangri-La* revealed the notion of a Golden Age which somehow had gone sour. The Biafran war and its suffering humanity were proof of just how sour things had gone.

Lying at the heart of *Lost Shangri-la* and subsequent coverage of the Biafran war was a sentiment referred to earlier by Hugh Gaitskell who began by saying, 'We are responsible for them . . .'. With Independence, of course, 'we' were no longer responsible for 'them' and the result was confusion, war and death, including the painful deaths of innocent children. Most viewers who watched reports of the war, could not help but be moved and wanted to know who was responsible. Analysis of events was done in terms of 'tribes' — Hausa and Yoruba against Ibo — or personalities — Gowon against Ojukwu. In the true style of Barthes' myth, the carpet of history was pulled from beneath the Biafra war. Some important issues were 'neglected' — the fact that, in the British interest, three nations had been pushed together and expected miraculously to become one; the fact that during the colonial period Britain had consistently played one ethnic group off against the other; that Britain had actively taken sides in the Biafran war itself. With the image of the stick-limbed child, all these considerations faded away. Even when the war was over and, contrary to all expectation, the victorious Federal government adopted a conciliatory position and did not indulge in an orgy of blood-letting, the memory that imposed itself, large and uncompromising, was that of the starving child, victim of circumstance, locked into an eternal cycle of dependency. The third great myth — that of black dependency — was thus fixed into the consciousness of the nation.

The implications of this myth must be looked at carefully. First, the child is, by definition, dependent — s/he depends for life itself on the responsible, caring adult world. The child dying of hunger is in a further stage of dependency, but inherent in this stage is the feeling that the adult world has not honoured its side of the contract. The symbolism works on a number of levels. The starving child can be seen as Africa itself, unable to get beyond childhood, looking to Europe for its salvation, even though Independence has severed the umbilical cord. From another angle, the starving child can be seen as the populations of Africa, suffering from the mismanagement and indifference of African leaders who are willing to allow things such as starvation to happen. Whichever way you look at it, the dependency myth neutralises the political debate as far as the West is concerned, and makes all intervention and aid appear to be acts of disinterested generosity. It also strips a continent of its dignity. I am not denying that many lives were lost in Biafra and more recently in Ethiopia, nor that Africa can shrug off all responsibility for its post-colonial difficulties. What I am saying however is that the dependency myth, with its roots in Britain's imperial past, has proved so sturdy, so resilient and so adaptable, that the residual impression is that the story of the starving child is Africa's one and only story. Television has served as an efficient agent of this myth which has not only interpreted Africa thus but also has had the ripple effect of representing black people in general in this way — child-like, incompetent, in need of help.

By the end of the Sixties, then, all three myths were firmly in place. The 1970 BBC Handbook singled out Olivier Todd's 'notable reports' from Biafra for special praise, while London Weekend Television did a programme about West Indians in Brixton called *Them and us* — with the inevitable troupe of black entertainers. The fact that one myth tended to be wholly separate from the other did not seem to matter and no one questioned the faintly bizarre spectre of a singing, dancing, rioting victim of malnutrition. All three thrived naturally·and simultaneously on the television screens. This was to be the pattern of the Seventies — but with a difference.

1970 was an election year, and whereas in 1964 Peter Griffiths had been something of an embarrassment to the Conservative party, this time 'race' was being talked about at the very summit of the party. The discourse was visionary and inflammatory and its high priest was Enoch Powell. He predicted that rivers of blood' would flow through England's green and pleasant land unless the 'coloured immigrants' were not only denied entry but also sent back home. Party leader Edward Heath had difficulty in controlling the haughtily intellectual Powell, especially as he seemed to have tapped into a huge groundswell of support within the country. Pundits have argued that Heath would not have won the election without Powell — there are arguments to be made on both sides. But in that same year, the Conservative party adopted an official policy of voluntary repatriation. The following year, the 1971 Immigration Act became law, further institutionalising the divide between those with 'patrial' connections with Britain and the rest — the black and brown 'non-patrials'. Things were looking grim for Britain's black communities.

Curiously, there was some fall-out from the entrenchment of this racist legislation which had a beneficial effect on these communities. Non-Powellite Tories again and again stressed how the new racist law would foster good race relations and be to the advantage of the black people already here. This was a totally unproven argument and was simply a forlorn attempt to humanize the Immigration Act. But it was an argument which, since Labour's two Race Relations Bills of the Sixties, was being used more and more. Powell had, by default, made people talk about the rights of Britain's black community. Britain was ceasing to be a land with some 'coloured immigrants' and struggling towards accepting itself as a multi-racial society. Television in the Seventies proved to be an important battle-field in that struggle.

Realigning the Myths (1971-1986)
I have made the point that the power of the images supporting the three myths about black people lay in the fact that they appeared 'natural' when in fact television was in the business of reinterpretation rather than reflection. I now move on to consider what place the three myths occupy within the concept of ideological hegemony which is, according to Gramsci, the dominant class's way of persuading the body politic to accept its ideology. There are two aspects of this process: firstly, the way in which the medium of television belongs to the 'ensemble of relations' which operates to the advantage of the state; and secondly, the way in which that 'ensemble of relations' can change, given the right pressure.

Whereas American television is constructed around market-forces and French television is clearly state-controlled, British television is founded on the laudable but somewhat nebulous notion of public service and acting in the public interest. The question might be asked — which public and whose interest? Clues are to be found within the structures of the organisations themselves and the typology of media people being 'the brightest and the best'. The fact that the controlling voices of the television organisations tend to come from the same class as the higher echelons of industry, high culture and politics has meant that, for the most part, the state has not had to exert pressure on the organisations and has simply left them to practise their own self-censorship.

The three myths about black people were only possible because television used ideological material from the external world to construct them. The reporter from a Biafran feeding-station was possibly not aware of his perpetuation of the dependency myth — his overt intention was probably humanitarian. But the effect was to reinforce the myth. The images ceased to be innocent and became, in Len Masterman's words, 'weapons used in the service of particular interests.[4] (It is interesting to see that Margaret Thatcher has been summoning the dependency myth — the starving child — as her moral justification for not applying sanctions against South Africa). The base line of all three myths was Britain's colonial experience in which black and brown peoples were dehumanized and made one-dimensional. The white working class 'consented' to these myths because being able to feel superior to someone else made their own exploitation easier to bear. So the only ones who did not 'consent' to those images were the black people themselves who were in effect excluded from the national experience. They were mute and could only watch the insidious images of themselves in silence. But change was on its way — very slowly at first but nevertheless irrevocably.

The early Seventies were marked by opposing propositions about black people. At one end of the spectrum there was the Tory Right with their spokesman Enoch Powell who, even after the 1971 Act, was still talking about immigration and repatriation. He and his followers were given an unexpected boost in 1972 with the expulsion from Uganda of thousands of Asian British passport-holders by Idi Amin. The repatriation theme took on another dimension during that same year when the streets of the nation's cities suddenly began to be plagued by a new peril — mugging. The first 'moral panic' of the Seventies was under way.

In *Folk Devils and Moral Panics,* Stanley Cohen analysed the moral panic arising from the Mods and Rockers of the late Fifties and early Sixties. He also used their model as the basis for a more generalised theory of manufactured public outrages or moral panics which he felt were inevitable 'because our society as presently structured will continue to generate problems for some of its members — like working class adolescents — and then condemn whatever solution these groups find.'[5] A decade after the nation had been treated to the spectacle of white working-class youth challenging social norms, the early Seventies gave rise to a new species of folk devil. The mugger was by definition black and amoral; in political terms he was a three-headed monster which conveniently fused the triple concerns of race, crime and youth. He was also the living vindication of the Powellite stand on immigration. The previous generation of immigrants had brought leprosy and alien cultures; their children now brought violence and fear. Stuart Hall has written in *Racism and Reaction*[6] how in general an ideology of indigenous British racism has often assumed the forms of a 'moral panic'. Here I am concerned with the media's role in particular.

Cohen insisted on the role of the media in the generation of the moral panic over the Mods and the Rockers, as 'an agent of moral indignation' and 'an important carrier and producer of moral panic'.[5] In their reporting and analysis of moral panic, he found the media guilty of using provocative and self-fulfilling techniques. 'The cumulative effect of such reports was to establish predictions whose truth was guaranteed by the way in which the event, non-event or pseudo-event it referred to was reported'. One much used method was 'over-reporting', where the seriousness of events was grossly exaggerated mainly through a mode of discourse relying heavily on 'melodramatic vocabulary and the deliberate heightening of those elements in the story considered as news'. A second media technique was 'symbolisation' with its use of 'dramatised and ritualistic interviews with 'representative members' of either group'. These techniques were particularly effective in television coverage where they could be combined with visual experience which far outstripped the actual experience in terms of impact. Reality became a pale imitation of the television version of events.

Television's handling of the mugging moral panic of 1972-73 followed the above pattern very closely. Although the corporations' handbooks give no indication that this panic existed outside the confines of 'news' (there is no mention of any documentaries on this subject at the time) I cannot overstress the power of news reporting, with its emphasis on eye-witness accounts and 'that-which-is-real'. Mugging, with its inherent association with black youth, fitted in neatly with the trouble-maker myth, literally in a parent-child relationship. The televiewer's perception of the black person as trouble-maker — whether as an unwelcome rival for jobs and housing or now as a perpetrator of street crime — was reinforced.

However, there was also pressure from the other end of the spectrum. I have referred to the movement which resisted unambiguous Powellite racism, mainly because it chafed against the concept of Britain as a tolerant society. This period saw the beginning of some initiatives which took into account the needs of the black communities and included the first tentative moves towards multi-cultural education in schools. In television there was a minor break-through of sorts. *Love Thy Neighbour* appeared on ITV in 1972. In the sense that it showed black people doing something other than singing, thieving or starving, it was a break-through. In the sense that it showed black people as part of the British scene, it was a break-through. But, like similar situation comedies which followed, it was fatally flawed. Some have argued that the white central character and his frumpy wife compared unfavourably with the efficient black neighbour and his decorative wife. However, the programme had a core of liberal idealism that said that the presence of black people could be justified only if they addressed the problem of prejudice and that prejudice was essentially an individual thing which could be eased away with laughter. *Love Thy Neighbour* took on (and even then timidly) the question of personal prejudice and left the more uncomfortable issue of racism quite alone. In the ideological battleground of 1972, a humorous black neighbour challenged the vicious young mugger on Britain's television screens. There was no contest — the mugger was far too virile an opponent to brook any liberal opposition. But there was an opponent at last.

By the mid-Seventies, the 'mugger-my-neighbour' syndrome had evolved into a confusing jumble of contradictory images. The three figures of trouble-maker, entertainer and dependant persisted, showing that part of their strength was in their ability to adapt. In addition to these, modest efforts were being made to rehabilitate the black image. The handbooks of one specific year — 1975 — illustrate how things had changed in a short time. The ITV handbook mentioned only two relevant programmes. The first was *Love Thy Neighbour,* indicating the continued success of the programme. The second was a play by Johnny Speight entitled *If there were not any blacks, you'd have to invent them,* which the handbook praised as being a 'hilarious but bitter attack on bigotry'. These two items represented different facets of the developing movement to include blacks in the broadcasting arena. *Love Thy Neighbour* hoped that the nation could laugh its way out of racism. It made people laugh but the racism remained. The very title of Johnny Speight's play revealed a fundamental dilemma which was also at the heart of its predecessor *Till Death Us Do Part.* In structuring the play around an overt bigot, the play offered the viewer the choice — of dismissing the bigoted view as nonsense or of agreeing with them. The possibility that the good intentions might backfire was consistently underestimated. But in comparison to *Till Death Us Do Part,* it did less damage as it was a single media event.

The BBC's 1975 handbook is fascinating in the way in which it highlighted the several factions at work within the Corporation itself. Special mention was made of the current affairs *Panorama* which featured the West Indian community in Brixton. *Man Alive* followed that same 'social awareness' tendency but personalised it by doing a report called *A Fighting Chance* on 'three coloured boys who through talent and hard work were breaking out of their environment'. These programmes spoke for those within the organisation who felt that the time had come to make black matters part of the broadcasting agenda. But the voice was tentative, isolated and spasmodic.

In contrast to this liberal conscience was poised the massive opposition of Light Entertainment which continued to churn out the three black myths in an almost unadulterated form. The same organisational hierarchy which applauded the efforts of *Panorama* and *Man Alive* also managed to congratulate the *Black and White Minstrels Show* for its 'pace, colour and entertainment value'. *Till Death Us Do Part* also merited a mention in the following way: 'Johnny Speight's scripts were funniest when they provided Alf Garnett and the members of his family with lines that were poignant rather than strident'. Were the viewers being asked to laugh at racism or feel sorry for the racist? I interpret that comment as another example of a lack not only of a consistent policy but also of a firm moral position.

Another programme with an openly racist bias — this time directed against Asians — was enthusiastically welcomed. It Ain't Half Hot, Mum was described as being set in 'a ramshackle Army unit in India in 1945'. The handbook accurately predicted the series' success, adding that 'the scripts were good enough to make people watch and laugh'. What was to be laughed at were the obsequious punkawallahs and similar left-overs from the Raj. In fact any brown (or brown-painted) person opening his mouth in this programme was guaranteed to raise a laugh; in the world of It Ain't Half Hot, Mum it was as though Indians had been created, with their quaint and curious ways of dressing and speaking, uniquely for the merriment of white people. Trial by accent had long been a feature of the British class system and when race was added, the equation led to an amplification of negative preconceptions and placed them even more on the level of unconscious reaction.

The final irony of 1975's programming, according to the handbook, was the inclusion of Athol Fugard's play about South Africa, Sizwe Bansi is Dead. It was important in allowing black actors a serious role on television — virtually unheard-of before. Screened on BBC 2, it was aimed at an intellectual minority audience. In terms of the organisation itself, it appeased that 'Arts' side of the liberal conscience which was at work in the Panorama and Man Alive programmes. But this tendency was in permanent and unequal struggle against the Light Entertainment brigade with its immense power and lack of reflection about how it was representing black people.

The point of looking in detail at the 1975 BBC handbook has been to show that on the television screens of that year there was no agreement on race. Whereas in the Sixties, the mythologies about black people were clearly delineated, by the Seventies, there was confusion. Beyond the broadcasting organisations the situation was similar, suggesting that the overlap between the views of the broadcasters and those of the politicians was more than coincidental. The range of opinion in the two spheres was strikingly similar. On the political Right, there still remained the indomitable legacy of Powell although, by the end of the Seventies, the man found himself somewhat in the political wilderness when he left the Conservative party. Going towards the Centre, there was the now familiar dilly-dallying of the Labour Party who, despite promises, never got around to doing anything about the 1971 Immigration Act but, by way of compensation, insisted on granting an amnesty to (a limited number of) illegal immigrants. Politically, the voice of the liberal conscience was heard in several ways. The Commission for Racial Equality replaced the toothless Community Relations Council. The 1976 Trades Union Congress conference heard speaker after speaker condemning racism, indicating that at least the official mouthpiece of the white working class no longer 'consented' to the treatment of black people in Britain. The last years of the Seventies witnessed the rise of the Anti-Nazi League and its flamboyant child, Rock Against Racism. In politics, then, as well as in television, the knee-jerk reaction to race so evident in the two previous decades was still there but coexisting with a movement, albeit insecure, towards recognising the black life in its midst. The three myths had realigned themselves and flourished — the trouble-maker was now a mugger, the entertainer was the black person whose very presence triggered off hilarity; the dependency myth crossed the African continent and settled itself in Amin's Uganda. Ranged against these were enlightened liberals, seeking change and speaking on behalf of the disenfranchised blacks. Because, despite Parliamentary democracy, that is what they were at the end of the Seventies — disenfranchised, represented by others, outside the consensus. But the Seventies had set the stage for real change, by allowing some cosmetic changes to occur.

The watershed year was 1979 with the election of a Conservative Government. Under the leadership of Margaret Thatcher, the party lurched to the Right. War was declared on inflation (and a peace treaty signed with unemployment). All of the 'soft' policies which had allegedly led the previous Labour government to their disastrous 'winter of discontent' were swept away in a flurry of national spring-cleaning. Most of all, the new government promised that Britain would be great again. A few years later, after the Falklands War, Mrs Thatcher chastised the faint-hearted who had not been willing to stand up and fight, with these words: 'There were those who would not admit it . . . but they too had their secret fears that it was true: that Britain was no longer the nation that had built an Empire and ruled a quarter of the world'. The essence of her concept of national identity was the rank exploitation of colonialism. She did not articulate this sentiment until she had been in power for three years but the black community was in no doubt about where she stood from the very beginning. Was she not the one who, in a pre-election speech, said how understandable — how natural — it was for 'British' people to fear being 'swamped by alien cultures'? Those carefully chosen words told black Britons all they needed to know about their new Prime Minister. The 'ensemble of relations' did not include the blacks, as far as the new government was concerned. This hardening of attitudes from the top provoked a corresponding reaction from the black community, especially the young. It would not be long before their voices would be heard as loudly and clearly as those who had so arrogantly called them 'alien'.

In the year of Mrs Thatcher's occupation of Downing Street, television continued to progress along the contradictory lines referred to earlier. There were two additions which are worthy of note. 1979 was the year of *Empire Road,* Britain's first drama series with an all-black cast and, more significantly, a black writer, Michael Abbensetts. It was a series that blazed briefly but then disappeared without a trace. The brevity of its run confirmed its experimental nature and although the programme-makers were at pains to make it easily digestible to the mainstream audience, as far as I am aware, there has been no black drama series that has since been given prime-time scheduling. Experimentation with current affairs coverage was also taking place at this time. London Weekend Television's Minorities Unit produces *Skin.* Tucked away at lunchtime on Sundays, this programme dealt with matters concerning the Afro-Caribbean community. In theory, these programmes should have signalled progress but as they were both curiously sanitised affairs, they managed to capture neither imagination nor audience.

Black life came leaping onto the television screens the next year with the riots/disturbances/uprisings of St. Pauls's, Bristol in 1980 and those of Toxteth and Brixton in 1981. It is pertinent to repeat the quote from Stanley Cohen about a society which continues 'to generate problems for some of its members - like working-class adolescents — and then condemn whatever solution these groups find'. The problems generated for black youth were not only in terms of physical and social deprivation but also in terms of a powerful sense of exclusion.

The black community had lived for almost three decades in political limbo — being alternately ignored, despised, harassed, feared, discussed and spoken for. The young blacks who took to the streets during those two summers entered the political arena by the most direct route. Their actions were perceived as destructive, mindless, anti-social and criminal — but without those deeply traumatic happenings, the likelihood is that black Britons would have remained hovering on the threshold of national life. More than a century before, black abolitionist Frederick Douglass had said to white America: 'Those who profess to favour freedom, and yet deprecate agitation, are men who want crops without ploughing up the ground . . . Power conceded nothing without a demand'.[7] It was the distress felt across the nation during those two summers as the American nightmare became the British reality which precipitated the massive soul-searching which followed. Without the pain, there would have been no change. From that point of view, the events of 1980 and 1981 were historically progressive.

It would be wrong, however, to imagine that the positive results of what I will term 'the events' were immediately felt. During the events of St. Paul's and Toxteth, the sensible black person kept a low profile and strenuously avoided newspaper and television reporters. For now the trouble-maker myth, after losing some of its mugging momentum, burst into a high-octane, technicolour life, evoking the purplest rhetoric from even prosaic journalists. The rioter slotted easily into the spaces formerly occupied by the mugger and the leprous immigrant. Stuart Hall described the process of slotting or 'mapping' thus: 'New, problematic or troubling events which breach our expectancies and run counter to our 'common-sense constructs' must be assigned to their discursive domains before they can be said to 'make sense'. The most common way of 'mapping' them is to assign the new to some domain or other of existing maps of problematic reality'.[8] The already well-established trouble-maker myth was given a disturbing new dimension.

Yet in that same year, in those same organisations, a curious thing happened: black faces started emerging from every crevice. Moira Stewart began to read prime time news; *Nationwide* seized upon a black female presenter Maggie Nelson; on ITN, Trevor Macdonald became more visible. The BBC introduced *Ebony,* a programme for Afro-Caribbean viewers. All of this activity coincided felicitiously with the arrival of Channel Four and its specific brief of representing minority interests. From this new source, the multicultural lobby was served by two programmes — *Black on Black* and *Eastern Eye* — which were screened on alternate weeks. The quality of these magazine programmes was variable, their main problem being that they tried to do the impossible — that is to tackle all things concerning black people in a forty-minute slot. Even so, these new programmes were important. Firstly, their existence was due largely if not wholly to the pressures on society which culminated in the events of 1980/81. Secondly, they gave a few black people the chance to train and learn their craft, in front of and behind the cameras. Lastly, their presence and that of a new crop of writers, presenters and comedians was evidence of a fundamental shift in British politics. In the years immediately following St. Paul's, Toxteth and Brixton, the mental horizon of Britain stretched to include black people. It is ironic that the entrenched attitudes of Thatcherism impressed on the black community the need to act for itself, defend itself and stake its claim to a more equitable share of the national pie.

And what of the three myths? It would be comforting to think that after the tentative moves away from them in the Seventies and then the breaking of new ground in the early Eighties, those hoary old myths could be laid to rest at last. On the entertainment side, the cruder manifestations of the myths have been reduced. Since the pioneering *Ebony* and *Black on Black,* the last two years have provided a variety of interesting and worthwhile programmes with the black audience in mind. And in the last eighteen months, *East Enders* is held up as proof that blacks can appear on mainstream television and have respectable, fleshed-out parts which allow them to be that most difficult of things — 'normal people'.

This would be the comforting, optimistic view of the present situation — that after a weary struggle in the world of television as in the wider world, black people have now gained access to the fullness of national life. I would argue, however, that one battle does not win the war and that although the events of 1980/81 did provoke changes, these were due less to some overdue sense of altruism and more to do with society's desire to preserve itself by accommodating and thereby defusing the perceived threat. Len Masterman said of hegemony that 'it must incorporate the views and interests of subordinate groups, making whatever concessions are necessary to establish equilibrium and win legitimacy, without compromising existing fundamental structures'.[4] In television, the debate now is about whether the concessions made will, qualitatively and quantitively, meet the needs of the black community.

Summary of Report on School-based Study
In an examination of black representations on British television during the period from July 1985 to June 1986, I tried to establish whether the figures of trouble-maker, entertainer and dependant still exist in some form or whether they have given way to the 'normal person', and to determine whether any new issues, not covered by the three-myth theory, are now manifest in the politics of black representation on television. The point of departure of all these issues was a school-based study carried out in May 1986.

Ostensibly, the aim of the study was quite simple — to elicit and monitor responses to nine chosen programmes* which reflected the newly enlarged black presence on T.V. However, it became clear that this blanket aim would have to be broken down into more specific objectives. These were: firstly, to discover what was successful and realistic in the mainstream programmes; secondly, to assess what was successful and accessible in the minority interest programmes; and lastly, to compare and contrast the responses of two school groups.

It is important to note the background and composition of the two groups. Both groups consisted of Sixth Form pupils from comprehensive schools. The Hailsham group came from a town of the same name situated between Brighton and Eastbourne. The pupils in this group were all white. The Plashet group came from a school in East London and were all either of Afro-Caribbean or Asian origin. Accordingly, the Hailsham group was seen as representing the mainstream perspective while the Plashet group was taken as the voice of the minority interest.

The nine programmes themselves were chosen to show the varied manifestations of the contemporary black television presence. They were multidisciplinary and were selected from all four channels with three clearly of 'minority interest', four from the popular mainstream, and two which did not clearly belong to either category.

The method of enquiry was carried out via questionnaires, log books and discussion. The three-pronged approach had the advantage of not depending on only one monitoring source so that the responses could be seen as coming from the subjective (discussion and written impressions in log books) as well as the objective (formal questionnaires) areas of experience.

The Findings
The point of the study was to test the three-myth theory but also to take into account any other data which the investigation revealed. Consequently, the first consideration was whether the figures of trouble-maker, entertainer and dependant were apparent to the two groups, followed by a description of 'any other business' thrown up by the study.

a) The trouble-maker
    Discussion centred around the black youth Kelvin Carpenter in the popular soap opera *East Enders*. In the particular episode used for the study, Kelvin had been behaving like a newly-converted revolutionary, although he never made mention of race. Both groups felt that Kelvin was not a trouble-maker, had no aura of menace and was being set up rather as an ecccentric. On a larger scale, both groups agreed that the black Carpenter family was seen as having troubles as opposed to causing trouble. In this, they were very much akin to the white families in the series. However the Plashet group felt that the black family's problems were less subtly explored than those of their white counterparts, giving rise to

* The nine programmes were: EastEnders, Albion Market, Top of the Pops, Club Mix, Bandung File, Ebony, King of the Ghetto and Hill Street Blues.

possible racist misinterpretations. So as far as this widely-watched programme was concerned, the case of the black trouble-maker was largely unproved. The reservations on the part of the Plashet group, however, did indicate that they were used to seeing black people as being represented as problematic elements in society.

b) The entertainer

Here entertainment was narrowed down to popular music and the focus was put on two programmes — the veteran mainstream *Top of the Pops* and the new ethnically-specific *Club Mix*. Debate turned about the music and images offered by these programmes. My view was that the only accepted role for the black entertainer was that exemplified by his or her use in *Top of the Pops,* where black music had been relieved of its identity and essentially co-opted into the mainstream of the popular music industry. There seemed to be no place for 'de-mythologised' black music — in other words — for music that retained strong links with black culture. Both the Hailsham and Plashet groups found the black music and images in *Top of the Pops* to be predictable — normal — even though the Hailsham group did not particularly identify with them. The Plashet group objected to the *Top of the Pops* formula for black music, in terms of quantity rather than quality. There was just not enough of it. When presented with *Club Mix* however — with its variety of black music, interlaced with conversation and satire — the reaction of the two groups was negative. Some of the Hailsham group found that this kind of 'segregation' was counterproductive. Although there were some pockets of enthusiasm, the Plashet group also rejected it on the grounds that in their effort to reflect the tastes of the young, black and British, the programme-makers had not quite got it right. So as far as the two groups were concerned, the pre-packaged, de-contextualized black musician/entertainer still retained pride of place despite attempts to dethrone him.

c) The dependant

Discussion about the black dependant myth found its reference point in the drama series *Prospects* which featured two young men, Pincey, white, and Billy, black, trying to break out of their deprivation mainly through 'fringe' business enterprises. The programme makers went out of their way to bypass the trouble-maker imagery by making Billy fundamentally non-aggressive while his friend Pincey emerges as a much more volatile and impetuous character. But in so do-ing, did they inevitably fall prey to the dependancy myth by making the white youth the leader and the black youth his malleable side-kick? The responses of the two groups were diametrically opposed. The Hailsham group did not perceive Pincey as the leader, considering that the strengths and weaknesses of the two characters balanced out. The Plashet group saw the relationship in terms of Pincey's clear dominance over Billy. To the suggestion that Billy had many positive qualities that Pincey lacked, they answered that no matter how much Billy was portrayed as 'Mr. Nice Guy' at every crucial decision, he took the lead from Pincey. Nowhere in the study was there a more striking divergence in the 'readings' of the images presented.

Realism versus Positive Images

The main issue to emerge outside the confines of the three-myth theory concerned what strategies should be used to portray black people more equitably. Both groups argued at length about what was realistic, although their respective perceptions were very different. Members of the Plashet group in particular felt that much that was on offer was not authentic and had little credibility at street level. At the same time, these same participants were not adverse to some social engineering, some positive images, to show black people in a better light. They were on the horns of a dilemma. They fervently wished to be portrayed as they were, but also as their very best selves. This conflict — felt by both the producers and consumers of television — between realism and positive images provided the most important unanswered question of this study.

Conclusions

The intention of the Hailsham/Plashet study was not to obtain categorical proof of the three-myth theory but to suggest movements in and around that theory from the twin perspectives of mainstream and minority interests. Within the limits of that framework, the study had several interesting things to say. It was clear to the participating pupils that there was a strong link between the imagery that was presented as 'real', in the form of news and current affairs, and that of the fictionalised texts of drama and Light Entertainment. This cross-fertilisation between television disciplines would have to be considered in any moves towards change. Secondly, the study showed that the mainstream group, though less critical of and less involved in the black television presence, accepted what was on offer and in all probability would accept more. Fears about the wholesale rejection of ethnically specific programmes by the mainstream did not seem to be justified.

As far as the existence of the trouble-maker, entertainer and dependant figures was concerned, the study indicated that, though less blatant than before, residual traces of them still persisted in the full range of television representation. On occasion they were just that, traces, but elsewhere they continued to flourish just beneath the new skin of change. The study also addressed the issue of the different interpretations possible in the face of one given image. The group coming from the minority communities read messages in some programmes which were entirely invisible to the mainstream group. This was not due to the cliché of oversensitivity but simply a different experience which the programme-makers had failed to credit with sufficient importance. Lastly, the study demonstrated that the contemporary scene was one of transition — from the ossified images of the colonial past to 1980's-style black representation. The decision as to whether to present black people on television 'realistically' or 'positively' was shown to be paramount in this, the next phase of the ideological struggle.

VIEWING LOG BOOK

NAME ....

Your viewing schedule is as follows:

Programme 1: Ebony (at school)
Programme 2: EastEnders — Thurs. May 8 BBC1 7.30 p.m.
Programme 3: Albion Market — Sun. May 11 ITV/TVS 5.00 p.m.

Programme 4: Prospects (at school)
Programme 5: Top of the Pops — Thurs. May 15 BBCi 7.00 p.m.
Programme 6: Club Mix — Thurs. May 15 C4 8.30 p.m.

Programme 7: Bandung File (at school)
Programme 8: King of the Ghetto — Thurs. May 22 BBC2 9.30 p.m.
Programme 9: Hill Street Blues — Sat. May 24 C4 10.00 p.m.

This log book is for the programmes that you watch at home. To keep the programme fresh in your mind, jot down a few notes on what actually went on,
in the section entitled 'Synopsis'. Would you then write down your immediate
responses, in the section entitled 'Impressions'. A few days later, you will receive
questionnaires which you fill out in the normal way.

References

1. *Mythologies,* Roland Barthes, Granada Publishing, 1973.
2. *Gramsci's Marxism,* Carl Boggs, Pluto Press, 1976.
3. *Immigration and Race in British Politics,* Paul Foot, Penguin, 1965.
4. *Teaching the Media,* Len Masterman, Comedia 1985.
5. *Folk Devils and Moral Panics,* Stanley Cohen, MacGibbon and Kee, 1972; 2nd ed. Martin Robinson, 1980.
6. *Racism and Reaction,* Stuart Hall, in *Five Views of Multi-racial Britain,* CRE, 1980.
7. Quoted in *Between the lines: how to detect bias and propaganda in the News,* E. Maclean, Black Rose Books, Montreal, 1981.
8. *Culture, Media, Language: introduction to Media Studies,* Stuart Hall, Hutchinson, 1980.

Black Independent Film in Britain: Historical Overview

by Jim Pines

The 1980s represent a kind of watershed in the history of black film-making in Britain. The emergence of a new generation of film and video practitioners whose work reflects a diverse range of thematic and formal concerns, has opened up new possibilities in representing black social, political, cultural and historical experiences in ways hitherto impossible to imagine. It is tempting to regard this as the beginnings of an emergent black U.K. film culture, although it is perhaps more realistic at this juncture to view these developments as important challenges to conventional 'race relations' and multicultural motifs which have characterised dominant representations of ethnic minorities in British films and television. Indeed, a number of recent black independent films and videos have exhibited a marked shift, thematically, from conventional race relations models, stressing instead modes of (black) film cultural practice which are rooted in the specificities of black cultural experiences. These developments have important implications not only for critics and theorists concerned with (black) British cinema and television history, but also for teachers wishing to incorporate these new themes into courses on 'racism in the media'. If nothing else, they challenge us to take black (oppositional) film/cultural work into fuller account when considering images of black experiences in the media.

While it might be useful for analysis, or in a teaching environment, to contrast dominant or mainstream representations with black-produced themes and images to highlight instances of, say, opposition, the danger of this approach in in possibly reducing the analysis to a simple pairing off of opposing types of racial imagery — not particularly useful in the long run. The relationship between black independent film cultural practice on the one hand, and dominant representations of 'race' on the other, is in fact a more complex affair which has yet to be properly theorized. In any case, black film/video practice has a cultural dynamic of its own which cannot (and should not) be reduced simply to the exegesis of oppositional practice; we need to develop ways of addressing this cultural dynamic in its own terms, without necessarily having to make constant reference to the dominant.

For example, a number of recent films and videos have explored the theme of black (British) history, drawing on archival footage and re-working the material in a non-realist documentary style. These 'experiments' with the historical documentary form are at one level questioning the primacy of documentary realism in representing black social and political culture. The significance of this becomes clearer when we consider, for example, the close relationship between the British documentary tradition on the one hand, and representations of Empire, 'race' and race relations in mainstream British media on the other — which has prevailed since the days of the Colonial Film Unit and Crown Film Unit in the 1930s, continuing up through the 1950s-60s cycle of documentaries on 'immigrant problems', to present-day television news and current affairs programmes dealing with race relations issues. In the context of race-related documentaries, therefore, we can identify clear expressions of oppositional practice particularly in the work of black independents who are concerned not only with content, but with formal questions as well.

From a slightly different angle, these history-based films and videos also represent an attempt by black cultural practitioners to reconstruct visually, black people's histories on a non-Eurocentric, anti-racist basis. Any degree of success, many black and Third World film-makers believe, will necessitate engaging in a different, radically politicized film, language — that is, a cinematic approach which is capable of expressing the complexities of black experiences including the ancestral past, the experiences of colonialism, immigration and settlement, as well as experiences which are specific to black people's lives in Britain. For many black film cultural practitioners, these experiences cannot be reduced to conventional race relations paradigms, nor can they be articulated honestly through the dominant modes of address. A radically different orientation is required.

Though culturally oppositional in its effects, this engagement with the formal aspects of film/video, in conjunction with (black) historiography, places greater emphasis on themes which are more closely concerned with black people's cultural identities as they themselves construct or define them. In other words, the critical terms of reference in this context are situated primarily within black cultural politics, especially as it has developed in the 1980s, and so do not depend on the problems of dominant representation. The inclusion of this kind of black-produced material in race media studies, therefore, engages one in critical approaches which in a very real sense go far beyond the limitations of 'race relations' and multiculturalism.

The tendency in race media studies to privilege 'dominant' or mainstream representatives and to concentrate on stereotypes (which is often framed by the notion of 'negative' and 'positive' images) remains a common practice, although there is a sense in which this has become less effective, methodologically, in the light of new themes and images recently emerging from the black cultural sector. But even in the context of dominant representation, recent archival-based research into race and ethnicity in British television has highlighted the importance of developing alternative critical strategies — for example, historical-based analyses which not only provide general accounts of how images of black people have changed over time, but also delineate particular themes within a historical framework like images of the black family in domestic sitcoms; the thematization of race issues in relation to popular/changing notions of 'Britishness'; the problem of 'white-ness' in Eurocentric racial representation; the complex relationship between race, gender, class and sexuality in media representation; the influence of documentary realism in film and television representations of British 'race relations', and how this relates historically and ideologically to the work of black film/video practitioners today; and so on. The emphasis in these studies is not 'race relations' per se, but rather the cultural and ideological mechanisms by which 'race' is constructed and mobilised in different genres of films and television programmes, and during different periods of black people's history in Britain.

The 1960's

Black independent film-making in Britain dates back to the mid-1960s, even before cultural funding bodies became aware that black people were interested in the cinema, let alone engaged in film production. Lionel Ngakane's allegorical short film *Jemima and Johnnie* (1964), was one of the earlier attempts to explore the dynamics of British 'race relations' in narrative fiction and from the black point of view. It follows the exploits of two children — one black, the other white — who happily run off together to play in the streets. Their 'disappearance' causes the distressed parents to join in the search for the children. the film's final image of unconditional friendship between the children, in contrast to the adults' uneasy inter-racial cooperation, struck an optimistic note invoking racial harmony in the face of prejudice and suspicion. The film achieves its effect not so much through the use of stereotypical (racial) narrative devices — despite the 'obviousness' of the story situation — but as a result of Ngakane's marvellous sense of cinematic expression, which we can easily identify as a stylistic feature of social realism prevailing in the British independent film movement during the 1950s-60s.

In fact, the propensity for cinematic experimentation, in terms of both content and style, was quite strong during the early period of black independent film-making, i.e. prior to the institutionalization of British 'race relations' which permeated all aspects of racial discourse and representation from the late-1960s onwards. Though only a short film, *Jemima and Johnnie* illustrates this very well, in the way that it develops the 'race relations' story cinematically and never allows the narrative to be hamstrung by the racial theme. In similar vein, though with quite different intentions, Frankie Dymon Jr's 'pop fantasy' *Death May Be Your Santa Claus* (1969), constructs a Dantesque narrative centring on the black hero's imaginary (nightmarish) journey through a world of politics, violence, alienation, and rediscovery. The film draws heavily on the themes and imagery of sixties cultural politics like Black Power, Che Guevara, the Underground Movement, pop culture, 'Flower Power', Vietnam, and so on, which are all worked into the non-realist narrative structure in a typically iconoclastic manner. Interestingly, the film was inspired by the director's involvement (as an actor) in Jean-Luc Godard's British film *One Plus One,* and aptly demonstrates how responsive black practitioners were to a wide range of film techniques and practices. Needless to add, this fascination with cinematic expression, touching in this example on avant-gardism, completely disppeared by the early-seventies, though happily aspects of it have reappeared in some recent works by a new generation of black film/video practitioners.

105

Both *Jemima and Johnnie* and *Death May Be Your Santa Claus,* in their different ways, show how daring early black independent film-making in Britain was in its approach to political themes and how inventive in its attitude toward the film process. Although a number of the film-makers had been trained at the London Film School, for instance, (now the London International Film School), renowned for its highly motivated students, the majority received no formal training but worked in other disciplines like writing and acting. But what they all shared was immense enthusiasm for the medium, and a burning desire to extend their creative energies into this otherwise inaccessibly expensive art form. Moreover, there was relatively little interest in documentary films, the real interest lying in feature-length production with a somewhat more commercial or entertainment orientation. This did not mean the abandonment of serious social issues, but rather the desire to incorporate these themes into narrative fiction on a fairly grand scale. Interestingly, the Hollywood entertainment film (especially with Sidney Poitier) and the European 'art movie' both provided useful, if not contradictory models.

Black film-makers started to receive some recognition by the early-1970s, but institutional support for black films was still notably lacking, with only the occasional race relations-supported project receiving significant funding from any major institution. The handful of black independents operating at the time continued to struggle in a characteristically entrepreneurial fashion, financing productions out of their own pockets or by other 'unconventional' means.

Horace Ove's engaging documentary *Reggae* (1970), for example, was financed by a black independent record producer. In sharp contrast to today, black film and video practitioners did not engage much in institutional funding politics. They tended to feel strongly alienated from these white-dominated structures and chose rather to remain independent. Cultural institutions for their part felt no real need to address the question of black film, since it never arose as an important issue during the debates then taking place about British film culture and the development of an independent film and video sector. So the gap between black film-makers and cultural funding bodies was enormous.

Pressure

The turning-point came when the BFI Production Board funded Ove's first feature *Pressure* (1974) — also the first British-made feature film by a black director. It is a classic 'race relations' drama which draws on a number of familiar themes — e.g. the 'immigrant problem' motif and the problem of assimilation — and reworks them into the film's documentary-like fictional narrative. In the context of the 1970s, the story of a British-born black school-leaver's disillusionment and growing politicization as he encounters rampant racism and discrimination, had a timely message which highlighted from a black perspective — for the first time in any British film — the contradictions and impossibilities inherent in the concept of 'Black British'. In this respect, certain aspects of the film can be 'read' as a critique of institutional race relations and of (British) society's failure to progress even in the light of a new generation of British-born black people, despite the influence of the race relations 'industry'.

Identity is a central theme in *Pressure,* most sharply articulated in the context of the boy's family. The black family is the locus of intense intergenerational conflict — an archetypal theme in sociological race relations — the conflict revolving around the British-born youth's sense of 'British-ness'. This identity is unstable, however, and gradually disintegrates as the story progresses. The youth is pulled in two ideologically opposing directions. His 'first generation immigrant' parents, especially the mother, try to impose a set of values and expectations based on an ideal notion of assimilation of the British-born progeny; an opposing set of values is represented by the boy's Caribbean-born militant brother, who constantly chides him about his lifestyle and exposes the contradictions and futility in 'trying to be like the English'. The youth's experiences in the outside world have a traumatic effect on his whole being and lead him inevitably to a 'non-English' identity position, which results in his politicization (i.e. identification with the brother's values) and his complete rejection of the parents' view of the world. However, the film's closing image of black political protest is less 'positive' than it might appear, being effectively more pessimistic.

1980s
Memelik Shabazz's *Burning an Illusion* (1981), which was also funded by the BFI, marked an important shift in terms of addressing 'race' and black cultural politics in black independent films. For a start, it is not concerned with black-white relations as such, nor with themes relating to multiculturalism, but focuses instead on various kinds of relationships within the black community, especially between men and women, and highlights the theme of black consciousness and cultural politicization. Like *Pressure,* the story centres on the political reawakening of the main character — in this case a black woman, whose initial social conformity and political naivete gradually evolve into an active black political consciousness. This transformation is framed by the young woman's relationship with her proud-hearted boyfriend whose arrest, imprisonment and ill-treatment by the authorities propel her into activist politics.

Whereas the identity theme in *Pressure* centred on the dissolution of 'Black British-ness', in *Burning an Illusion* it is built around the notion of black identity being defined essentially within its own terms of reference, i.e. in the context of 'the black community'. The question of 'British-ness' therefore does not arise — it has no relevance in terms of the film's representation of black experiences. Thus the theme of racial victimization — i.e. the image of blacks as 'victims' so familiar in race relations discourse — is not a major concern here, despite its appearance at key moments in the story, but functions more as a catalyst to drive the plot along. In other words, black-white interactions — which are always problematical — affect relationships primarily within the black community or between black people, so compelling 'the community' to define its identity more sharply for the sake of its own survival. By stressing such intra-ethnic or intra-black community concerns, *Burning an Illusion* helped introduce a more militant tone to representations of black experiences. It also captured much of the mood of a new generation of British blacks who were to challenge the whole basis of British race relations by the early-1980s.

Both *Pressure* and *Burning an Illusion* are landmark films which reflect the major concerns of the period in which they were made. But the years separating them also indicate the extent to which black independent film-making has been marginalized in Britain, especially in terms of feature film production. Ahmed Jamal's *Majdhar* (1984) and Horace Ove's *Playing Away* (1986) are the only other notable features that have come out of the black independent sector in recent years, although the latter might well qualify as a 'mainstream' film by virtue of its million-pounds-plus budget! *Majdhar* is especially interesting because, like the two previous black features, it focuses on the theme of (cultural) identity, but iñ an Asian context: the story concerns a young Pakistani woman who is forced to adopt a new lifestyle when she is abandoned by her unfaithful husband and left to fend for herself. Her new 'independence' leads to a series of 'discoveries' about the world and, especially, about 'western' (British) attitudes and lifestyles which she gradually begins to adopt herself, though only after a great deal of confusion.

Though without quite the same political thrust as say, *Burning an Illusion, Majdhar* is similar in its (male-oriented) representation of black women's identity and politicization. This is an important issue which should be addressed in any analysis of the film(s). It is not a question of simply placing these black independent films in opposition to mainstream or dominant representations, however useful this operation might be, but rather going a lot further analytically and examining how the films are constructed in order to determine what they signify. This means, in effect, shifting the focus from race relations/multicultural concerns, to dealing with the films in terms of their own cultural and ideological dynamic.

Beyond 'Race Relations'

Sankofa's *The Passion of Remembrance* (1986) best illustrates the way in which recent black independent film and video in Britain has evolved beyond the confines of conventional race relations and multicultural representation. Formally, this intriguing film about the history of black people's struggle in Britain is a departure from problem-oriented documentary realism, addressing instead broader themes relating to black British experiences through the creative use of sound and images. The 'story' is constructed around a series of dramatic moments, in which characters' personal histories intertwine with the history of political protest in ways that defy simple explanations based on race politics alone. The film makes extensive use of archival footage, which it re-processes and re-presents in the form of montages celebrating political struggle and solidarity. These documentary moments are framed by narrative vignettes of black family life, social encounters, interactions, and relationships which cut across generational differences and highlight and depth and diversity of black experiences without resorting to stereotypical conventions.

The drama is set against the harsh backdrop of Britain in the 1980s, but the film is not particularly concerned with the 'British crisis', nor for that matter with the race relations crisis. It focuses on the theme of black people working through and (re-)defining their own identities for themselves, i.e. not in relation to the dominant. This is built around the idea of historical memory and how our sense of the past — historic moments in black people's political struggle — is brought to bear on the present. As the film's title suggests, these reverential moments of remembering are fraught with painful ambiguities, in the sense that each successive generation attempts to immortalize its own contributions to history and to imbue its own struggles with highly charged symbolism, which subsequent generations are compelled to live through. While acknowledging the essential importance of this often mythologised historical past, *The Passion of Remembrance* nevertheless invites us to reappraise precisely what it entails in terms of how black people define and experience their reality, psychically and politically, and to consider its implications for the future. Thus the hitherto neglected issue of black women's role in political struggle — i.e. the relationship between black women (the mythical tea-makers) and black men (the mythologised action figures) — becomes a critical one, which the film explores with overwhelming intensity. What emerges is an engaging critique of black political culture from largely a black feminist perspective. Black themes and images are recast in ways quite new to British film and television representations.

Like their earlier experimental documentary *Territories* (1984), Sankofa's *The Passion of Remembrance* breaks new ground in representing black experiences in British cincema. The film's narrative thrust subverts conventional modes of racial representation, but it also opens up the possibility for the emergence of radically new cultural themes and images, based on a deeper understanding of the complexities of black cultural life. It presents a formidable challenge for both practitioners and audiences in the way that it addresses questions, not only of race and anti-racism, but also of class, sexuality, gender and, perhaps most interesting of all, cultural perceptions within black communities which black people themselves must begin to take on board politically.

Sankofa Film & Video Collective — along with other black workshops like Black Audio Film Collective, Ceddo Film & Video Workshop, Retake Film & Video Collective — are part of the new generation of independent film and video practitioners whose work is rooted in the cultural politics of the 1980s and expresses an originality in style and content which at times has been innovative. This resurgence of black independent film culminated in three major works in 1986 — *The Passion of Remembrance,* Black Audio Film's award-winning documentary *Handsworth Songs,* and Horace Ove's *Playing Away.* These films reflect the diversity of approaches which now defines black independence in Britain; although it has to be said that the most interesting innovations, formally speaking, have tended to come from the grant-aided workshop sector.

The Marketplace

However, it would be a mistake to dismiss the non-workshop independents, or evaluate their contributions pejoratively because of their relatively mainstream orientation. The fact is, this sector is not 'protected' or cushioned by a structure of grants and subsidies and, therefore, is obliged to compete in the commercial marketplace. The nature of their practice, by definition, does not allow them the 'space' for experimentation, although their interventions are important in terms of penetrating mainstream media structures (e.g. in the area of employment in the film and television industries) and de-marginalizing black film and television production. Indeed despite institutional support for black film and video, which has increased considerably in the past couple of years, the problem of cultural and professional marginalization remains a critical issue which affects black practitioners as a whole, irrespective of their creative proclivities. The whole of the black independent film/video sector has to engage in institutional funding policy issues and struggle to secure greater access to otherwise limited resources.

This has led to several new initiatives within the black independent sector around film/video distribution and exhibition. The wider circulation of black and Third World films is a crucially important area and is being addressed with a sense of utmost urgency. In terms of the development of black film culture, it is as important as production, involving practitioners in the complex process of audience building. Of course there is no sense in which we can conceive the black audience as a homogeneous entity; the reality is the opposite. Black film and video practitioners are therefore having to think seriously about ways of addressing these different (black) audiences, and about how to promote different kinds of black films. It is no longer a matter of simply showing the films, but rather building into film programming strategies some form of film educational practice, to enable audiences to participate directly in the cultural debates around black independent film and video.

This work has already begun to take shape in for example, the screenings and distribution-related projects organised by Sankofa Film & Video Collective, and in the activities of Vokani Black & Third World Film Circuit, a black film exhibition 'agency' based in the West Midlands. Several (white) independent venues like BFI-supported regional film theatres are also making an effort to include more black and Third World films in their programmes. But perhaps the most significant development has been the growing number of community-based venues across the country such as social clubs, community centres, and cultural associations, which are becoming increasingly involved in film exhibition and other media education-oriented activity. In fact, this has been one of the most fertile areas of growth within the ethnic film/video sector in the past couple of years, encompassing a fairly broad audience of mainly, but not only, young black people. These community-based venues are particularly interesting because they represent a potentially stable network of exhibition outlets, where the whole range of (film) cultural issues can also be taken up and developed. The cultural, as well as commercial implications of black film distribution and exhibition are therefore quite far-reaching.

These new developments point to the emergence of a clearly distinguishable black film and video sector in Britain, which encompasses not just production but also distribution, exhibition, educational work, and critical practice. It is this sense of cohesion — which has been evolving steadily since the early 1980s — that prompts one into thinking in terms of an emerging black film culture in this country. Obviously, the sector comprises disparate groups and practices, whose creative expressions are informed by different histories and cultural experiences. But this should not detract from the real advances which have been made within the black independent film and video sector and their effect on the wider (British) cultural scene. Moreover, although the pervasiveness of dominant representations, along with institutional marginalization, have tended to impose serious constraints on black film practice historically, e.g. by pigeonholing it in 'race relations', the signs today are that these constraints are gradually being whittled away by black cultural practitioners themselves. How a black (oppositional) film or videotape achieves this structurally is as important an area for study as the exegesis of dominant modes of (racial) representation.

Reflections on The Language of Racism; The Legacy of Colonialism; Prejudice and the Press

by Bhikhu Parekh

1. THE LANGUAGE OF RACISM (Extracts from *Colour, Culture and Consciousness,* George Allen and Unwin, 1974).

'Race'

Let me begin by registering a protest against the language used to describe the black community. It is amazing how often the term race is used to describe the situation in Britain. Britain is said to be a 'multi-racial society'; she enacted a — 'race' relations act, setting up a 'race' relations board; and her social idea is to achieve 'racial' harmony. Now there are several grounds on which the term race is objectionable. First, on any racial typology, Indians and Pakistanis belong to the *same* race of Caucasoids as do the British and therefore there is simply no question of race relations so far as they are concerned. As for West Indians there has been much 'racial' intermingling between them and the British. The free sexual relations of the British settlers in the West Indies with their black slave women have meant that nearly one-fifth of Jamaicans and Barbadians have some white blood in them. The reverse process, although not always mentioned, has also occurred. Over ten thousand negro slaves in London, after their emancipation, intermarried with the white community and became biologically assimilated. One wonders how much negro blood courses in British veins.

Apart from its empirical inaccuracy in the British context, the term race is, as is generally recognised, highly misleading. It is basically a biological concept and probably has some taxonomic value for the biologist although, in view of so much racial intermixing over centuries, even this is doubtful. When used in politics the term is particularly obnoxious. To a layman ill-versed in scientific controversy, it suggests that each racial group is a distinct and unique biological unit, the patterns of behaviour and thought of whose members are determined by their genes. As acknowledged by most biologists, however, the fact is that the genes men share in common are overwhelmingly greater than those that make them physically distinct, and that human behaviour is capable of considerable adaptation. The term race suggests further that racial mixing and mating are undesirable, and there is no evidence for this whatsoever. What is more, given the past history of European States, the term evokes powerful emotions and images and renders dispassionate discussion of relevant issues difficult.

'Coloured'

Like the language of race, the language of colour too is inappropriate and misleading. The non-white population is universally referred to as 'coloured'. The basic objection to this term is that every man is coloured, white being a colour just as much as black or brown. To confine the term coloured to non-whites is to suggest that white is in some sense so different a colour as not to be a colour at all. Why the whites are not called coloured is difficult to say. Perhaps an unconscious racism is at work here. To accept white as a colour is to acknowledge the white man's shared humanity and equality with men of other colours, and, since throughout their long encounter with non-whites the whites have treated them as animals or as children, they perhaps cannot bring themselves to accept that they belong to the same species as the 'coloured'. Whatever the explanation it is obvious that to call a man 'coloured' is to suggest that he is reducible to his colour, that his colour is the only significant thing about him, that colour, like leprosy, is a disease which the poor man suffers from and from which the white man is miraculously exempt. If some people are to be called coloured, then fairness demands that those not called coloured should be called colourless!

'Immigrants'

Sometimes the so-called coloured people are referred to as 'immigrants'. This term is less offensive than the other two, but it too is misleading. British history is a history of successive waves of immigrants. It is not therefore clear why only the members of the 'coloured' community should be called immigrants. It might be rejoined that they are so called because they are recent arrivals — but then so are many whites. In fact, since 1945, two out of three immigrants in Britain have been white, and yet, as is well known, in newspaper headlines and government records the reference to immigrants invariably means a reference to the 'coloured' immigrants. What is more it is not true that the 'coloured' people are recent arrivals. Although a very large number of 'coloured' people have arrived in Britain in recent years, a fairly large number have been resident here intermittently for over 400 years. The *Gentleman's Magazine* in 1764 put their number at about 20,000 in London alone. Since the population of London then was probably 650,000, the 'coloured' people amounted to nearly 3% of the total population. Already in 1788, Philip Thicknesse, a former army officer in Jamaica, was saying that 'London abounds with an incredible number of these black men, who have clubs to support those who are out of place . . .' and who are to be seen 'in every country town, nay in almost every village'. When many West Indians, initially brought to Britain as slaves or servants, were emancipated, they got absorbed into British society and have lived here ever since. Indians started coming to Britain at the turn of the century, and quite a few of them have been resident here since the First World War. It is also odd that the children of recent immigrants should be referred to by that strange and self-contradictory expression 'second-generation *immigrants*'. Since they are born and raised in Britain, by no stretch of imagination can they be called immigrants.

'The Host Community'

Sometimes immigrants are referred to as 'guests' and the local community as their 'hosts'. Although those using these terms are well-meaning men, clearly they have not thought the matter out carefully. To call a man a guest is to suggest that he is temporary and will not only leave one day but can also be 'persuaded' to leave if he overstays his welcome. In other words, to refer to immigrants as guests is to place them under a moral obligation to leave and, by implication, to confer on their hosts a moral right to throw them out should they fail to do so in time. Men who have no intention of leaving the national 'household' and who wish to become members of the national 'family' can hardly be called guests. Further, the language of guest and host not only imposes obligations on each party that it does not wish to accept, but also forces them into an artifical relationship which is difficult to keep up for long and which prevents the emergence of a natural and healthy relationship. As long as immigrants regard themselves as guests, they continue to expect their hosts to take the initiative and do not explore the ways in which they can adjust to the wider society. Also, as long as the wider community looks upon, or is made to look upon, itself as a host, it is constrained, even blackmailed, to feel concerned about men who do not really mean anything to them. The language of 'guest' and 'host' is obnoxious for another reason as well. Immigrants were encouraged or allowed to come to Britain to do the menial and dirty jobs which the natives shunned. Most of them eke out their livelihood by working as sweepers, cleaners, cooks and factory workers, and live in pretty miserable conditions. To call those men guests who live by serving their masters, who cook for, serve and wash their masters' dishes, who live in what are sometimes no better than servants' quarters, and who are sometimes treated with undisguised contempt, is a perverse and inhuman joke.

The point of this terminological exercise was to show that the apparently innocent and even well-meaning terms contain an ideological bias and can appear highly offensive to those they are meant to describe. For example, although he is often described as a second generation immigrant, the Asian child feels that he is not at all an immigrant, but a first generation Black Briton. As such he is free from the 'guest complex'. He does not think that he should feel grateful for the privilege of being allowed to live in Britain. Britain is his home. He belongs to it, and it to him, just as much as it belongs to his white compatriots. Consequently, he does not feel the need to justify his existence, that is, to prove that he is a worthy member of the country, and makes claims on the country his parents never thought of making. Further, unlike them, his standards of comparison and points of reference are drawn from Britain. He judges his job, house, income, opportunities, and the like by British standards, and demands equality with his white compatriots. Unlike his parents who, under a mistaken sense of gratitude and insecurity did not press their demands for justice and fair play and either relied on the whites to fight for them or wallowed in self-pity, the young black Briton insists upon fighting his battle himself. Because the level of expectation and the sensitivity to discrimination have increased, he feels discriminated against far more acutely than they did. Unlike them, his image of the British is based not on colonial experience but on his day to day contacts. He is therefore free from his parents' deep-seated feeling of inferiority and insecurity in his dealings with the native British, and feels much less inhibited in standing up for his rights.

'White Society'

If Britain is defined as a white society, and a Briton as a white man whose mother tongue is English and whose kith and kin are settled in Australia, New Zealand, Canada and South Africa, then the non-white minority, and for that matter even the Continentals, and Americans settled here, are bound to feel, and are bound to be regarded by the rest, ultimately, as outsiders, as at best only partial members of the national 'family'; clearly persons who do not speak the same tongue, nor share the same physical features, and do not have the same relatives cannot be said to belong to the same family. The national family therefore needs to be redefined to accord with social reality. Only when it is acknowledged as a matter of course that a Briton is not by definition white but could be black, brown or yellow, that he might speak Swahili, Mandarin or Hindustani as his first, and English as his second, language, and that his 'kith and kin' might be found in Bombay, Barbados and Ibadan as well as in Salisbury and Wellington, can the non-white minority feel as authentically British as the native, and can be so accepted by the latter. Naturally the radical revision of its self-image is painful to any community, especially to one so homogeneous and insular as England, but there is no alternative if the ideal of pluralistic integration is taken seriously.

'Prejudice' and 'Racism'

Most social psychologists interpret racism as a form of prejudice one 'race' entertains against another, and argue that, although it represesnts an extreme form of prejudice, it is essentially the same type of phenomenon as the prejudices encountered in other walks of life — the prejudices, e.g. which the middle class has against the working class, the Englishman against the Frenchman, or which some men have against long-haired or bearded or dark-haired men. The black man is, it is argued, an archetypal *stranger*, and that the white man's prejudice against him is no more than an extreme form of prejudice he entertains against strangers. This view seems to me to totally mistaken.

Prejudice is a partial rejection of a man on the basis of his real or supposed specific or specifiable characteristics. A white man may be prejudiced against a black man because he thinks he is lazy, sexy, dirty, mean, unclean, unintelligent, etc., even as a black man might be prejudiced against a white man because in his view he is selfish, inhuman, merciless, devious, emotionally undeveloped, etc. Since prejudice is based on some assumed characteristic of the victim, it can be countered by showing that he does not in fact possess this characteristic, or that it is not really obnoxious, or that he can be helped to get rid of it. Racism belongs to a very different category. It involves a *total* refusal to accept the victim as a full human being entitled to the respect due to a fellow human being, and implies that his belonging to a particular race has so corrupted his humanity that he belongs to an entirely different species. A white Southerner in America is not merely *prejudiced* against the negro; he *rejects* the negro's humanity and refuses to acknowledge that they both belong to the same species. To say that Hitler was *prejudiced* against Jews or that his prejudice differed only in degree from my prejudice against, say, a bearded or a red-haired man is totally to misunderstand and misrepresent the basic issue involved. What Hitler did was to refuse to accept Jews as his fellow human beings and looked down upon them almost as worms that could with moral impunity be trampled upon. Colonial powers, similarly, did not just entertain prejudices against natives, but saw them as belonging to a different species, to an altogether different level in the scale of civilisation. The examples of the treatment meted out to the immigrant discussed above reflect a similar attitude. Racism, to put the point differently, is not the same as racial *prejudice*, and it degrades and dehumanises the victim in a way that ordinary forms of prejudice do not.

Combating racism, then, involves not simply ending discrimination or eradicating prejudice but something totally different; it involves securing from the white community a full recognition of the humanity of the black man who, although deficient in this or that respect as all human beings, white and black, are, is still a human being with dignity and pride and entitled to proper respect and regard. Racism therefore cannot be combated in ways that social

115

psychologists have proposed for eradicating prejudices, since what is required here is not to establish the simple point that the black man possesses or lacks some specific characteristic on which the white man's prejudice is based, but to get him to appreciate their shared humanity. It is this failure to comprehend the distinctiveness of racism that is largely responsible for much of social psychology's inability to suggest effective ways to combat it. Indeed, as long as it remains *social* psychology, that is, as long as it remains rooted in the assumptions derived from the study of isolated individuals or of groups within the *same* cultural milieu, and remains innocent of the historical dialectic of the political relations between different communities, it is by its very nature incapable of understanding the phenomenon like racism which is, as we shall presently see, historical and political in its origin and nature.

2. THE LEGACY OF COLONIALISM (From *Colour, Culture and Consciousness,* 1974).

Racism was a result of the dramatic historical encounter between the white and the black man in a colonial context, and can only be understood in historical terms. The image of the black man as an inferior creature was a product of several factors of which two deserve mention. The first was economic and the second cultural. Colonialism was by its nature a master-servant relationship and was fundamentally exploitative in nature. Colonies were largely suppliers of raw material and consumers of imperial industrial products; and the native bourgeoisie, such as it was, played a subordinate role to imperial interests. Not only did colonies remain poor but their economy remained tied to the European economy and was seriously distorted. The simple fact that even after decades and, in some cases, centuries of colonial rule they are still very poor and undeveloped is a sufficient proof of this. The vast disparity between the level of existence of the native and his European master, and their relationship of command and obedience, made it impossible for the two to meet on equal terms. Each knew his place and kept to it.

The second, cultural, factor carried the process further and turned economic subservience into cultural and moral inferiority. Convinced that they represented the highest level of human civilisation, the British (and for that matter Europeans) defined the civilised man in familiar liberal terms, and predictably the non-European peoples turned out to be uncivilised. Since a civilised society was defined as one that had a strong and centralised state, a firm sense of national identity, a competitive capitalist economy and a high level of technology, and a civilised man as one who had drive and ambition, who was competitive, individualistic, calculative and ruthless in the pursuit of his interests, non-European societies and their members were by definition uncivilised. Non-European societies naturally found these ideological definitions impossible to resist. No doubt, there was some resistance and scepticism in the beginning, but it collapsed before systematic European indoctrination carefully carried out by educational, legal, political and economic means. To be fair, the natives themselves were sometimes a willing party. They were impressed by European self-confidence, power and energy and were only too eager, as the biographies and autobiographies of their leaders show, to imbibe the ways of thought and life that had made these possible. So gradually the black man began to internalise European values, and with these, the European image of him. The white man said that the black man's religion was superstitious, that his morality was primitive, his social and legal institutions backward and his traditions uncouth, and the black man agreed. The bewitched native, judging himself on the basis of European values and ideals, felt that he could not respect himself if he failed to live up to them. Since these values were not an outgrowth from, and therefore unsuited to, his temperament and background, he naturally found it difficult fully to live up to them. However hard to tried he failed, thus reinforcing his own and his master's belief that he was naturally, inherently, an inferior creature.

Since racism was a product of, among others, these two powerful and mutually complementary forces of economic and political power and cultural domination, the answer to it obviously does not lie in analysing the white and black man's personality structure and asking how they can be made less 'authoritarian' and 'deferential' respectively, nor in hoping to eradicate the white man's 'prejudices' by giving him more information on the black man's cultural and personal background, nor in exhorting both to treat each other as brothers, nor in trying to *prove* to the white man that the black man is, for example, clean, healthy, intelligent and 'civilised'. In trying to see the latter as an acceptable human package this last approach not only perpetuates the repulsive initial inequality at another level but also degrades him even further. While all these and other methods may succeed in establishing better relations between isolated members of different races, the problem of racism is too profound to be tackled by such simpleminded ahistorical and apolitical approaches. If what we have said above is correct, the answer, if we may so call what is no more than a tentative suggestion, is to be found in radically altering the politico-economic and cultural relationship between the white and the black man which generated racism in the first instance.

As long as the black man remains wretched and powerless he is unlikely to command any respect. Unless therefore the immigrants settled in Britain can organise and become a powerful force in British economic and political life, they are unlikely to be taken seriously. Further, the destiny of the black man in England is integrally tied up with the Third World, in that the latter's success or failure inevitably affects the way the white community looks upon him. As the changing British images of the Chinese, the Japanese and the Jews during the past two decades show, the respect enjoyed by an individual follows the power and success of his nation. Unless therefore the countries of the Third World acquire economic and political power such that they cannot be taken for granted, that is, unless they undergo profound political and economic changes and succeed in totally redefining their parasitic relationship with the West, the black man's demand for equality and respect will be met with nothing more than patronising condescension at best and downright contempt at worst. People who lack the will to take charge of their destiny and to stand up for their rights may be flattered for their 'moderation' and 'civilised' behaviour by those whose interests they serve, but they never evoke respect.

At the cultural level the black man's demand for the full recognition of his humanity rests on his ability successfully to recreate his identity and to assert his individuality at the deepest existential level. Men who have no pride in their history and its heritage and are content to conform to others' image of them are culturally insubstantial and lack the necessary basis of self-respect. Recreation of identity is an extremely complicated and painful process, requiring a patient and intelligent recomposition of one's historical heritage by putting together the scattered fragments of the ruptured past.

Centuries of contact with Europe have left deep marks on the black man's consciousness, which he simply cannot blot out or wish out of existence. Indeed as the black man begins to rediscover his past, he is bound to find that not everything there is valuable and worth preserving. Of some of his customs and institutions, he is bound to feel ashamed (e.g. treatment of women, or of the socially and economically underprivileged).

He is also bound to find that his pre-colonial past is not a golden age as he fondly believes; along with much that is great and worth cherishing, it was also disgraced by tyranny, oppression, violence and exploitation, comparable in their magnitude and inhumanity to those perpetrated by the imperial powers. Indeed, the more he digs into his past, the less contemptuous he is likely to be of his colonial heritage, and the more he is likely to realise that some European influences have been for the good, and that he should therefore incorporate them into his heritage. The answer to European cultural hegemony, in short, is not to be found in the black man's aggressive and undiscriminating assertion of his native traditions and values but in going beyond and transcending European culture by recreating his identity on the basis of the best that *both* his own society and Europe have to offer.

So far as the white community is concerned, it is inconsistent of it to claim to abhor racism, and to do nothing to remove the very conditions which foster it. If it is *seriously* worried about its racism, it should therefore do all in its power to help the black man achieve economic and political power and cultural self-respect. It could stop treating meanly the representatives of the Third World settled in its midst as successive British governments have done, and show them respect and humanity. It could go further and end its exploitative relationship with the Third World, and help its members achieve decent human existence. It must stop thinking in terms of foreign 'aid' which, far from helping poorer nations, is really a process by which they help the rich nations sustain an ever-rising standard of living, and join them in a spirit of partnership in combating the terrifying economic legacy of colonial rule. At the cultural level, the white community can encourage the black man to develop his own distinctive identity by taking sympathetic interest in his culture, social institutions, beliefs and historical achievements. And this it can do only if it stops imposing culturally biased standards of evaluation on the Third World, reflecting the familiar divine pretension of the West to define and create the black man in its own image, and acknowledges that each community has its own distinctive mode of life which, subject to certain universally operative moral principles, is entitled to equal respect.

Lack of any real concern in Britain and elsewhere for the dire economic predicament of the Third World, and the cultural naricissism underlying academic, journalistic and other approaches to the Third World offer little ground for optimism. If lucky, we might succeed in creating better 'race relations' in Britain, but we are unlikely to end racism.

3. PREJUDICE AND THE PRESS (Article for *New Society,* 7 Nov. 1986)
British newspapers, including the best of them, have not shown much care and sensitivity in reporting racial matters. Two recent events have sharply brought this painful truth to the attention of even those otherwise inclined to doubt it.

Ever since the sixties it has been widely recognised that a local authority with a sizeable proportion of Commonwealth children should make requisite provisions to help overcome the difficulties they are likely to face in their environment. In order to help and encourage a local authority to do so, section 11 of the Local Government Act, 1966, entitles it to receive 75 per cent of the salary cost of the extra staff appointed by it. As is widely known, several local authorities have for years been improperly using the section 11 money to appoint general staff and allocating the money saved to other purposes. Despite years of complaints by the blacks, nothing was done.

During the last five years the Rampton, Swann and Eggleston reports have all highlighted the gross underachievement of ethnic minority children, and pointed to such factors as low teacher expectations, inadequate teacher attention and stimulus, lack of role models, poor regard for the children's culture and identity, and ethnocentric curriculum as among its major causes. Brent Council developed a set of proposals to deal with the situation and applied for a staff of 177, 103 to be placed in schools, 66 to be engaged in curriculum development projects and eight in the Directorate of Education. The proposals were prepared by its Conservative administration, had all-party support, were widely known, and had, after suitable revisions, been approved by the DES and the Home Office in April this year.

All of a sudden a storm broke loose. We were told the following by all the tabloid and some quality newspapers:

1) Brent was going to appoint 'race advisers'.
2) The 'race advisers' were really 'spies' reporting on their colleagues.
3) They were 'thought police' and 'commissars' who will tell our children what to think.
4) They represented a backdoor attempt to initiate a 'political revolution'.
5) Brent's ideas were all 'left-wing' and reflected the crazy educational philosophy of the 'looney left'.
6) Since Brent is now Labour-controlled, its actions reflected Labour's policies and showed what it would do if it came to power.

7) The whole thing was 'suddenly' contrived and a 'shock' to the innocent British public.

8) Brent had violated section 11, for the latter was only meant to appoint English language teachers.

Now (1) was false as Brent was appointing teachers, not race advisers. (2) was a distortion bordering on a lie for, although this may occur, it may not, and this was not the intention. (3) was entirely untrue because periodic revision of the curriculum is a part of a local authority's responsibility, was recommended by the three government reports mentioned earlier, and the new curriculum is open to HMI's scrutiny. (4) was mischievous, as a mere 177 among several thousand staff can obviously do little, they are organisationally responsible to head teachers, and they have clearly allocated responsibilities. (5) was wrong because the ideas came from the three 'liberal' reports and were conceived by Brent's Conservative administration. (6) was a mischievous and disgraceful way to malign a party and serve the interests of its opponents. (7) was totally false, for the Brent proposals had been known for nearly a year. (8) was a distortion, because section 11 covers a wide area. The Brent proposals do have obvious limitations and require critical examination. Misrepresenting and denouncing them, or mixing them up with a discussion of the case of Maureen McGoldrick (the headteacher suspended for alleged racism) was hardly the way to do so.

Thanks to these falsehoods and distortions, Brent might lose the posts. More importantly the black minorities are bound to feel deeply offended. When 'their' money was misused no one listened to their complaints. But now it was being put to what appeared to be good use, and their children seemed likely to progress, it looks like being taken away, and a demand made to abolish section 11 itself. They also feel that when their affairs are the subject of discussion, truth, sensitivity, and mutual respect apparently do not count.

The picture was little different when the visa requirement was imposed on visitors from five Commonwealth countries. The requirement was discriminatory; a case for it had not been made out; neither the governments concerned nor the Commission for Racial Equality had been consulted; and no provision had been made to send adequate and trained staff to the countries concerned. with a couple of exceptions, no newspaper took up these matters. When around 2,500 Asians arrived, the tabloid newspapers were awash with denigatory headlines. 'Asian flood swamps airport', screamed the Express. '3,000 Asians flood Britain', shouted the Sun. 'Migrants flood in', echoed the Mail. The Sun, in a six-inch headline, called them 'liars'. Only the Independent and the Guardian agreed that the scenes at Heathrow were a 'disgrace' to Britain.

Once again, the newspaper reports contained falsehoods and distortions. The Asians were visitors not immigrants; a very large majority of them had a right to come; many came sooner than they had intended because of the uncertainty of the government policy; and the chaos was a result of inadequate planning and warning. Tremendous inconvenience was caused to their sponsors travelling from long distances, about which not a word was said, and the entire Asian community was subjected to most vicious moral mugging.

When the press twists facts, tells lies, declares a cold war on a section of the community, uses editorials as party political broadcasts and subjects its readers to a daily breakfast of raw prejudices, it undermines the basic pre-conditions of democracy. By systematically misrepresenting the speeches of public figures, it not only vitiates public debate but also terrorises them into silence. The freedom of the *press* then becomes an enemy of the freedom of *speech*. Further, when the press reduces complex arguments to mischievous cliches, shuts out inconvenient opinions and becomes little more than an industry manufacturing beliefs and opinions, the freedom of the press becomes an enemy of the freedom of *thought*. Thought is integrally related to speech. Speech is not an expression or objectification of a pre-existing thought, but its very content and condition of existence. As social beings we first learn to speak and then think. Thinking is a form of speaking to oneself, and necessarily presupposes a world in which men constantly speak to one another. When speech is threatened, the capacity to think too is threatened. The press creates the world of public and political speech. And when that world is systematically distorted and vulgarised, the community's capacity for political thought is gravely endangered. Its capacity to think, reflect and reason is weakened, and reduced to little more than playing around with inert cliches and static images.

One would have thought that the Press Council had a vital role to play here. As a Council for and not merely of the press, it has a supreme responsibility to protect the integrity of public discourse, nurture a free flow of information and ideas and preserve public confidence in the press. In racial matters its record so far has been rather patchy. Most of its adjudications relate to complaints about whether or not a newspaper was right to disclose a person's colour in criminal cases and riots. Sometimes it has dealt with offensive cartoons. And on rare occasions it has adjudicated on complaints about articles lacking 'balance, sensitivity and care'.

Surely all this is hardly enough. Complaints about the disclosure of a man's colour are rather trivial. Far more important issues relating to how we talk about each other and how much we respect truth and objectivity are at stake. The Press Council could periodically mount investigations of its own into the way certain types of event and groups of people are reported and commented upon. It could also issue guidelines, a kind of code of practice, in areas where it thinks the press has a tendency to slip up. And it must really do something about the absurd situation when the force of its adjudication can be undermined by the newspaper concerned publishing and ridiculing it.

The freedom of the press is not only one of the vital conditions but also one of the essential constituents of democracy. The old nineteenth century arguments for it are no longer relevant to the vastly changed economic and political context within which a modern democracy functions. Further freedom of the press is qualitatively different from freedom of speech, and the arguments traditionally advanced in defence of the latter cannot without serious qualifications be extended to it. The press represents a specific form of speech, namely one that is public, organized, printed and hence relatively permanent, controlled by the owners of newspapers and hence both selective and censored, reaching out to a vast audience and hence politically powerful, and invested with the moral authority popularly accorded to the printed word. As such, it wields a kind and degree of political power and moral authority not available to other forms of speech. Being wholly unlike the freedom of the individual to speak as he likes, freedom of the press requires a different kind of justification. The former can be a natural right; the latter cannot. And the former may be intrinsically desirable, whereas the latter can only have an instrumental value.

The democratic form of government is rightly based on the suspicion of political power and aims to tame and render it publicly accountable by such devices as the separation of powers, dispersal of power, the system of checks and balances and the periodic election and removal of government. There is no reason why the press should be treated differently. It is odd to be suspicious of the government but not of the press, to be sensitive to the dangers of one form of political power but not another. John Stuart Mill thought that society posed as great a danger to individual liberty as the state, and that the traditional focus of political debate needed to be expanded to include it as well. Hitherto we have thought of the press as the custodian of liberty and necessary to check the government. We know that it in fact sometimes works in close co-operation with the government, and/or gangs up against dissent and either wears it down by systematic misrepresentation and indoctrination or blocks its emergence. The press is a paradoxical institution. It is an economic enterprise, privately owned, at least partially motivated by profit and subject to the constraints and compulsions of the market. At the same time it is also a public and political institution, discharging the vital function of determining the character and content of the public realm, filtering and forming the shared body of political knowledge and shaping the manner in which citizens think and talk about political life. Its economic and political dimensions make different, even conflicting, demands, and there is no guarantee that the latter will always be given priority.

We need to ask if it is wise to allow private and publicly non-accountable individuals or agencies to exercise political functions and wield enormous political power. It is, of course, true that in a liberal democracy the industrialists and others too exercise considerable political influence. The case of the press, however, is different. Unlike them it does not merely seek to influence the Government but also to determine the character of public life and the way people think and feel. It therefore affects the very roots of political life and cannot be treated as an ordinary industry. The freedom to influence beliefs and opinions is wholly different from and must be subjected to more stringent constraints than the freedom to produce soap and washing machines. Until we find better alternatives, we may have to continue with the economically propelled private ownership of a vital and inherently public institution. However, we should never lose sight of its inherent dangers, nor of the need to find more effective ways of coping with them.

In most democratic countries, the freedom of the press is generally subject to no other constraints than those imposed by the law of libel. In its current form the law only applies to individuals not groups, which can therefore be maligned with impunity. Further it only applies to named or easily identifiable individuals but not to those darkly hinted at. A newspaper claiming that all Africans are cheats, all Asians devious and liars and all Jews rapacious, is subject to no constraint. The law of libel gives no protection to a helpless ethnic group and a political party subjected to wilful and grossly mischievous misrepresentation. We must find ways of combining the freedom of the press with proper respect for individuals and groups and the integrity of public discourse.

Attitudes, Race Relations and Television
by Gajendra Verma

A leading broadcaster[1] has claimed that the role of television in maintaining national spirit and morale in times of crisis and difficulty is crucial. He may be right. The role of television clearly stands above that of other forms of mass media. Hartmann and Husband[2] found that, for the children and adolescents they interviewed, television was undoubtedly the most important source of information about the world. They argue that the important effect of the mass media is not that watching television makes us more violent or permissive or racist, but that the media throw some features into sharp relief, obliterate others, select and limit the issues which are worthy of consideration or recall. The mass media do not determine attitudes, but they do structure and select information we may use on which to base decisions about what attitude is appropriate. For the mass of people, of course, this process is hardly rational or conscious. Attitudes themselves are ill-formed and may be focused by the images and attitudes of the mass media. It is possible, too, as Halloran and his colleagues have argued[3] that television and other news media serve to support already formed prejudiced opinions, in that adults and children who are already prejudiced recall more readily news items and programmes whose content is racial. The same programme can also mean different things to different observers. The influence of television programmes may be both subtle and indirect.

123

Television becomes important as children grow older. In a study of 11 national and cultural groups, Lambert and Klineberg (1967) found that six-year-old children report a primary dependence on their parents for attitudes about other ethnic groups. Children of ten and older, however, report a greater dependence on television and reading materials. What this implies is that children can learn racial concepts, and racial terms of abuse which they would otherwise have been ignorant of. A case in point is the influence of the TV series *Love They Neighbour* which portrayed a white bigot who heaps racial abuse upon his neighbour. The programme was meant to be funny. The Area Round-up Column of *Race Today* reported in May 1973 that a primary school headteacher in Fife, Scotland, said 'that children in his school had made a coloured worker's life a misery, calling him names like 'coon' and 'sambo', having picked them up from the programme *Love Thy Neighbour*. A Thames TV spokesman said that all the evidence they had showed that people were overwhelmingly in favour of the programme both as entertainment and as good race relations — 'by using humour it takes the heat out of the colour question'. It could be said that the programme created a 'colour question' in Fife and in other areas where there are very few coloured immigrants.

Carlin has noted that 'Racial clowning is the classic defence against humiliation and physical attack . . . there is the Latin American clown, who is always smiling; there is, as Conor Cruise O'Brien again has pointed out, the Irish clown, who is always drunk; there is the Asian clown, the Babu; there is the Negro clown — we know him well. There is — or was — a Jewish clown. All racial clowns are sooner or later celebrated on the musical comedy stage'.[4] These clowns are celebrated too, on our TV screens, and serve to reinforce the stereotypes of the majority. In recent years, television's treatment of other cultures concerns the Arabs. Characters are either wealthy stumblebums in situation comedies or unprincipled terrorists in so-called dramas.

Both BBC and ITV continue to show a variety of old films, which portray Africans and American Indians as untrustworthy savages, fit peoples for subjugation and civilisation by the white man. A new genre of TV programmes has appeared on British screens in recent years — specially produced ficitional programmes for TV which have been made in America in a new era of apparent racial enlightenment. A detailed content analysis of these programmes has been made by a group of American researchers.[5] A number of the programmes analysed have been shown on British TV. The formal roles assigned to the characters varied considerably. Males, both white and black, were represented as professionals or semi-professionals e.g. educators, policemen, firemen, detectives, ranchers. Females of both races were portrayed as teachers, secretaries and housewives, whereas white females also took on such roles as nurses, counsellors, detectives and newspaper owners. Formal role-status, say the researchers, was not completely equitable but represented a substantial movement toward equality compared to role assignment during the earlier years of television. Citing research which shows that children's positive and negative attitudes toward their own and other races can be influenced by the specific ways in which racial characters are portrayed on television, Donagher et al conclude that the new wave of television dramas may have served to transmit a new wave of stereotypes, but these stereotypes are still ones of black inferiority.

Current statistics show that children spend a great deal of time watching television. A piece of research[6] was conducted to ascertain the effects of a television series specifically designed to influence racial attitudes.

Kemelfield evaluated the effects of programmes transmitted in schools TV service for 9 to 12-year-olds on the lives of children in other cultures. The programmes were shown to two groups of children, one in an area of immigrant settlement, and one in an area without immigrants. In general, the programme was well received, and also effective in achieving its aims of 'encouraging appreciating and tolerance of people of different creeds and races now living in Britain'. For example, of the subjects in the low contact area, 39% thought that 'Pakistanis are usually as clean as English people', before seeing the programme, compared with 75% of those questioned after seeing it. There was one exception to these results, in white children in one school in an area of high immigrant settlement, where 28% of pupils were, in fact from Pakistan. Here, all the children's pre-programme knowledge was generally greater, but their post-programme answers suggested that in certain areas they were reacting to their own knowledge of their Pakistani peers rather than to the programme content. After viewing the programme, white pupils in this high contact school appeared to be more sensitive to the possibilities of culture clashes (e.g. over different diets) with Pakistani children. Clearly the effects of television are complex, as are the effects of teaching about race relations in schools,[7] but TV programmes can have, in certain circumstances, a considerable influence on attitudes. If programmes transmitted by school television can affect attitudes in positive ways, it seems probable that programmes transmitted at other times can also affect attitudes. Unfortunately, there is not as much research on the issues as would be desirable.

British television's coverage of the 'Third World' fosters 'mythic reactions' as opposed to historical explication of complex social reality, by evoking irony, scepticism and fascination. Having examined coverage of the recent developments in South Africa, terrorism in Europe and race relations in Britain, one is forced to conclude that television coverage is constrained by its structural limitations as a medium. These result in trivialisation of complex social issues into stereotyped conflicts by personification of nations and issues, with prominence given to violence rather than to underlying social or political conditions.

The interweaving of 'entertainment' and 'information' on the TV programmes cultivates a 'knowledge' of reality based on facts that are often learned from fictional dramas. Although most of us have never been in an operating theatre, a courtroom, a prison or a space programme control centre, we have formed certain images of the way these look and operate, based on 'facts' learned from mass media descriptions.

Television makes specific and measureable contributions to viewers' perceptions of reality. But that 'TV reality' is often synthetic and distorted, suited to the stylistic and dramatic requirements of the medium. Thus it has been pointed out that '. . . the more time one spends 'living' in the world of television, the more likely one is to report perceptions of social reality which can be traced to television's most persistent representation of life and society'.[8]

For the majority of people, television is the prime medium of entertainment, instruction and information. The written word comes a poor second. Television is essentially a visual medium and the spoken word serves to explain or reinforce the messages that the images convey. It is arguable that, in many cases, the words are redundant and that the best television requires few or none. (It shares this with film. It is very noticeable that old films have their characters engaging in a great deal of dialogue which does nothing but repeat messages that have already been conveyed more effectively and quicker by the images. One can almost date a film by the density of the dialogue — the more recent it is, the more the producer allows the images to do the work.) Thus in the current (June 1986) inter-racial conflict in South Africa, the image of the hacked body of the TV reporter, his blood seeping through the hastily applied bandages, indistinctly seen for a few seconds as he was being taken to a distant hospital, is likely to be the one element of that news coverage that remains in the minds of many — indeed most — of the viewers. They will be unlikely to remember which of the two groups of black Africans was responsible, or indeed see it as a significant issue; they will be unlikely to place it in the total context of the South African situation, even if they (or indeed any one) knew it; what will remain is the image of that mutilated body — soon to die — and with it, perhaps, a sense of outrage that a man who was simply doing his job could be so treated by men who stood to benefit from his work. And we scarcely need to observe that this very public murder, naively committed in circumstances of maximum publicity was indisputably the work of a black South African. The message of indiscriminate savagery could hardly be more effective conveyed. Of course, we all know that repressive regimes practise the most appalling cruelties on those whom they repress; that men and women die unspeakable deaths every day as consequence of organised, deliberate and cold-blooded torture. But these acts are carried out in secret places from which no pictures emerge to be carried round the world on television. The deaths of Steve Biko and many like him remain shrouded by silence and, faced by the immediacy of the image of the dying reporter, it is difficult to bring all these events together.

Lest there should be any doubt, we are not seeking for a moment to attempt to justify the death of that reporter. What we are trying to emphasise is the way in which a single image, on the screen for perhaps three or four seconds, can so potently occupy the minds of viewers and can create associations that will, unconsciously perhaps, inform attitudes towards black people in social and political contexts far removed from South Africa. The death of Steve Biko and many like him is just as much a fact. The difference, the crucial difference, lies in the way those facts are presented and this, in turn, affects the nature and distribution of the knowledge of those facts and, hence, the way in which they can modify a white community's response to a black presence.

Nor do we suggest that this item should not have formed part of the news from South Africa. Given the nature of television, it is inconceivable that any editor would have deleted it, or should be expected to do so. The problem central to the medium is that, by its nature, it is capable of creating very potent images which convey very powerful messages but that these images cannot readily be placed in a rational context within the news programme in which they are first presented. For the viewer who has a pre-existing framework of knowledge and understanding, these images can, as it were, be tamed, they can be harnessed in ways that make them a force for constructive action. Without that framework they can be projected onto quite other situations and become destructive. Nor is the problem solved by attempting to contextualise the item in a later programme. Most of the audience of *New at Ten* will not turn over later that night to, shall we say, *Newsnight*, where, if the BBC has picked it up quickly enough, some talking heads might try to make some sense of a situation that almost defies analysis. Talking heads make 'bad' television and, however well they talk, it requires a special kind of training, not given to the majority of viewers, to derive the kind of pleasure that makes them turn to it in the first place and stay with it in the second.

How do we depend on the media?

The media represent a vital source of information which is informed by belief and values so as to construct a representation of the reality which surrounds us. The nature of that representation varies according to the medium and the editorial policies of those in positions of power in the organisation.

Race and race relations are issues of controversy. They arouse strong emotions in many of the general public, of whom the editorial staff are part. There is thus a positive feedback from public to medium and back to the public such that strong emotions are likely to, and often do affect the ways in which these issues are presented. From an analysis of a large amount of data on racial attitudes drawn from a number of national and local surveys of prejudice in Britain, the evidence is that at least 20% of the population are hard-line racialists, wanting little contact with minorities, and desiring the suppression of rights and, ultimately, their repatriation. Some 60% hold a broadly assimilationist position, offering minorities some acceptance if they give up their 'alien' languages, religions, dress and customs in the face of superior British culture, and even this often at the price of accepting subordinate roles without close contact with the majority group. Only about 20% of the population accept a broadly pluralist position, accepting minority cultures as valuable contributions to a multicultural society.

It is not surprising therefore that, consciously or unconsciously, the emotional cues contained within the presentation of news prompt negative responses towards ethnic minorities. The sensitivity of the issues involved makes this kind of response the more powerful. For example, the emphasis of the media in the area of race relations changed substantially from a habitual concern in the 1960s with the number of black people entering the country to the problems associated with their presence, that is to say, from being an 'external threat' to becoming 'the outsider within'. Thus, part of the media representation of reality is to do with representing black people as essentially different from the mainstream of society. For example, Councillor Ajeeb, Bradford's first Asian Lord Mayor, was shown at prayer at the time of his election to Mayor. That in itself would be unusual for a white politician. It is an activity that few of the electorate would regularly engage in and there are few votes to be won from it but, more significantly, it was prayer addressed to an 'alien' deity.

For those living in all-white areas of the country — and they are in the majority — direct knowledge of the kind that can only be acquired by living with and personally interacting with members of ethnic minorities is not available. Their knowledge of race relations is confined to what they can glean from the media.

The reporting of news and current affairs is not simply a matter of collecting facts, whether about race riots or anything else. Facts do not exist in a vacuum but can acquire meaning only when located in a wide ranging set of assumptions about the nature of reality. Which facts are brought into sharp focus — or reported at all — depends on which set of assumptions are held by the editorial staff as well as by the medium in which they are operating. Similarly, at the receiving end, there is a tendency for the reader, listener or viewer to interpret 'race-related' ideas in ways that are congruent with an already existing point of view. Where there is conflict, ideas that do not support existing points of view are ignored or suppressed. Of course the editorial staff are likely to be similarly affected and events which conform to their sense of 'reality' have a better chance of being reported than those which conflict with it.

The criteria suggested by the Independent Broadcasting Authority are:

a)   confronting differences
b)   identifying differences
c)   endorsing differences (e.g. by using multiethnic resources to illustrate the values of other cultures)
d)   absorbing differences (e.g. by using non-white people in normal situations without implying any other differences)

These, together with the NUJ guidelines on race have led to cosmetic improvements in the treatment of race in the media but the news process has not been materially affected. For example, the National Front is still permitted to masquerade as a legitimate participant in British politics and stories about it and 'white hostility' are placed in an entirely different 'framework' which has its origins in conceptions about freedom of speech. Quite properly, this freedom is jealously preserved but there is an apparent failure to distinguish between a proper freedom within the law as enshrined in the Race Relations Act and a quite spurious freedom to insult and, by insulting, to generate inter-group conflict. Journalistic assumptions about what constitutes 'good' news in the area of race relations tend to result in their concentrating more closely on the manifestations of these conflicts rather than on the reasons for them. This is not surprising since journalists handling news and current affairs will naturally concentrate on unusual, dramatic and difficult situations because of the impact they carry while they, or their superiors, are reluctant to dilute that impact by including in the story, didactic passages that seek to place the events in context. Even if they do, problems then arise as to which context to use — should it be free speech, or community relations, or equal rights, the liberal tradition, or what? Each will serve perhaps as a framework within which the story can be constructed, but each will result in a different product. In the end, the decision is likely to be taken on the basis of assumptions about what the reader or viewer will prefer and thus existing attitudes will be reinforced as we have seen earlier.

It is tempting to argue that the media should help correct the distorted picture held by the white majority about ethnic minorities and that they should play a responsible part in creating a just and harmonious society in which the whole concept of race relations becomes redundant. Unfortunately, our analysis suggests that its very nature and the relationship it has with its public are such that it is ill-equipped to do so. The way television functions means that it tends to maintain, cultivate and exploit beliefs and attitudes already held rather than undermine or alter existing perceptions. That is not to say that it has no part to play.

The reporting and discussion of many important issues in Britain and the World seem to be unduly dependent on the concept that 'newsworthiness' or 'topicality' derives from 'conflict' or 'drama'. As a result many issues reported and discussed in the media tend to become distorted. In issues relating to a multiracial society, this concept of presentation tends to heighten difference rather than to stress the points of harmony. In consequence, there is an urgent need to sensitize opinion, not merely among those in British public life as a whole, but particularly among those who control or influence the policy-making and day-to-day decision making processes in the media.

Note: This paper draws upon and develops Dr. Verma's Annex A to Chapter Two of the Swann Committee Report, *Education For All.*

References

1. Frank Gillard quoted in The Times, 19 Sept. 1975.
2. *Racism and the mass media.* Hartmann and Husband, Davis-Poynter, 1974.
3. *Mass media and social attitudes.* Halloran, Hartmann and Husband, SSRC Newsletter, 1974.
4. *Clowns for all races,* M. Carlin, *New Society,* Jan 9, 1975.
5. *Race, sex and social example: an analysis of character portrayals on inter-racial television entertainment,* P. Donagher et al, Psychological Reports, 37, 1975.
6. *The evaluation of schools' broadcasting,* G. Kemelfield, *New Society,* June 1, 1972.
7. *Teaching about race relations: problems and effects,* Stenhouse, Verma and Wild, Routledge, 1982.
8. *The mainstreaming of America,* Gerbner et al, Journal of Communications 30, 1980.

The Raj revival

by Salman Rushdie

(Article in *The Observer,* April 1984)

Anyone who has switched on the television set, been to the cinema or entered a bookshop will be aware that the British Raj, after three and a half decades in retirement has been making a sort of comeback. After the big-budget fantasy double-bill of 'Gandhi' and 'Octopussy' we have had the blackface minstrel-show of 'The Far Pavilions' in its TV-serial incarnation, and immediately afterwards the grotesquely overpraised 'Jewel in the Crown'.

I should also include the alleged 'documentary' about Subhas Chandra Bose, Granada Television's 'War of the Springing Tiger,' which, in the finest traditions of journalistic impartiality, described India's second most revered Independence leader as a 'clown'. And lest we begin to console ourselves that the painful experiences are coming to an end, we are reminded of David Lean's film of 'A Passage to India'.

I remember seeing an interview with Mr. Lean in *The Times,* in which he explained his reasons for wishing to make a film of Forster's novel. 'I haven't seen Dickie Attenborough's 'Gandhi' yet,' he said, 'but as far as I'm aware, nobody has yet succeeded in putting India on the screen.' The Indian film industry, from Satyajit Ray to Mr. N.T. Rama Rao, will no doubt feel suitably humbled by the great man's opinion.

These are dark days. Having expressed my reservations about the 'Gandhi' film elsewhere, I have no wish to renew my quarrel with Mahatma Dickie. And in defence of the Mahattenborough, he did allow a few Indians to be played by Indians. (One is becoming grateful for the smallest of mercies.)

Those responsible for transferring 'The Far Pavilions' to the screen would have no truck with such tomfoolery. True, Indian actors were allowed to play the villains (Saeed Jaffrey, who has turned the Raj revival into a personal cottage industry, with parts in 'Gandhi' and 'The Jewel in the Crown' as well, did his hissing and hand-rubbing party piece; and Sneh Gupta played the selfish princess, but unluckily for her, her entire part consisted of the interminably repeated line, 'Ram Ram').

Meanwhile, the good-guy roles were firmly commandeered by Ben Cross, Christopher Lee, Omar Sharif, and, most memorably, Amy Irving as the good princess, whose make-up person obviously believed that Indian princesses dip their eyes in black ink and get sun-tans on their lips.

Now of course 'The Far Pavilions' is the purest bilge. The great processing machines of TV soap opera have taken the somewhat more fibrous garbage of the M.M. Kaye book and puréed it into easy-swallow, no-chewing-necessary drivel. Thus, the two central characters, both supposedly raised as Indians, have been lobotomised to the point of being incapable of pronouncing their own names. The man calls himself 'A Shock', and the woman 'An Jooly'.

Around and about them there is branding of human flesh and snakery and widow-burning by the natives. There are Pathans who cannot speak Pushtu. And, to avoid offending the Christian market, we are asked to believe that the child 'A Shock', while being raised by Hindus and Muslims, somehow knew that neither 'way' was for him, and instinctively, when he wished to raise his voice in prayer, 'prayed to the mountains'.

It would be easy to conclude that such material could not possibly be taken seriously by anyone, and that it is therefore unnecessary to get worked up about it. Should we not simply rise above the twaddle, switch off our sets, and not care?

I should be happier about this, the quietist option, if I did not believe that it matters, it always matters, to name rubbish as rubbish; that to do otherwise is to legitimise it. But 'The Far Pavilions' is only the latest in a very long line of fake portraits inflicted by the West on the East. The creation of a false Orient of cruel-lipped princes and dusky slim-hipped maidens, of ungodliness, fire and the sword, has been brilliantly described by Edward Said in his classic study 'Orientalism', in which he makes clear that the purpose of such false portraits was to provide moral, cultural and artistic justification for imperialism and for its under-pinning ideology, that of the racial superiority of the Caucasian over the Asiatic.

Paul Scott was M.M. Kaye's agent, and it has always seemed to me a damning indictment of his literary judgment that he believed 'The Far Pavilions' to be a good book. 'The Raj Quartet' and the Kaye novel lift their central plot motifs from earlier, and much finer novels. In 'The Far Pavilions', the hero Ash ('A Shock'), raised an Indian, discovered to be a sahib, and ever afterwards torn between his two selves, will be instantly recognisable as the cardboard cut-out version of Kipling's Kim. And the rape of Daphne Manners in the Bibighar Gardens derives just as plainly from Forster's 'Passage to India'.

But because Kaye and Scott are vastly inferior to the writers they follow, they turn what they touch to pure lead. Where Forster's scene in the Marabar caves retains its ambiguity and mystery, Scott gives us not one rape but a gang assault, and one perpetrated, what is more, by peasants. Smelly persons of the worst sort. So class as well as sex is violated; Daphne gets the works.

It is useless, I'm sure, to suggest that if a rape must be used as the metaphor of the Indo-British connection, then surely, in the interests of accuracy, it should be the rape of an Indian woman by one or more Englishmen of whatever class. So much more evocative to conjure up white society's fear of the darkie, of big brown cocks. You will say I am being unfair; Scott is a writer of a different calibre than M.M. Kaye. What's more, very few of the British characters come at all well out of the Quartet — only Barbie, Sarah, Daphne, none of the men. (Ms Kaye, reviewing the TV adaptation, found it excessively rude about the British.)

In point of fact, I am not so sure that Scott is so much finer an artist. Like M.M. Kaye, he has an instinct for the cliché. Sadistic, bottom-flogging policeman Merrick turns out to be (surprise!) a closet homosexual. His grammar school origins give him (what else?) a chip on the shoulder. And all around him is a galaxy of chinless wonders, regimental *grandes dames*, lushes, empty-headed blondes, silly-asses, plucky young things, good sorts, bad eggs and Russian counts with eye-patches. The overall effect is rather like a literary version of Mulligatawny soup. It tries to taste Indian, but ends up being ultra-parochially British, only with too much pepper. And yes, Scott is harsh in his portraits of many British characters; but I want to try to make a rather more difficult point, a point about *form*. The Quartet's form tells us, in effect, that the history of the end of the Raj was largely composed of the doings of the officer class and its wife. Indians get walk-ons, but remain, for the most part, bit-players in their own history. Once this form has been set, it scarcely matters that individual, fictional Brits get unsympathetic treatment from their author. The form insists that *they are the ones whose stories matter,* and that is so much less than the whole truth that it must be called a falsehood.

It will not do to argue that Scott was attempting only to portray the British in India, and that such was the nature of imperialist society that the Indians *would* only have had bit parts. It is no defence to say that a work adopts, in its structure, the very ethic which, in its content and tone, it pretends to dislike. It is, in fact, the case for the prosecution.

I cannot end this brief account of the Raj revival without returning to David Lean. Here are three passages from an interview with him in the *Guardian:*

1) Forster was a bit anti-English, anti-Raj and so on, I suppose it's a tricky thing to say but I'm not so much. I intend to keep the balance more. I don't believe all the English were a lot of idiots. Forster rather made them so. He came down hard against them. I've cut out that bit at the trial where they try to take over the court. Richard (Goodwin, the producer) wanted me to leave it in. But I said no, it just wasn't right. They wouldn't have done that.

2) As for Aziz, there's a hell of a lot of Indian in him. They're marvellous people but maddening sometimes, you know. . . . He's a goose. But he's warm and you like him awfully. I don't mean that in a derogatory way — things just happen to him. He can't help it.

3) One other thing. I've got rid of that 'Not yet, not yet' bit. You know, when the Quit India stuff comes up, and we have the passage about driving us into the sea? . . . I thought that bit rather tacked on. Anyway, I see it as a personal not a political story.

Forster's lifelong refusal to permit his novel to be filmed begins to look rather sensible. But once a revisionist enterprise gets under way, the mere wishes of a dead novelist provide no obstacle. The recrudescence of imperialist ideology and the popularity of Raj fictions put one in mind of the phantom twitchings of an amputated limb. The continuing decline, the growing poverty and the meanness of spirit of much of Thatcherite Britain encourage many Britons to turn their eyes nostalgically to the lost hour of their precedence. Britain is in danger of entering a condition of cultural psychosis, in which it begins once again to strut and to posture like a great power while, in fact, its power diminishes every year. The jewel in the crown is made, these days, of paste.

Anthony Barnett has cogently argued, in his television essay 'Let's take the 'great' out of Britain', that the idea of a *great* Britain (originally just a collective term for the countries of the British Isles, but repeatedly used to bolster the myth of national grandeur) has bedevilled the actions of all post-war governments.

It was Margaret Thatcher who, in the euphoria of the Falklands victory, most plainly nailed her colours to the old colonial mast, claiming that the success in the South Atlantic proved that the British were still the people 'who had ruled a quarter of the world'. Shortly afterwards she called for a return to Victorian values, thus demonstrating that she had embarked upon a heroic battle against the linear passage of Time.

I am trying to say something which is not easily heard above the clamour of praise for the present spate of British-Indian fictions: that works of art, even works of entertainment, do not come into being in a social and political vacuum; and that the way they operate in a society cannot be separated from politics, from history. For every text, a context; and the rise of Raj revisionism, exemplified by the huge success of these fictions, is the artistic counterpart to the rise of conservative ideologies in modern Britain.

No matter how innocently the writers and film-makers work, no matter how skilfully the actors act (and nobody would deny the brilliance of, for example, the performances of Susan Wooldridge as Daphne and Peggy Ashcroft as Barbie in the TV 'Jewel'), they run the grave risk of helping to shore up that conservatism, by offering it the fictional glamour which its reality so grievously lacks.

Reflections on Recent TV Coverage of Africa

by Zeinab Badawi

I was born in the Sudan, but I have lived in England since I was three years old. As far as working in television goes, I am treated as an insider — foreign, but so anglicised that I could be regarded as British. However, particularly after the experience of filming in my home country, the Sudan, with a British TV crew, I would see myself more as a Sudanese with some inside experience of British television, than as a television journalist with some experience of Africa.

In 1986 I spent 4 months in the Sudan doing the research for a television series on the developing world. It was an ambitious project, a joint venture between ITV, CBC — the Canadian Broadcasting Corporation — and TV New Zealand which also included filming in Brazil, India and Bangladesh. I remember jumping for joy for when I first learned of my involvement. I thought that at last this would be my chance to do something worthwhile on a topic which is very close to my heart. I also welcomed the opportunity to travel extensively around my own home country, for up until then my experience of the Sudan was limited to a privileged life in the capital — Khartoum — where my relatives live. However, I must confess, sadly, that there are real difficulties about working on programmes about Africa for British television: not that we cannot aspire to more worthwhile coverage of Africa, indeed we *can* do much better than we are at present, but what a British person and what an African person is likely to consider as good TV coverage of the continent are two different things.

As with most things it is easier to identify the negative rather than the positive aspects, but one positive thing to be said about TV coverage of Africa today is that it is better than that of say 25 years ago. Earlier TV coverage of Africa was born of a negative attitude towards Africans, and gave rise to negative effects. Africans were seen as a colonised people. Their own culture, identity and history were not really recognised as being valid or important. So coverage of Africa was usually viewed from a position of overt imperial authority, racial superiority and cultural chauvinism. No pretence was made to cover this.

With the end of the empire, one might have hoped for a change, and certainly there is evidence of a more enlightened and positive approach. Kenyan historian Ali Masrui gave us the BBC series *The Africans* — programmes from an African viewpoint; some programme makers are making a determined effort to find Africans to sum up the situation for them on location, instead of wheeling in the customary ex-patriate from some aid organistion. However what I find disturbing about recent TV coverage of Africa is that an apparently enlightened approach gives rise to some unpalatable side effects: cultural superiority is still presupposed, only now it is more subtle.

To me the 'Band Aid' initiative is an obvious example. I recognise that most people responded to the 'Band Aid' appeal out of genuine humanitarian motives, and certainly many poor desperate people were helped. But what I am concerned with are some of the *images* and *impressions* created by TV coverage of 'Band Aid'.

Firstly, it confirms the general problem of the media that it spends much more time responding topically and superficially to events, than to prompting education and greater understanding. It seems that Africa only hits the news when there is a coup, war or famine occurring. As a journalist I can understand why we want to look at such events, but what we should be doing is putting them in context, to show how in reality such things are symptoms of complex political, social and economic issues. As the famine has ended in the Sudan, so media attention has receded. What of the country's new government — a democracy restored after 17 years of dictatorship? What efforts are the Sudanese making to pick up the pieces of their shattered lives? Why exactly did a famine occur? A well informed picture of African politics depends on a steadier flow of coverage. After all, the Sudan is the largest country in Africa, colonised for about fifty years or so by the British. Events in the Sudan have largely gone unreported in the British media TV and newspapers. For instance we have had a civil war raging in the country for 30 years or so in which the British had played a significant part when they were governors of the land: this is not reported. I believe more people have died in this war than in the entire Arab/Israeli wars and it costs the Sudanese Government close on $1M a day to meet this war going. Who knows about it? Nobody does. But Sudan hit the headlines in 1985 as soon as people were starving to death.

Secondly, because 'Band Aid' in television terms was such a magnificent spectacle with its rock star involvement, the whole enterprise just became one big media hype.

The great attention it received *exaggerated* the importance of aid in the development process of Africa, and tended to confirm a false impression that Africa's problem can be solved if the West pours lots of charity into it. 'Band Aid' was a spectacle made by the West for the West, and Africa was the junior partner. I was in the Sudan when 'Sport Aid' was being initiated, and I was amused to see that its launch coincided with the month of 'Ramadan' when most African Muslims — certainly the majority of Sudanese — fast between the hours of sunrise and sun-set. Unlikely that anyone there would brave such a run. Soon after I arrived in England, I was surprised at my own feelings of how irrelevant I thought all those ardent runners in London were to the reality of life in remote villages of the Sudan.

However, the most disturbing aspect of TV coverage of 'Band-Aid' for me was its negative portrayal of the relationship between the West and Africans — and this is very important because it determines how the West views Africans. Of all the pictures I have seen of 'Band Aid' and its 'subsidiaries', the one that sticks out in my mind is the one of Bob Geldof, K.B.E. looking like a latter day Lawrence of Arabia, walking in the desert with hundreds of black hands tugging at his robes — welcoming this white saviour in their midst. TV deals in imperialist stereotypes today, just as it did 25 years ago. The impression such an image left me with is: 'Africans starve to death — for whatever reason — and it is the West, this time in the guise of Bob Geldof, which comes to their rescue'. They are portrayed as passive and helpless, spectators to their own destiny — the West is the superior partner.

Ah, you may well say, the enlightened view, the correct 'Channel 4' approach is to put all this into context and explain that is it the *West* , in alliance with corrupt African elites, who are responsible for the plight of these famine victims. In their book *Television and the Ethiopian Famine,* Greg Philo and Robert Lamb applaud Michael Poole's argument in the 'Listener' that 'famine is a problem of underdevelopment. To see the problem in its proper context we need to analyse international trade, colonial ties, and other factors which make developing countries dependant on world markets which are controlled and orientated to the needs of the developed economies'. By helping Africa, this 'enlightened' view holds that the West is simply putting back into Africa what is has effectively plundered. But in my opinion, there are still dangers in this view, because it undermines the notion of responsible indigenous government, and it *still* has the West talking from a position of superiority — the ball is still in the court of the West — and again this reinforces 'imperialist' stereotypes.

Another example of how a well-meaning aim can reinforce racist and imperialist stereotypes is the Channel 4 programme *A Man Made Famine* broadcast in May 1986. It seemed thoughtful and commendable enough, in showing that it is women who account for 85 per cent of Africa's food production. African women are portrayed as courageous, industrious and caring for their children against all odds. The African male did not come out well at all. He was seen as lazy and irresponsible, abandoning family for city life, thus confirming some of the British audience's view of African culture as being backward and unfair. A victory for feminism unwittingly becomes a tool for cultural chauvinism.

I think there will always be a problem in making TV programmes about Africa for British television. This is mainly because most people here lack alternative information and first hand experience of Africa. They cannot put things into context and so will always be viewing in a vacuum — a vacuum in which any pre-existing stereotypes or prejudices are left uncorrected. This was the problem I encountered when making a film about the Sudan. In an account of why the Sudan suffered in the mid 1980's, I would wish to outline the wider context of international terms of trade, but then lay much blame at the door of ex-President Nimeiry and earlier governments. However, such an approach for a British audience could easily be boring because they would feel remote from such a programme, it would not relate to them. Worse, if they did watch it, prejudiced views such as 'Well, it's all their own fault that they starve, because they are backward, undemocratic people given to tyranny etc', might be reinforced especially as it is unlikely that such a programme would be made unless there were enough 'distended bellies and emaciated arms', or some other gruelling spectacle to be filmed. Thus Africa poses a particular challenge in how to make popular and interesting coverage which avoids these pitfalls.

Out in the Sudan, the only way that I could persuade the Sudanese that the intrusion into their lives was justified, was by assuring them that yes, the new Sudanese government would see the film and be made aware of their plight. It was of no consequence to them that people here in the West would be better informed about them, or indeed that Westerners would be impelled to donate more to 'third world' charities. Indeed on several occasions we encountered stiff opposition, or at least reluctant acquiescence, for our filming — not from the authorities, but from these poor, desperate people themselves. They quite rightly judged that the real power which could do something to alleviate their sufferings was their *own* government, not another 'Bob Geldof'. Robbed of everything, I felt we were now robbing these people of their dignity, by putting them up as a spectacle in a medium ever conscious of ratings.

If programmes about Africa are to be broadcast at prime time and not relegated to the fringes of television viewing, there has to be a 'good story' which can appeal to a wide audience. For me there is all to often a contradiction between what I deem to be a 'good story' as a broadcaster, and what I find acceptable as an African. Take the BBC programme in the *40 Minutes* series, about female circumcision in the Sudan, shown in 1983. It was a true enough account of this abominable practice of female genital mutilation, which often results in horrendous mental and physical suffering. Still commonly practised in the Sudan, the whole exercise fills me with anger. Yet I doubt if I could co-operate in the making of such a programme for British television, because it would almost inevitably evoke dealings in the language of racism and cultural superiority. I say this because *whenever* I am asked where I was born, to my reply of 'The Sudan' I get one of only three responses: 'Oh, that's where you have all those starving people'; 'Oh, that's where women are mutilated'; 'Oh, that's where criminals have their hands chopped off' — referring to ex-President Nimeiry's introduction of 'Islamic' punishment for thieves in 1983, which got a lot of media attention at the time. Implicit (and even on occasion, explicit) in their words is the idea 'Aren't you one of the lucky ones then, to be living in the (civilised) West'.

Perhaps some patronising and ill-informed attitudes will remain, unless some degree of control is insisted upon over what is filmed by Western TV companies. I do not condone censorship within these countries — but perhaps there is a case for curbing the irresponsible pressures to sensationalise and over-simplify on the part of external agencies. A few years ago a West German producer gained permission from the Sudanese government to 'make a programme about Sudanese culture'. The programme subsequently broadcast in the West concentrated essentially on the ancient 'sport' of 'Nubian Wrestling' — bloody even by Roman gladiators' standards. Many West Germans could be pardoned for thinking that the Sudanese are a bloody, barbaric race after watching such a programme. Wonderful for the TV ratings, but not so wonderful for we Sudanese who live in the West.

As a Muslim, I find British people's image of Islam is that it is a very 'backward' religion; there is usually a wholesale rejection of the principles that Islam stands for, partly because TV and the media in general misleadingly focus on the fundamentalist Islam found in Iran. For the Shi'ite Moslems there, the role of the clergy is very elevated, but the majority of the Moslem world, some 90%, belong to the other sects which do not have any clergy as such.

People often say to me, 'What do you have to do when you go to your own country, do you have to wear a veil and what do you do about your Ayatollahs?', and I have to explain that we do not have any Ayatollahs in the Sudan. I am always having to explain that one must not focus only on negative aspects of Islam: for example, people always think Islam is particularly oppressive to females because of the veil and the fact that men have four wives and so on and so forth. This distorts the picture: most women in the Islamic world really believe in Islam and are quite happy to live by its principles.

People here also constantly ask how I put up with having to marry someone I have never clapped eyes on. I have to explain that while arranged marriage may not be suitable for me personally, that does not imply it is in itself a bad institution. Members of my own family have opted for the system of parentally guided marriage and that has been fine for them. If you ask most people what they think in relation to Asian women in Britain, they will say 'an arranged marriage' largely because the media seem somewhat obsessed with the subject of arranged marriages. TV perpetuates attitudes of cultural superiority when it focusses on the issue of arranged marriages because it tends to portray only the negative side of it — by focussing on the dilemma of some Asian women who reject such a marraige. This serves to discredit the entire notion, because what TV omits to tells us is that studies have shown that the majority of young Asians in Britain actually approve of parentally guided marriages; and, even when an Asian woman rejects an arranged marriage, she is only rejecting a particular aspect of her culture, she is not turning her back on the entire Asian culture.

Let me summarise why I feel so often that what is wonderful for the ratings is not so wonderful for those of us from Africa living in Britain.

It is understandable that in Britain television priority will go to domestic rather than foreign issues, and that foreign issues will only displace domestic ones if they are judged to be a 'good story', which will appeal to a wide audience. The trouble is that 'good stories' all too often seem to fall into one of only two categories: the 'cultural kaleidoscope' or the 'compassion seeking'. The 'compassion seeking' programmes, i.e. the famine type programmes, always view Africa's problems from a Western perspective: they try to awaken feelings of guilt at the West's economic superiority, and ask 'What can *we* do?' TV coverage of schools doing their 'bit' for Ethiopia and the Sudan is copious, and apparently oblivious to the degree of paternalism which can be fostered amongst school children towards their African counterparts. I hope I have highlighted the problems with the 'cultural kaleidoscope' approach.

No doubt it will go on, as it is not easy to resist a 'good story', but as an *African* some stories will be easier for me to resist than for my British colleagues. Television is controlled and owned by the West. Television news as supplied to most Third World countries is compiled from material from Western news agencies — mainly 'Visnews', 'UP-ITN', and 'CBS Newsfilm' (Columbia Broadcasting System). Advancement in the television industry is low on the list of priorities for most African governments — not surprisingly. Thus they cannot yet present themselves in their own terms on television. At the same time the West is selective about what it shows of Africa on television, and still presents it in Eurocentric terms and assumptions. The world might be seen as an 'electronic village', but it is still the West looking at Africa, not the other way round. Thus TV coverage of Africa will from an African viewpoint be merely a 'voyeuristic' exercise, at least while white European teams make programmes for white Europeans audiences without involving authentic African perspectives and analysis. I need to be convinced that we can justify TV coverage of Africa on 'global village grounds', because I cannot really explain why a British audience should be more concerned with problems abroad rather than with domestic ones, unless of course there is some sort of spectacle to behold. The latest development in say a domestic industrial dispute *will* take precedence over a foreign story in the news bulletin, unless the foreign story becomes 'good copy'. The famine in the Sudan and Ethiopia — long predicted — did not hit our screens until the problem had reached a severe magnitude.

I do not believe we can justify responsible and better TV coverage of Africa on the 'global village' grounds. The only way I can do this is to remove my 'African hat' and put on my 'British one'. From the *domestic* point of view I think it is dangerous to consider TV coverage of Africa in isolation from the immigrant communities in Britain. Since the way Africans (and Asians) are portrayed in the international arena reflects on the image of black people here, the issue becomes a domestic racial issue — and that affects all Britons directly. Black 'immigrants' have been a major concern in domestic politics. So if blacks abroad are for example seen as starving, helpless, and in need of Western assistance, it can reinforce in *some* British people's minds the idea that black immigrants *here* are fleeing economic hardship from their own poverty stricken countries. They are the 'needy outsiders, who take up jobs, scrounge off social security and live in luxury off the council etc'. Such opinions are hardly a recipe for racial harmony.

You may feel that I have arrived at a not very startling conclusion through a rather circuitous route. As an insider working in British television, I say that TV coverage of Africa *should* be handled more sensitively, because of the connotations that has for domestic racial issues, and *not* out of some notion that we work in an 'electronic global village' where we all link hands — because then, I repeat, from an *African* viewpoint it becomes merely a voyeuristic exercise.

SECTION THREE

Classroom resources for teaching about the role of the media

Media Studies in Primary School

by Laura Sparrow

1. QUESTIONING BASIC ASSUMPTIONS

Before we attempted to initiate Media Studies at Sparrow Hill, we worked together for a considerable time to determine its relationship to our curriculum. We recognised that though as teachers we may feel at home with television, we often fail to apply to it the kind of critical skills which we employ elsewhere. With television, we seldom examine or analyze our responses to what we see, or do so in only a limited form, and we fail to perceive the media as an active, performance based, interactive medium. As teachers, we take far too much for granted and receive information too passively. In drawing parallels between ourselves and children, we attempted first to clarify precisely how *we* fail to get to grips with what we view; only then were we clear about what and how we should teach the children.

There is still considerable confusion among many primary teachers between teaching about the content of programmes, which is often their only previous association with using television in school, and teaching about processes and skills necessary for analyzing how the medium functions. In addition, teachers' own personal views about how television functions as a cultural transmitter need to be challenged and reconstructed according to a set of agreed criteria.

It is our experience that primary teachers tend to withdraw from the notion of teaching about television because they all too quickly assume that it will be perceived by parents and others as basically a noneducational activity. They need to be persuaded that if they choose only to attend to the content rather than the teaching of skills of/for analysis, using television in school will be largely unproductive. In many ways it is all too easy to steer clear of the whole area.

Many primary teachers still see television as no more than an extended teaching resource for project work, developing children's knowledge, and helping to compensate for an experiential shortfall. In taking such a position, teachers run the risk of operating with incorrect assumptions linked to deficit theory. To assume that through the process of presentation, an accurate understanding of a particular content is achieved, is naive and uncautious.

Information children have received might be so distorted and mistaken that they could as well have had no information at all. Having a true notion about how a lock works, for instance, is vitally linked to seeing pulleys, levers and water levels moving in sequence. Viewing this process on television may be no more useful to a young child in providing a clear concept of 'lock' than a written description from a book. Because children have seen specific content on television, teachers may all too readily assume that an understanding is achieved, and so not attempt sufficient clarification and feedback.

It seemed to us that the relationship between young children and television is much more abstract and problematic than the relationship between children and books. Children, over an extended period, can be made to appreciate that books are written and designed for publication. Having frequent direct experience of this process of book production, as most children in primary school should, they eventually come to acquire a notion of scripting, drafting, editing and finished version. By providing writing' workshops, writing corners, and injecting print into an environment which is saturated with written stimulus, most children become literate about the use of books, confident in their usage, and develop enough interest and skill to join the 'Literacy Club' which affords them access to mainstream culture.

We decided to teach television as the end product of a particular process which, like literacy, is drafted, scripted, edited and produced, such that there are set criteria for judging its effectiveness and its effect. We attempt to teach children that writing is a powerful form of communication which can be used for many crucial purposes: complaining, making lists, taking notes, exchanging messages, explaining processes, gathering information, making statements, and expressing feelings. To us, it seems essential that children should apply the organising skills which they are learning about in writing to analyzing what they see on television. Although the analysis does not necessarily involve much writing, it is closely related to getting children to focus on structure, content and production. We attempt to give them the analogous tools of analysis of television. Their responses have indicated that they are both capable and eager to enter into such discussion, and as viewers, they are extremely willing to develop and apply critical skills.

2. MEDIA STUDIES AND STRUCTURED PLAY

Although it took a long time to decide how to integrate Media Studies into our primary curriculum, we were determined to implement it in a way which would spring from direct, first hand experience. This meant that we had to present the topic through other means than children sitting passively watching television. We wanted to focus children's attention on the social construction of the images of graphics, video and print. We wanted to inform them about the process selection, rejection, manipulation, suppression and construction of those images. We were hoping to provide an undersanding of actual technical processes involved in production and transmission. We were attempting to make children aware that images are the result of conscious choices made by people according to a variety of ideological, cultural and commercial criteria.

As a route of access into television which would be motivating for children, we decided to set up a television studio as a play area. In it children learn about social, technical and curriculum processes and their component parts, and come to understand that the world is made up of interdependent features which require that people communicate, collect and exchange information, and share one another's contributions.

In the 'studio' children aquire specialist vocabulary, technical language, social dialogue; they absorb processes and retain new information. They discover that they themselves help to direct and define their own learning and that their creative production is essential in building up the studio. They come to see that their work becomes a learning resource for others; they come to perceive themselves as 'experts'.

Teachers planned related classroom topics like communication, entertainment, electricity. The explicit interlinking of topic-based classroom investigation resulted in reinforcing the learning going on in the Studio, just as the learning going on in the Studio served to strengthen the concepts and skills, developed in the classroom.

In this way there was considerable coherence to the term's work for both teachers and children. Media Studies was easily and naturally slotted in. Children understood why they were investigating the effects of lenses and prisms as these related to the Studio, even though they might be working in the classroom. In the Studio, children might plot the floor coordinates for filming a short scene from a soap opera which they may have written in the classroom. A continuity of process and a strong relationship between many different curriculum activities, all concerned with the same basic theme, Television, established a clear frame of reference for real learning.

3. THE TELEVISION STUDIO AT SPARROW HILL
PLANNING
Far in advance of setting up, we made detailed plans of our aims and objectives. We drew up skills charts for specific areas which identified aims for children's learning. We attempted to identify the skills which would develop our aims. Then we considered activities which would develop these skills. Finally, we considered the resources which we would need. The more small detail and actual equipment there is, the more the 'play' feels authentic to the children and so worthy of their attention and interest. Here are some examples from Viv Dawson's Language Skill Chart for the Studio:

Broad Aim: Writing

To provide opportunities for children to identify and use relevant style and form for a varied audience in order to fulfill a variety of functions.

Skills
A8. Reading: Prediction of outcomes
B8. Writing: Summary
C8. Speaking: Express self

Activities

A8. Complete story-line of soap opera	B8. Collate/summarize/select news
What will happen if . . .	list storylines for EastEnders
devise questionnaires, predict outcome,	plot and subplot
select and order picture sequence story	synopsis of plays/books
C.8 Introduce programmes	
Brainstorming	
Selecting ideas for scripts/	
programmes/designs	
'voice over' videos	

Resources		
A.8 Storyboard	B.8 Real items	C8. Plans/Maps
Picture sequences	Continuity photos	Drawings
Matrix sheets	Scripts	Real items

LAYOUT

Our layout was designed to stress the cross referencing of departments so children would appreciate how necessary it is for people to work together to produce a successful transmission.

1) Reception
Children dealt with enquiries and security, studio rental and technical costs.
2) Studio Floor
A floor matrix enabled camera positioning and direction.
3) Control Room
Banks of discarded equipment and hardware provided levers and control knobs.
4) Newsroom
Desks were stocked with typewriters, and had maps, globes, clocks.
5) Design Department
Housed drawing equipment, real items of plans and models.
6) Wardrobe Department
Borrowed props and costumes from a local theatre company enhanced response. Dummies, mirrors and makeup were provided.
7) Production Office
Dealt with programming and style, casting files and production notes.
8) Sound Effects Department
Housed conventional and unusual materials for making sound tracks.

MEDIA STUDIES DISPLAY

We decided to use wall display as a means of informing about production techniques and to focus attention on the use and manipulation of images in the media, in terms of bias and stereotyping.

We mounted costumes on walls and wrote accompanying questions which asked children to think about common associations with respect to use of colour, texture, style and gender.

We mounted large advertisements, handbills, film posters, fashion pictures, and asked children to consider at whom these materials were being specifically targetted. Advertisements with particular image stresses were dissected with questions, arrows and comments. Production techniques were queried.

Perspective and the physical effects of changing visual perspective were examined by camera work. Children measured and made a display to illustrate differences between close-up, mid-shot, and long-shot.

Much of the display work stressed the importance of the shift of perspective, in both the physical and attitudinal senses. A large display on 'The Media' attempted to identify how different processes work together to determine how images are constructed and interpreted in different contexts. It pointed out some of the features which function to help images produce particular effects.

This included a section on the image, and how images can be used ambivalently, to alter or distort meaning (what is selected). There was also a section on wording and the use of text and print. This questioned how the size and style of lettering and wording alter meaning and stress (what is stated). Another section examined what is left out or understressed, and the hidden meanings which images successfully or unsuccessfully transmit (what is the message?).

Finally, we had a display of many different newspapers which compared their functional usages and varying readership. We examined their coverage of one event on a single day.

It was interesting that many of our parents spent a great deal of time studying the display on 'The Media'.

ACTIVITIES IN THE STUDIO
Reception
This area was equipped with signing-in book, copies of The Stage newspaper, telephone and typewriter, index box in which visitor's passes were filed alphabetically. These stimulated social negotiation and appropriate professional language ('Can I help you, which studio would you like to book, how many technicians will you require, what equipment do you need?'). Children signed in and out, exchanged passes and filed them, filled in forms and signed letters, wrote queries, requested space, made appointments involving using diaries, calendars and time, and conducted interviews.

Studio Floor
Positioning of actors, cameras, lights, and props created opportunity for spacial language, language of direction, and language of negotiation. The floor was marked out with a taped matrix, and children worked on camera angles, three hundred and sixty degree rotation, use of coordinates for plotting, use of close-up, mid-shot, or long-shot, the use of autocue and the presentation and performance of particular programmes. Because the performance levels of children altered as they grew more experienced and skilled on the Studio Floor, their expectation of their own performance continually increased. If a child made a mistake, the director simply called 'cut', and the children did a retake. All the children accepted the legitimate need to try again, but better and harder, with each new take. We saw a fascinating development of some of the less confident readers and speakers as they had a go at broadcasting. They clearly recognised that there was very little personal risk and a lot of enjoyment involved with Studio Floor performance.

Children also were responsible for designing and building cameras, different styles of lighting equipment, sound booms, autocue, and recording instruments.

Having designed and built them, they were then expected to instruct others in their use.

Production Office
In this department children worked on programming, scripting, and designation of people, sets and equipment to productions in progress. Activities were largely concerned with analyzing the pattern of actual programming output, comparison of channels, and programming a week or day's broadcasting by cutting up T.V. and Radio Times. Matrix work, in which the children had blocks of time to fill with selected programmes slotted in according to different criteria, was used extensively. We examined styles of programming output and compared how stations targeted their audiences according to time of day, gender, age and interest. Children conducted surveys to establish how many people in school watched television and discussed how these results related to how and when programmes were transmitted.

We established a clear notion of audience, presentation and style. Children were encouraged to create, edit and script new programmes. They were also expected to function in role to decide what was needed for specific productions on the Studio Floor. They had experience of coordinating technicians, actors, sets, floor plans, and scripts. They examined real scripts written for television, noted how directions are indicated, and thought about how to produce sets, sound-tracks, atmosphere and style.

Many real items were used in this area. Actors' profiles from a casting agency were studied by the children and used as prototypes for a children's profile folder in which they presented their own skills and abilities for an agency. This proved to be an excellent self-esteem activity, particularly for children who could write 'I can speak three languages fluently and have travelled a lot'. (Many teachers tried to get jobs from this department but were generally unsuccessful.)

The discussion of plots, characters, locations, programmes and productions were all duly recorded and available for later reference. Some were taken on to development and some were not, depending on their viability. 'Werewolf' was a very popular and promising programme which was worked out extensively on paper but which unfortunately never got into production.

Wardrobe and Costume Department
The costumes and props which we acquired from colleagues in the theatre were a strong boost to the success of this area. What was on offer to children was so creative, imaginative and delightful that teachers were found dressing up from time to time.

The focus of this department was to get children to appreciate concepts of style and appropriateness of scene. Children were encouraged to understand that styles are conscious social constructions formed on the basis of commonly agreed criteria. Within this context they discussed makeup, colour, gender, culture and race. They considered the relative exclusion of particular groups of people in parts of the media, such as women, ethnic minorities, and the disabled.

Dummies were provided for dresssing in different kinds of role or production. Varied set requirements and costume specifications had to be attended to by children, such as laying out an outfit for a daytime scene in Dallas or Coronation Street. Children were asked to design makeup for actors in specific productions such as Dracula or Star Trek.

Design Department
Work was focussed on style and presentation of images. Discussion centred on how products are designed and packaged, and how productions are designed for targeted audiences.

The targeting of advertising was especially valuable in this respect. There was a wealth of printed materials on offer for cutting up and setting into groups and sets. Adverts aimed at women, men, girls, boys, were compiled. The incidence of such categories in ads was counted and charted. Children were asked to draw their own conclusions about advertising assumptions.

Children also worked on story sequencing through pictures from comics. The investigation of image, sequence and emphasis served to illustrate how meaning and interpretation is mediated through captions, order and stress.

Sound Effects Department
The work in this area contained a great deal of scientific investigation. There was a range of instruments and recording equipment available. There was also junk for experimenting with the production of sound. Children worked on conductivity, electricity, and pitch.

4. DEVELOPMENTS FROM MEDIA STUDIES
What went on in the Studio and as a result of the Media Studies work was so creative, imaginative and inventive, and such an example of the effectiveness of open ended learning, problem solving, and extending children's levels of confidence, that it is difficult to extract only a few examples.

a) Magic Music
A group of children improvised a short musical sequence for a production which was entitled Magic Music, which indeed it was. They performed it for appreciative audiences and realized that if they were going to perform the piece over a period of time, it would be essential for them to transcribe it. They had extended discussion about how best to construct a working score.

b) Sparrow Hill Square
The children were adamant that any network worth its salt would have a block buster of a soap opera. As we had spent time comparing the signature tunes of different soaps very early on in the Studio (in order to analyze their styles with a view to understanding what it was they were attempting to convey through the music) from the beginning of the project one group was concerned with writing 'Sparrow Hill Square', a multicultural soap.

149

They defined characters, locations, events. They devised a system for recording this information and devised a schemata of relationships. We were particularly impressed by their use of arrows to indicate the cross referencing of relationships.

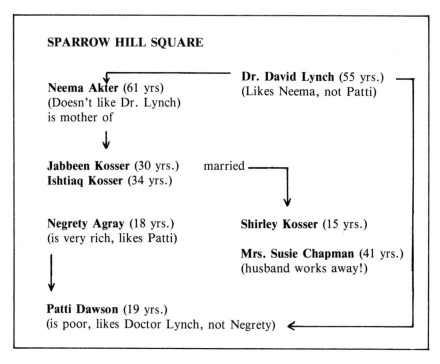

SPARROW HILL SQUARE

Neema Akter (61 yrs)
(Doesn't like Dr. Lynch)
is mother of

Dr. David Lynch (55 yrs.)
(Likes Neema, not Patti)

Jabbeen Kosser (30 yrs.)
Ishtiaq Kosser (34 yrs.)

married

Negrety Agray (18 yrs.)
(is very rich, likes Patti)

Shirley Kosser (15 yrs.)

Mrs. Susie Chapman (41 yrs.)
(husband works away!)

Patti Dawson (19 yrs.)
(is poor, likes Doctor Lynch, not Negrety)

The children drew plans of the square and sketches for locations. They also defined characters, pictures of scenes, and events.

Event 1
Dr. David Lynch tells Neema Akter he likes her. Neema tells her granddaughter Shirley.
Shirley promises not to tell anyone but she breaks her promise and tells Patti Dawson, her friend.
Patti likes Dr. Lynch and he had said he likes her, but now she has found out that he was lying to her.

ਤ

THE BLACK AND WHITE MEDIA BOOK

Personal Histories of Characters in Sparrow Hill Square
Negrety Agray: Age 19
Family Details : All died in Mexican earthquake.
Personal History: Born in Mexico. Came to England age 18. Supposed to come at 17 years old but had to play in the World Cup for Mexico.
Information: Speaks American English and Pakistani. Plays for Manchester United. Lives in a big house with servants in.
Personality: Kind and not bad tempered.

We felt that the perceptive and well considered features of this soap opera was on par with much of what we see at night on television, which is remarkable considering the authors were only 7-10 years old.

c) The Weather Forecast

A group of girls worked on broadcasting forecasts, with map and symbols. As one might well imagine, they started off with the most outgoing child as the presenter, a less outgoing child as the director, and the least outgoing child as the camera operator. As they progressed we observed that they exchanged roles. Cyrah, the least outgoing child, is shy, and her confidence with using English is very limited, although her understanding is good. The other girls encouraged her to present the weather in Punjabi and praised her efforts. After several attempts in Punjabi, she felt sufficiently confident to attempt the broadcast in English as well. This entire process of role exchange and social negotiation was undertaken by the children with no external adult intervention.

d) Television News

Thirty children successfully managed to organise a news broadcast from the earliest stages of pre- production to final cut. There was almost no adult intervention, save Viv Dawson shouting out twice, 'Quiet now in the Studio, this is costing us money. Only the director may speak now'. The children directed, recorded, filmed, performed, rolled autocue, worked the control room and silently observed, understanding all the features involved in production. They functioned with skill and professionalism, as defined in their own terms of reference. It is worth noting that when the children discussed who would read the news, two people volunteered who would have been identified as 'remedial' readers in most schools. We were interested that during this negotiation no one voiced any reason why they should not be chosen. The video which we have of this broadcast is not impressively slick or polished. It is not clearly recognisable as a practised performance, like a play. Nevertheless, it is their own work and a tremendous testimony to their learning achievements.

151

e) Bias and Stereotypes

We examined photopacks which depict non-stereotypic families, including, in positive roles, disabled people, black and Asian people, the elderly, single parents, and women.

We compared these with stereotyped pictures which children cut out from magazines or found in books.

We looked at television programmes and tried to analyze how black and Asian people were portrayed and in what circumstances.

We studied photopacks of Asian people in stereotypic situations and compared them with equivalent images of white people, questioning how the ethnicity of the people within the picture affected our responses.

To illustrate bias in production, we used the *Guardian* television ad which shows three shots (1) in close-up, an aggressive looking youth is seen running down a street, (2) in mid-shot, he violently pushes a man aside, (3) then in wide shot, an unsafe structure collapses where the man had been standing. The shift of perspective proved a useful model for study of our tendency to stereotype individuals and to make assumptions about their behaviour in un-conscious and inappropriate ways. This ad also demonstrates the degree of inbuilt bias which is operating through the use of camera and selected angles. It stresses the degree to which how the camera is used mediates the sense which we make of events presented to us.

5. THE POWER OF HIDDEN MESSAGES TO CHILDREN

Much of our group work is focussed on enabling children to value themselves and others, and our environment both in school and outside. The work on implicit and explicit messages is fundamentally linked into our multicultural process work. By examining stereotypes and bias, and omission and rejection of images, the notion of hidden messages and their power to influence our attitudes and our responses becomes clear.

By introducing Media Studies we have broadened our curriculum and made accessible many new areas for consideration and analysis. In supplying children with the necessary tools to deconstruct the images presented to them through the culture of the mass media, we hope to strengthen their ability to reflect upon what they see in an informed way.

Through the children's sheer hard work and daring endeavours we are as much involved in the interactive business of learning, and learning how to teach, as they are in teaching us how they learn. Media Studies has been a tremendous resource for investigating the power of communication, social negotiation, and cultural exchange.

References and materials we found useful:

Teaching the media L. Masterman; Comedia 1985
Making sense of the media, Hartley, Goulden, O'Sullivan; Comedia
Teaching about Television, L. Masterman; Macmillan 1980
The World in Birmingham (photopack) 1982: Development Education Centre, Gillett Centre,
    Selly Oak Colleges, Bristol Road, Birmingham B29 6LE

The friendly classroom for a small planet, P. Prutzman et.al.; Avery
Eyeopener-one and two, A. Bethell; Cambridge University Press
Viewpoints, A. Bethell; Cambridge University Press
Doing things in and about the home (photo pack); Maidenhead teachers centre
Women, J. Moran; Edward Arnold
Hidden Messages; Birmingham Development Education Centre
What is a family? (photo pack); Birmingham Development Education Centre
Values, cultures and kids; Birmingham Development Education Centre
Working now; London Borough of Brent (photo pack)
Just like us (photo pack); ILEA
Feelings (photo pack); ILEA
Multicultural Photo Pack; Edward Arnold
Joining the Literacy Club, F. Smith; Abel Press, Victoria B.C., 1984
Introducing Media Education in Primary School, Paul Morrison; Leicestershire Media Ed. Project, Leicestershire Centre for Education and Technology, Herrick Road, Leicester LE2 6EJ
Teaching packs from B.F.I. Education, 21, Stephen Street, London W1P 1PL (01-255 1444)
Catalogue of materials from Triangle Media and Arts Centre, Aston University, Birmingham B4 7E7
Comedia Catalogues: 9, Poland Street, London W1V 3DG
Concord Films Council Catalogue: 201, Felixstowe Road, Ipswich, Suffolk (0473-79300)
Another practical account of anti-racist approaches to media education in the primary/junior school is given in *Making Snap Decisions?* in *Multicultural Education Review* (Issue No 8, Winter/Spring 1988, available from Education Support Service, The Bordesley Centre, Stratford Rd., Birmingham B11 1AR).
Whose Image? (teaching pack, 1989) Tindal School, Balsall Heath, B'ham B12 9QS.
Aspects of Africa (photo pack 1988) Manchester DEP 061-445 2495.

Racism and Comics
by Brian Thompson

School assignment:
'Do comics and teenage magazines truly reflect Britain's multi-ethnic society? Illustrate your answer with examples from texts, pictures and cartoons, wherever possible. Indicate how improvements might be made.'

Brian Thompson May 1985

Children's comics and magazines form only a small part of the socializing information to which children are exposed. However, they remain strategically important in the formation of historical and social consciousness. As the World Council of Churches study guide, *Racism in Childrens and School Textbooks*[1] concluded:

> To the extent that racism in books conditions children of the dominating group so that they cannot relate to people of other 'races' their human potential is stunted.

153

Rae Alexander's article in *Racist and Sexist Images in children's books*[2] states that a book should be excluded if it contains even one negative stereotype, if it fails to provide strong characters as role models or if it is inappropriate for use in an all-Black classroom, an all-White classroom or an integrated classroom. However she then says:

> Underlying these criteria was my own experience with many teachers who are insensitive to the racist content of books or who are not equipped to handle such material adequately in the classes. The tragedy is that so many teachers fail to expose racist material for what it is and they fail to make use of it as a basis for discussing prejudice.

The value of an assignment such as this is that it causes us to stop, look and reflect, to contemplate on the state of things as they are and came to be.

Fifteen years ago Dorothy Kuya gave me, as part of a small group in Arundel Comprehensive School, a similar exercise. The process of racism awareness was started as I re-read some of the books I was then using in History lessons, with criteria to locate racist assumptions and ideas which I was not previously aware of. I had never read Malcolm X, Julius Lester, Eldridge Cleaver, Angela Davis, George Jackson or even Martin Luther King, so I was not qualified to make any kind of judgement about the books, except with reference to Dorothy's list.

What happend hit the solar plexus of my bleached white consciousness and changed my life!

Ten years ago David Milner in *Children and Race*[3] presented the following conclusions based on surveys of comics:

> They encouraged outdated and dangerously hostile views of foreign nations, and non-white peoples are largely omitted from comics and derogated in their few appearances. While comics are fantasy materials, we have seen that they have real consequences, and their present treatment of black people can only foster ignorance and divisiveness in a multi-racial society

In his book *Children and Race — Ten Years On*[4] he adds:

> A new generation of science fiction comics commands an increasing share of the market. It is interesting that the writers' projections for the next millenium are beyond even the extreme Right's wildest dreams: an exclusively white world save for the extra-terrestrial beings who have taken over the villain's role. '2000 AD' includes no Black characters as such although one of its heroes is Black Hawk (once a Roman Centurion . . . now a gladiator in a savage alien arena!) whose ancestry is unclear though probably not entirely Caucasian. Of contemporary fantasy comics Wonderwomen and Superman occasionally include background Blacks.

The comic *2000 AD* is published by I.P.C. and sells in South Africa. The white future might appeal to their outlook so the market determines the product. It feeds racism.

Milner refers to Jennie Laishley's analysis of comics *Can comics join the multi-racial society?*[5]:

> Jennie Laishley looked at this issue by analysing some sixteen comics over a six month period; 162 issues examined including comics for very young children, boys' comics, teenage girls' magazines and a general knowledge magazine. When most comics contain at least five stories, it is significant that only twenty stories from the entire sam-

ple featured any non-white figures at all. Of these 'eight treated these characters in a wholly unfavourable fashion, that is, they were represented as evil, treacherous, violent or stupid. Three stories included characters who although not treated in a strongly unfavourable manner, were nonetheless represented as rather limited stereotypes. Two stories included a single non-white in the background of the story who had little or no personality, and two further stories included characters who had a personality of their own but whose status was subordinate to the white hero or heroine of the tale'.

Children are especially vulnerable to subtle conditioning, particularly when they are not presented with anything which challenges the stereotypes, life-styles and roles which are presented. (As any advertiser will confirm). If seeing is believing, then what are our children led to believe when they read their regular diet of comics today? Have things improved since Laishley's study in 1972?

I examined all the 23 comics and teenage magazines available at W.H. Smiths on Saturday April 27th, 1985. Pop magazines like 'Jackie', 'Melody Maker' and 'New Musical Express' have a number of Black people from the pop world, also sports magazines and comics such as 'Match' and 'Shoot' which reflect the rising number of Black footballers. However, none of the pop or sport comics/magazines include Chinese, Asian or Arab Black people. The specialisation of the magazines fits the Black people portrayed neatly into the stereotype of entertainers and sportspeople.

While the number of stories with Black people in them has improved, out of 274 stories which sold to millions of children in Britain, 249 comprised exclusively White European people, with no recognition of the 'multi-racial' composition of Britain or the world in which we live.

Dorothy Broderick in *Images of the Black in Childrens fiction*[6] says:

> While there are many reasons for reading, two of the fundamental reasons have to do with the readers' search for self-identification and their need to learn about persons different from themselves.

It can be argued that mainstream British comics give White children the wrong impression about their significance in the world's population — a false sense of importance. Does their over-representation lay the basis for eurocentrism, racism and the potential for the 'White God complex'?

If you have Japanese ancestry for instance, and happen to live and go to school in England, then in April 1985 you would have found someone like you in only three stories. Your white peer group would see Japanese people

a) attempting to shoot an innocent hero
b) attempting a so-called traditional suicide
c) attacking a 'Golden Boy' White European who has beaten him in a sprint.

The character in b) is prevented from killing himself by a white European who utters the words:

> You stupid Nip . . . cut out
> that Kamikaze craziness!

a. 'Victor'
b. 'Battle Action Force'
c. 'Eagle & Tiger'
d. 'Dandy'

1. Beano 1985
2. Tin Tin 1933
3. Comic Cuts 1933
4. Beano 1983
5. Beano 1985

5.

157

And if you have Chinese origins, then White children will see you presented as an exaggerated stereotype running a Chinese laundry, or else not at all as this is the only Chinese character in all the 274 stories.

The pictures that follow paint a sorry tale of the state of 'public information' in Britain. In the hands of private enterprise, nearly 60% of the market analysed is supplied by one, non-unionised, company.

The *Beano* presents us with a gross 'throwback' from the 30's era of racist stereotyping similar to the drawings done for *Tin Tin* and *Comic Cuts*. Lord Snooty's friend is like a Black 'picaninny' jelly baby with a white face reminiscent of the B.B.C. 'Blacked up Minstrels'. The 'girl' says nothing. The two other 'Black' people in the comic have speaking parts.

However, Benjy in 'Ball Boy' is a secondary role and is simply drawn as an updated version of the 'Blacked up minstrel' with the black face and white lips. When this character first appeared about 3-4 years ago he was a black stereotype who used the expression 'man' as often as 'Little Plum' used 'Um'. A scene which shows Benjy's father shows the consistency in the drawing style. The long and noble struggle of the indigenous American is horrifyingly demeaned in 'Little Plum'. No further comment is necessary.

Next in this racist continuum we see black people, again in secondary roles, as characters who are drawn as White people but with some shading. Two of the characters in *Buster* and *Whizzer and Chips* have Afro hair and one can only assume that the others are meant to be Asians. There is no character development or other indication of their origin except in *Pepper Street* where a symbol of traditional dress is worn.

The stereotype of an Arab with limitless money is reinforced by the character in *Whizzer and Chips* named Mustapha Million. Drawn as a European but wearing traditional Arab dress he spends his time spending money on his English friends.

We now reach the point where a more acceptable portrayal of black people is seen. The characters in *Roy of the Rovers* are recognisable and identifiable for Black and White children. Their role is again secondary and undeveloped and again a kind of 'sporting blacks' stereotype, however it is refreshing to see a Black boy on the front cover.

Apart from the 'murderous Japanese' character, the *Victor* represents a Black British footballer and an Arab family. The drawings are much better than other comics so far, but again it is a very simple stereotyping of Arab life which is portrayed.

Last but not least are the only two stories where a Black person appears as the central character (apart from Little Plum). In both cases some aspect of life as a Black person is considered and the drawings are of a relatively high standard. The range of characters in *Look In's* 'A Team' is particularly good. However, both *Warlord's* 'Rayker' and *Look In's* 'A Team' present us with a Black Superman. B.A. Baracus is an exotic media creation which has a life of its own and children can buy B.A. masks behind which they can talk gruff and act tough.

1. 'Buster'   2. Ibid.   3. Ibid.   4. 'Whizzer & Chips'   5. Ibid.   6. Ibid.   7. Ibid.
8. 'Roy of The Rovers'   9. Ibid.   10. 'Victor'   11. Ibid.
All bought on April 27th 1985

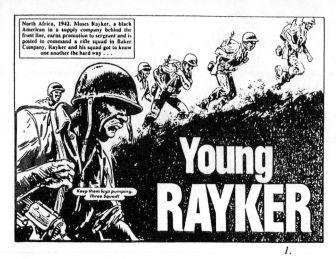

1. 'Warlord' 1985
2. 'Look-In' 1985
3. Ibid
4. Ibid
5. Golden Legacy 'Lewis Latimer & Other Black Inventors' 1976
6. Amar, Chitra, Katha 'Prithviraj Chauhan' 1981

'Young Rayker' actually confronts white racism in the army when a Black man is a sergeant in charge of white platoon. The message for black children is to take a 'Charles Atlas' course and learn to kick sand back in your oppressor's face. 'Young Rayker' then is the best of a bad bunch. Not one story out of the whole 274 would pass the Alexander test and it could be argued that comics which have no black people in are better than those that degrade or misrepresent.

While they remain privately owned, it is difficult to say how improvements can be made. *Golden Legacy* (published in USA) and *Amar Chitra Katha* (published in India) seem to be getting somewhere and children I have taught value them greatly. If comics are going to be able to serve a wholesome content to children, which gives proper representation of black people, the publishers have to employ black staff and set up procedures of accountability to advisory groups within the minority communities. Generally speaking, action within the media struggle is limited and demands huge amounts of energy and a supportive network of friends, colleagues and allies to create an oasis in the desert. However, in this work I can vouch for the practical value of the ACER catalogue,[7] the checklists by the NUT[8] and the Council on Inter-racial books for children. (Pp.164-168).

While publishing power remains in the hands of a tiny, undemocratic white elite, it is necessary for educationalists to engage in the social, economic and political struggle for truth and justice. The alternative is to adopt the ostrich position which as Salman Rushdie has observed,[9] invites 'a kick up the backside'.

References

1. *Racism in Children's and School Textbooks* World Council of Churches, 1978, p.26.
2. *Racist and Sexist Images in Children's Books* Rae Alexander, Writers and Readers Publishing Cooperative, 1975 p.10.
3. *Children and Race* David Milner, Penguin 1975 p.73.
4. *Children and Race — Ten Years On* David Milner, Ward Lock p.94-95.
5. as above p.94; see also *Images of Blacks are Whites in the children's media,* by Jennie Laishley, in *White Media and Black Britain* ed. C. Husband, Arrow 1975.
6. *Image of the Black in Children's Fiction* Dorothy Broderick, Xerox p.6.
7. *Images and Reflections* ACER, 1985
8. *In Black and White* NUT 1979
9. *The Empire Within* Salman Rushdie, C4 (see pp.41-2).

Also
    Catching them Young Bob Dixon, Pluto 1977.
    Anti-Racist, Anti-Sexist Drawings Natalie Ninvalle, Sheba 1984

Checklists for identifying racist imagery and thinking in books and the media

Compiled by John Twitchin

Introduction

Full sets of guidelines are available in *The slant of the pen: criteria for the evaluation of racism in children's books,* ed. R. Prieswerk, World Council of Churches, Geneva, 1980, and reprinted in the first issue of *Children's Book Bulletin,* June 1979, and *Resources for multicultural education: an introduction,* Gillian Klein, Longman Resources Unit, 1984, for Schools Council.

This chapter offers a selection of other guidelines and checklists which complement each other and which teachers have found helpful in assessing the books and materials they use in schools. (A basic reference here is *Reading into racism — bias in children's literature* by Gillian Klein, Routledge, 1985 which also provides guidelines, as well as strategies for dealing with bias in literature).

Some perhaps obvious points on the checklists that follow:

1. They are not offered in support of censorship; after all, some bias of one sort or another may be unavoidable. The aim is to draw attention to materials that least risk reinforcing racist assumptions.
2. They are not offered to help teachers locate racist books in order to throw such books out. It would be naive to imagine that children will not come across such materials outside school, so the aim is to *use* the racist books to help children to see for themselves what is racist about them. (As *Racism the 4th R,* the ALTARF film (see page 68) shows, young children can spot unreal stereotypes and negative images more quickly than perhaps some teachers). Thus the task is to find ways of teaching the content of the checklists to the pupils, so that they can identify racist imagery wherever they come across it.
3. They are included here in the hope that teachers will relate the ideas in the checklists to the television and films their pupils are watching — after all, the brute reality is that the bulk of pupils will be watching more TV than they will be reading books. *The Black and White Media Shows* give a range of TV clips for analysis in class, as well as referring directly to books like *Robinson Crusoe.* (Several of the drama extracts were chosen because they feature children for pupils to identify with).

   Every evening's television is giving scope, either in terms of 'good' or 'bad' practice for teachers to develop children's powers of critical awareness of what these checklists can reveal about the ways black people are often represented — if represented at all, that is. Older pupils of course would encouraged to go on to reflect on why such checklists should be necessary; why they seem to have been ignored by many film and television producers; what would be needed for them to be acted upon by publishers, TV organisations and film makers.

4. One 'easy' way of teaching the checklist is simply to stick a copy, perhaps of a simplified version, into the inside cover of certain books — under some 'Racism Warning' title. This will alert readers to what they might otherwise miss. Even simpler would be to place offending books together in a part of the school library labelled 'racist museum section'. Many teachers will initially assent to this as 'a really good idea' (not, one hopes, because they think that will obviate the need for classroom work on racism in the media) but as soon as they suggest it in school, a range of apparently reasonable difficulties are likely to be raised:

'But if we do that with the racist books we should do it with all the sexist books too — and that's at least half the library'. 'But the books were re-catalogued only last year with the help of that parent group — we can't rearrange them again so soon'.

It is by such rationalisations for inaction that institutional racism works to keep black people's due rights a matter of low priority in white dominant structures. This will be clear to any group which has worked through the exercises on institutional racism and the assumptions that fuel it, as outlined in Section 1.

Children will be educated most by the sense they have that the teachers are sharing what as adults they are learning in applying the checklists to books and the media both in and out of school, and by how they see teachers applying the implications of these checklists to the way the school is run as a social organism.

An article in *Issues in Race and Education* outlines how Holland Park School organised a system for reviewing books — called 'Book Look'. If any member of the school came across any racist or sexist ideas in a book, they were asked to fill in a form about what elements of it are racist or sexist. They also could recommend that the book be given a 'Book Look' sticker to alert other readers to the fact that someone is disturbed by its contents. Such an approach could be adapted for use in the primary school classroom in a simplified form, for example each book could have a reference card filed in a box. The class could design a checklist of questions to ask about any book. When the children have read a book they refer to the checklist. If there is anything striking in the book to which they want to alert others, they write it on the file card. This is a quick reference system for other children to use. The questions might include:

— *Are the main characters boys, girls or both?*
— *Are there any Black or Asian people in the book?*
— *Are there groups of people who are treated badly?*
— *Do you like the pictures?*
— *Did you find any racist or sexist comments?*

Reading another child's review may alert children to the prejudices of a book or it may encourage them to read a book which otherwise might have been ignored.

A letter to *Multicultural Teaching* journal (Spring 1986) from Brenda Keyte, Librarian at Dick Sheppard School, London SW2, indicates how this idea has been taken up:

> I was interested to read in MCT 4.1 (Summer 1985) the Report on the 'Book Look' method of dealing with the tricky problem of some books having racist/sexist ideas, images, bias, yet not being dreadful enough to discard. I have a large poster on the wall behind the issue desk, where it catches the eye, stating, 'THIS LIBRARY AIMS TO BE NON-RACIST AND NON-SEXIST. Please tell Ms Keyte if you find anything which offends. See the Equal Rights File'. This file is a loose leaf binder kept on the catalogue cabinet, containing forms rather similar to Holland Park School's. There is also a slip stuck in the book above the date label. The system has created much interest amongst the pupils and I feel that the discussions it has provoked have increased their awareness.
>
> I strongly recommend it to all other librarians who are troubled by stocking such titles as *Uncle Tom's Cabin* and *Little Women,* etc.

CHECKLISTS

Study of the following checklists will help (a) teachers and librarians (b) children and all other library users to identify what is offensive and racist — not only in books, but in the feature films and the television they watch.

In Black and White: a checklist for teachers, Shirley Darlington.*

- Do not pass over or ignore a racist concept or cliché in a textbook; if you have decided to use the book, point out its inadequacies and false assumptions and use it to stimulate discussion.
- Do not use books which would cause offence to ethnic minority group pupils by derogatory references which suggest the inferiority of minority groups.
- Point out stereotypes: do not allow them to pass unchallenged, and be ready with counter-examples which show other attributes of personality and achievement of the ethnic group in question.
- Look carefully at illustrations; do they correctly represent the ethnic group depicted? Are these illustrations realistic, and not caricatures?
- Check that books do not either by text or illustration reinforce the image of a power structure in which white people have all the power and make all the decisions, with ethnic minorities functioning in subservient roles. Black people should be shown in all kinds of jobs, reflecting their increasingly important role in our society.
- In stories about children, the question should be raised whether the non-white child has to strive harder for acceptance and, in friendships, whether he or she has to do most of the understanding and forgiving.

- Check whether there are people in the story with whom black children could identify, thereby enhancing their self-concept and self-esteem.
- Assess whether the book is factually accurate and ensure that it does not perpetuate the myth of white superiority. Books about urban life should contain reference to minority groups.
- Ask these questions: Is the book written from the standpoint of a multi-cultural society? Does it recognise cultural diversity? Are its moral assumptions those of parity of esteem between people of different ethnic groups?
- Could a child of any ethnic group retain his or her cultural pride and dignity whilst reading it?

* *Guidelines on racial stereotyping in textbooks and learning materials,* 1979, National Union of Teachers.

Checklist from *The changing world and the primary school,* Centre for World Development Education.*

1. Choose books which give a sensitive, sympathetic portrayal of people with an emphasis on the fact that they are real people. Avoid stereotypes.
2. Books should recognise that other cultures have their own values; they should not be judged exclusively through British eyes against British norms. Wherever possible, people from other cultures should be given the opportunity to speak for themselves.
3. Information should be as up to date as possible taking into account that societies everywhere are changing and that to dwell on quaint exotic traditions is not presenting a true picture of life in that society.
4. Characters from non-European origins should not always be represented as the underdogs, or in need of help; they should also be shown in positions of authority and responsibility.
5. Any book which in some way portrays a society, whether in fiction, history or the contemporary world, should present fairly the cultural and social mix of that society. This is equally important whether portraying life in Liverpool, Nairobi or the Outer Hebrides.
6. Where issues of poverty or struggle are touched on, recognition should be given to the fact that the wealth of some countries is due to the maintenance of poverty in others and that this poverty cannot be dismissed as due simply to incompetence of the poor. (A similar relationship exists within countries as between them).
7. Where issues of conflict arise they should be handled openly and not glossed over as if no problems existed.
8. Books should make clear the interdependence between people and nations and the influence that actions by one have on others.
9. Books should encourage a sense of the individual's ability to influence events.
10. Books should be attractive and clear to use so that children can readily find the information they require.

* C.W.D.E. 128, Buckingham Palace Road, London SW1 9FH

Ten Quick Ways to Analyse Children's Books for Racism, Council on Interracial Books for Children, New York.* (This American checklist can be adapted to suit the British context).

1. Check the illustrations: Look for stereotypes. A stereotype is an over-simplified generalisation about a particular group, race or sex, which usually carries derogatory implications. Some infamous (overt) stereotypes of Blacks are the happy-go-lucky water-melon-eating Sambo and the fat, eye-rolling 'mammy'; of Chichanos, the sombrero-wearing peon or fiesta-loving, macho bandit; of Asian Americans, the inscrutable, slant-eyed 'Oriental'; of Native Americans, the naked savage or 'primitive' craftsman and his squaw; of Puerto Ricans, the switchblade-toting teenage gang member. While you may not always find stereotypes in the blatant forms described, look for variations which in any way demean or ridicule characters because of their race.

   Look for tokenism. If there are non-white characters in the illustrations, do they look just like whites except for being tinted or coloured in? Do all minority faces look stereotypically alike; or are they depicted as genuine individuals with distinctive features?

   Who's doing what? Do the illustrations depict minorities in subservient and passive roles or in leadership and action roles?

2. Check the story line. The Civil Rights Movement has led publishers to weed out many insulting passages, particularly from stories with Black themes, but the attitudes still find expression in less obvious ways. Some of the subtle (covert) forms of bias to watch for:

   Standard for success. Does it take 'white' behaviour standards for a minority person to 'get ahead'? Is 'making it' in the dominant white society projected as the only ideal? To gain acceptance and approval, do non-white persons have to exhibit extraordinary qualities — excel in sports, get A's etc.? In friendship between white and non-white children, is it the non-white who does most of the understanding?

   Resolution of problems. How are problems presented, conceived and resolved in the story? Are minority people considered to be 'the problem?' Are the oppressions faced by minorities and women represented as causally related to an unjust society? Are the reasons for poverty and oppression explained, or are they acccepted as inevitable? Does the story line encourage passive acceptance or active resistance? Is a particular problem that is faced by a minority person resolved through the benevolent intervention of a white person?

3. Look at the lifestyles. Are minority persons and their setting depicted in such a way that they contrast unfavourably with the unstated norm of white middle-class suburbia? If the minority group in question is depicted as 'different', are negative value judgements implied? Are minorities depicted exclusively in ghettoes, barrios or migrant camps? If the illustrations and text attempt to depict another culture, do they go beyond over-simplifications and offer genuine insights into another lifestyle? Look for inaccuracy and

inappropriateness in the depiction of other cultures. Watch·for instances of the 'quaint-natives-in-costume' syndrome (most noticeable in areas like costume and custom, but extending to behaviour and personality traits as well).

4. Weigh the relationships between people. Do the whites in the story possess the power, take the leadership, and make the important decisions? Do non-whites and females function in essentially supporting roles? How are family relationships depicted? In Black families, is the mother always dominant? In Hispanic families, are there always lots and lots of children? If the family is separated, are societal conditions — unemployment, poverty — cited among the reasons for the separation?

5. Note the heroes and heroines. When minority heroes and heroines do appear, are they admired for the same qualities that have made white heroes and heroines famous or because what they have done has benefited white people? Ask this question: Whose interest is a particular figure serving?

6. Consider the effects on a child's self-image. Are norms established which limit the child's aspirations and self-concepts? What effect can it have on Black children to be continuously bombarded with images of the colour white as the ultimate in beauty, cleanliness, virtue, etc., and the colour black as evil, dirty, menacing, etc.? Does the book counteract or reinforce this positive association with the colour white and negative association with black?

   What happens to a girl's self-image when she reads that boys perform all of the brave and important deeds? What about a girl's self-esteem if she is not 'fair' of skin and slim of body?

   In a particular story, is there one or more persons with whom a minority child can readily identify to a positive and constructive end?

7. Consider the author's or illustrator's background. Analyse the biographical material on the jacket flap or the back of the book. If a story deals with a minority theme, what qualifies the author or illustrator to deal with the subject? If the author and illustrator are not members of the minority being written about, is there anything in their background that would specifically recommend them as the creators of this book?

8. Check out the author's perspective. No author can be wholly objective. All authors write out of a cultural as well as a personal context. Children's books in the past have traditionally come from authors who are white and who are members of the middle class with one result being that a single ethnocentric perspective has dominated American children's literature. With the book in question, look carefully to determine whether the direction of the author's perspective substantially weakens or strengthens the value of his/her written work. Are omissions and distortions central to the overall character or 'message' of the book?

9. Watch for loaded words. A word is loaded when it has insulting overtones. Examples of loaded adjectives (usually racist) are: savage, primitive, conniving, lazy, superstitious, treacherous, wily, crafty, inscrutable, docile and backward.

10. Look at the copyright date. Books on minority themes — usually hastily conceived — suddenly began appearing in the mid-1960s. There followed a growing number of 'minority experience' books to meet the new market demand, but most of these were still written by white authors, edited by white editors and published by white publishers. They therefore reflect a white point of view. Only very recently, in the late 1960s and early 1970s, has the children's book world begun even remotely to reflect the realities of a multi-racial society.

Actions you can take —

Discuss the bias in books. Make a point of discussing with your children and other members of your family the hidden messages and implied values in books.

Organise parents and teachers. Find other interested parents and teachers to analyse library books and classroom materials.

Hold consciousness-raising meetings. Plan school-wide meetings with speakers on racism and hold workshops for school administrators, teachers, parents, and students. Make sure there is substantial non-white input to such meetings.

Urge classroom innovation. Suggest that students join with teachers to critically analyse their textbooks for bias. This in itself can be an educational classroom experience. (There is no need to censor books if teachers will openly discuss stereotypes with students).

Suggest special treatment in the library. Urge the school librarian to point out racist passages to students. Suggest that books which are particularly offensive be placed on special shelves and clearly identified as racist.

Sensitise those who buy books. Pinpoint responsibility for book purchasing in schools and libraries and take special care to involve these people in consciousness-raising efforts.

Write to book publishers. Complain to book publishers: cite book title, page number, and the offensive passage. Send copies of your letter to the local newspaper and urge other parents and teachers to do likewise. (Citing specific examples of racism can be highly consciousness-raising for a community.)

*The Council on Interracial Books for Children, 1841 Broadway, New York, NY 10023, U.S.A.

A checklist for syllabuses, Godfrey Brandt.*

1. Does the syllabus represent a global view? And does it open up opportunities for the development of a global analysis of local and national events?
2. Does it relate to the children's experience in any way?
3. Does it offer an interactive and dynamic approach to phenomena?
4. Does it challenge racially defined phenomena and phenomena that seek to perpetuate the dominant power relations within society?
5. Does it open up the opportunity for pupils' *critical* engagement with the subject matter?

6. Does it provide the opportunity for pupils to extrapolate ways of challenging bias, racism, sexism, class dominant and other forms of oppression?
7. Does it address specifically to any, all or some of the 'building' blocks of racism and other forms of oppression?
8. Does it positively acknowledge the history of struggle of black and other oppressed people against their oppression?
9. Does it contribute towards the overall aims of equality, justice and emancipation?
10. Does it give validity and legitimacy to the knowledge, experience and language of the learners rather than operating a predetermined notion of the nature of knowledge?
11. Does it explicitly acknowledge and identify the perspectives of the 'authors' of materials?
12. Does it acknowledge the contribution made by Black people to the country's history, culture and development?
13. Does it leave room for change, adjustment and new questions?

* Drawn from *Community Conflict and the Curriculum,* paper for NAME conference, 1986. Godfrey Brandt writes as a black academic from London University Institute of Education who has been senior education officer, Arts Council, since 1986. Detailed implications of the above questions are spelt out in his book *The Realisation of Anti-racist Teaching,* Falmer Press, 1986.

Race relations in schoolbooks: a checklist of positive messages, Robin Richardson.*

A schoolbook is non-racist if it has *both* these characteristics:
1. It reflects, supports and affirms, as distinct from ignores or rejects, the identity, experience and concerns of ethnic minority pupils or students.
2. It criticizes and challenges, as distinct from reflects and reinforces, false beliefs about white (or European, or Western) superiority in white pupils or students.
The following list explains and illustrates these two main points in greater detail. The list is in principle relevant to pupils and students of all ages, including the very youngest. It summarises the main positive messages about 'race' and international affairs which schoolbooks should be presenting.

A. 'Race' and 'Race Relations'
1. 'Race'
   It is not stated or implied that human beings can be divided into biological 'races', and words reflecting this false belief ('Caucasian', 'Asiatic', 'Negro', 'coloured' etc.) are not used.
2. Opposition to racialism
   Racialism — the twin false beliefs that (a) races exist and (b) whites are superior — is opposed and criticized, both as personal belief and as political doctrine.

169

3. Opposition to racism

Racism — the combination of (a) unequal power structures (b) discriminatory procedures and (c) prejudices — is opposed and criticized.

4. Migration

It is emphasized that the black people came to Britian in the 1950s and 1960s primarily because their labour was needed by the economy. Many were explicitly invited or recruited.

B. References to Black People

(The term 'black' is a political term, not a biological term. Its use implies that racism is the basic phenomenon to be named, not cultural differences, and that opposition to racism is a basic political struggle. In this sense, in contemporary Britain it refers *both* to Asian people *and* to Afro-Caribbean).

5. Control and decision-making

Black people are shown as in control of their lives and environments, and with intentions, desires and ideals, not merely as passive victims.

6. Their own words

The views and perspectives of black people are presented or quoted in their own words, and in their own categories and definitions.

7. Everyday life and values

There are examples of warmth, care, love, laughter, kindness, in the descriptions of family life and everyday relationships of black people.

C. References to 'Other' Countries and Cultures

(The term 'other' here means in principle other than the main culture of the school; in practice in Britain it means non-British, and non-European or non-Western.)

8. Multicultural, multiracial 'West'

Britain and the United States, and also most West European countries, are shown as multicultural, multiracial, multilingual, multifaith societies. They are not all-white, not all-Christian, not all monolingual.

9. Meanings

Customs, lifestyles, traditions and beliefs in other cultures are shown as having value and meaning for the people concerned, not as exotic, peculiar or bizarre.

10. Generalizations

Generalizations about all or most people in another country or culture are not made or implied. On the contrary there is emphasis on diversity within other groups.

11. One World

It is clear that many apparently localized, smallish-scale events in the modern world are in fact influenced by, and may themselves influence, events and trends elsewhere.

12. Religion

Christianity is not shown as the only true religion, the only source of valid religious insight and experience. Religions other than Christianity are described in their own terms and categories, not with Christian or Western terms.

13. Interaction and learning
People in other countries and cultures are portrayed as people from whom 'we' can learn — their values, their experience of life, their insights, their politics.

D. References to the 'Third World'

14. Poverty and politics
It is not implied that poverty is merely the absence of Western goods, nor that poverty is mainly a consequence of climate and environment, or of ignorance.

15. Science and technology
Scientific and technological achievements are not shown as exclusively Western or European neither in the past nor in the present.

16. History
'Third World' countries and cultures are shown as having a long history and tradition — they were not merely 'discovered' by Europeans.

17. Liberation and struggle
Struggles by black and 'Third World' people against oppression are shown and evaluated from their own points of view, not merely dismissed as disorders, riots, revolts, insurrections, etc.

18. Language
The language avoids insulting or patronizing terms — for example, 'coloured', 'tribe', 'native', 'primitive', 'hut', 'superstitious', 'witch-doctor', 'chief', 'jabber'.

19. Heroes and heroines
People who are considered and admired in 'Third World' countries as heroes and heroines are described in these terms, and their influence and inspiration are clear.

E. References to Particular Issues

20. Islam
Islam is shown as a religious tradition of great depth and insight, and as a major cultural influence and civilization. It is not implied that Muslims are typically 'fundamentalists' or 'fanatics', and terms such as 'the rise of Islam', implying threat, are not used.

21. South Africa
It is not implied that apartheid is merely a matter of segregation — separation in housing, cinemas, parks, railways etc. The inequalities and injustices of a political and economic nature are emphasized, and there is reference to South Africa's economic links with Western countries.

F. General References

(These last points are not *directly* related to racism and non-racism. It is probable, however, that a non-racist curriculum will have these features also, at least.)

22. The role of women
    In all countries and cultures, and at all times in history, women are shown as half of the human race, and their work and actions as essential. The word 'man' is not used to refer to all human beings. Traditional gender roles are shown as man-made (sic), not immutable.
23. Conflict and its resolution
    Human beings frequently, even typically, disagree and dispute with each other, they are in constant conflict. This reality is not glossed over, but resolutions of conflict which are (a) non-violent and (b) just, are emphasized also.
24. The media
    There are frequent reminders that newspapers and television over-simplify and distort — for example by ignoring long-term underlying causes of events, by concentrating on personalities and trivialities, by seeking to entertain rather than to explain, and by flattering and reinforcing the prejudices of the audience.
25. 'Ordinary' people
    The vast majority of human beings are 'ordinary' and always have been — not monarchs, rulers, politicians, aristocracy etc. Their experience and outlook are attended to and respected, both in the past and in the present.
26. Bias
    Everything is biased. Every book, talk, lesson, course, syllabus and topic in schools is biased, and so is every list such as this.

*Reprinted from *Journal of Moral Education,* Vol. 15 no. 1, Jan. 1986. Robin Richardson is Principal Adviser, Brent LEA.

Criteria for Assessing Bias in Non-Fiction Books on South Africa
Beverley Naidoo.*

We need to consider:
● what material has been selected and what has been omitted
● how material is presented.

Historical Information:

(i) Is the pre-colonial period coveed or does the histroy of South Africa begin with 'diseovery' by Europeans? Is evidence of Iron Age settlements included, or is it claimed that black and white arrived in South Africa at the same time?

(ii) Is there an appreciation of traditional African societies and life-styles? Or are they regarded simplistically — as 'primitive', 'barbaric', 'uncivilised', 'inferior', at best 'exotic'?

(iii) Is the experience of slavery dealt with adequately?

(iv) Is the focus on European personalities while black lives are omitted or treated as marginal? Is the history of resistance included?

(v) Are people stereotypes? Are Africans resisting invasion portrayed as 'savages', 'war-like', 'treacherous', 'hostile' — while white colonists and trekkers are 'noble', 'courageous', 'brave'?

Is it implied that only white people were worthy and capable of handling power?

(vi) Does the writer portray the colonial relationship as bringing the advantages of Western civilisation, education and technology to Africans, while exploitation is minimised?

Geographical and Contemporary Information:

(i) Is reference made to apartheid? Is it defined by the South African Authority's definition as 'separate development' or is it shown to be a system of domination?

(ii) Is the focus on positive concepts like industrial development, agricultural output and economic progress, while negative features of the system are omitted? What attention is given to the contrast between white privilege and black poverty? (e.g. with reference to wages, housing, education, health, welfare).

(iii) Are the living conditions of Black South Africans falsified or justified? (e.g. presented as 'better than in the rest of Africa').

(iv) How is the 'pass' system portrayed — as a forced labour system or merely as the control of movement? Is the destruction of family life mentioned?

(v) How are the bantustans presented — as areas confined to under-development and the provision of cheap labour for the developed 'white' areas, or as areas for 'separate ethnic development', or 'independent states' with 'self-government'?

Is it shown how millions of black South Africans are being denationalised by being assigned to bantustans?

(vi) Are democratic claims made about changes in the political system, or are these changes carefully examined?

(vii) What is said about methods of dealing with political opponents, including trade unionists? (e.g. indefinite detention without trial, torture, banishment, censorship).

(viii) What is said about the South African Government's relations with other African states? (e.g. its involvement in Namibia, Angola, Mozambique and the other neighbouring states).

(ix) Is there an examination of the extent of western investment in South Africa, and a discussion of its consequences?

173

Biological Information:

(i) Are racial stereotypes promoted? Or does the author show how the categorising of people into 'distinctive races' and 'separate ethnic groups' is used to maintain control by the government?

(ii) Is it acknowledged that there are South Africans who reject racial categorisation and regard themselves not as 'Xhosas', 'Zulus', 'Tswanas', 'Indians', 'Europeans', 'Coloureds', etc. but as 'South Africans'?

Cultural Information:

(i) Is the focus on white culture, or is reference made to black South African culture, without it being treated as 'exotic'?
(ii) What reference is made to literature and art which provide critical comment on the society?

References and Sources:

(i) Are only establishment books and organisations referred to for further information?

(ii)Are only establishment sources of information and illustrations used?

Visual Information:

(i) Are the illustrations biased towards historical events and characters significant only to the ruling minority?

(ii) Do the illustrations promote stereotypes?

(iii) Do the images suggest industrial and agricultural prosperity, without revealing the poverty of black workers?

(iv) Are the stark contrasts in education, health and welfare revealed? Or do the pictures feature progress made in selected black areas?

(v) Are there pictures which bring out the effect of apartheid regulations? (e.g. the 'pass' system, demolition of homes, and transportation to 'home-lands').

(vi) Do pictures legitimise bantustans as 'independent republics'?

Statistics:

(i) What areas of life do the statistics cover? Only those which suggest over-all progress, or also those which reveal privilege and poverty?

(ii) Is there an awareness tht official statistics now omit information about millions of denationalised black South Africans who live in areas declared 'independent', where rural poverty is most intense?

From Censoring Reality, available from British Defence and Aid Fund for Southern Africa (BDAFSA), Unit 22, The Ivories, Northampton St., London N1.

Using Video Resources in PSE courses on racism in Britain

by Alec Roberts

Bohunt School in Liphook is a purpose-built 11-16 Community Comprehensive which takes in about 1200 children from villages in Mid-Hampshire. The area is predominantly white, middle class and *in* employment. It has been described as part of 'the soft underbelly of Britain' because the national recession in the late 1970's and early 80's and the cut backs in Government expenditure have not had a dramatic effect on the majority of people in the area.

There are very few black people in Mid-Hampshire, and consequently, until 1983, such notions as anti-racism and multiculturalism were ignored by most teachers in the school. However, with the deepening awareness of the need for change by a few members of staff coupled with the greater exposure to multiculturalism in all levels of education (work for INSET by B.B.C. Continuing Education Dept., G.C.S.E. National Criteria, The Swann Report, Anti-Racist work in Brent), a group set about exploring why the school needed to be concerned about challenging racism.

We soon saw a need for building into our non-examination personal and social education programme, modules of work which revealed how racism operates in different contexts. This eight week course in the 5th year builds upon another running in the 4th year which involved discussion on:— the distinctions between racism and prejudice; between immigration and emigration; the history of slavery and apartheid; and something of what it feels like to be in a minority.

Our 5th year course must also be seen in the context of our school policy on anti-racism. This short document was welcomed by our School Governing Body and became in February 1987 part of the fabric of the school and its community. Teachers introducing this and other courses lower down the school do so in the knowledge that the Management Team endorse its contents and back up teachers when they challenge students over racist issues.

Week One

Aims

1) Before discussing media and showing the video we think it is important to remind groups of the difference between Racism and Prejudice.

2) This lesson aims to heighten the awareness of the students to the racism inherent in such institutions as the B.B.C. and I.T.V. and to show that much of this racism is unintentional and part of our taken-for-granted assumptions about society. However, because the television is such a powerful means of communication it *has* the power to formulate and maintain racist attitudes.

Method

(A) Recap on work done in the 4th year entitled Multicultural Britain: What is Prejudice? What is Racism? What is Stereotyping? The video *Black* (see pp.17 and 40) which included the Blue eyes, Brown eyes experiment in the U.S.; the old 1950's newsreels of West Indians arriving in Britain; the young black people of today talking about achieving identity through personal struggle. Remind group of *why* groups such as the West Indians were invited to come to Britain after the war. Remind them of apartheid, of Nelson Mandela, of *Country Lovers* — the film they watched.

(B) Explain that today and throughout next 7 weeks we will be focussing on Britain and racist thinking by white British people towards those of different ethnic origin — most of whom are British.

The course starts with Racism in the Media because *The Black & White Media Show — part 1* (see p.42) shows on television programmes watched by many students. It would be useful *before* starting the programme to ask the group to chat for a few minutes about Lenny Henry and his success as a comedian. Why is he so popular? Does he have something original to offer? How does he compare with Little and Large? The Two Ronnies? Russ Abbot? Can you think about one of the funniest sketches Lenny Henry has taken part in? Why was it funny? Do you think he is aware of his position as a black comedian? How, do you think, this will affect writing and production techniques? (Note: this course was devised for a group of students who are predominantly white).

A

**Tape section . . . L. Henry to end of M. Grade's first interview.
1) Why is L.H. ashamed of the image he created in *O.T.T.*?
2) What is the difference between L.H. now and when he was in *O.T.T.*?
3) What does M. Grade mean by 'everyone has his own inner prejudices'?

B

**Tape section . . . *Carrott's Lib* . . . (stop the tape before the comments on *Carrott's Lib.*)
1) Why would black people find this offensive?
(The implications of ridiculing the frustrations of young black people. It visually portrays black people as violent and this reinforces a dangerous stereotype).

C

**Tape section . . . from end of *C.Lib* to end of *The Chinese Detective.*
1) Why is 'wog' an offensive term?
2) Should writers of TV programmes show characters fighting against prejudice?

Before showing Section D, it is advisable to show the Bob Hope picture in freeze frame and ask the students to discuss their thoughts and feelings about it in the light of some of the ideas which have been mentioned in the programme so far.

One way of approaching this is to ask students in groups of 3 or 4 to write down what they notice about it. Bob Ferguson's comments on the video will probably underline and reinforce ideas which the students suggest.

D

**Tape section . . . from end of *Chinese Detective* to end of Aunt Jemima
1) Where does prejudice come from?
   a. Our own language, 'black' words.
   b. Visual representation . . . the Bob Hope pictures.
   c. Black people as figures of fun.
2) Having watched the first half of the video *The Black and White Media Show,* distribute the 'Golliwog' worksheets: 'I love my golly' (see page 207). Ask the group to split into pairs and read through the information. There is only one question to be answered: 'What is wrong with golly?'

Week Two

With the start of Week Two's work, we are trying to shift the focus to empathy with a person from an ethnic minority. Where do racist ideas and images orginate? How are they perpetuated? Why are they rarely challenged? Do schools have a role to play here or should teachers keep out of this?

Aims

1) To continue the broad aims of the first week's work but to focus more specifically on the way the media can portray an event with a racist bias.
2) To raise questions about the need for more responsible media coverage of issues which involve the emergent power of minority ethnic groups.

Method

(A) Recap on last week's video which mentioned *Carrott's Lib,* Lenny Henry, *The Chinese Detective* and joky, paternalistic images of black people.
(B) Now watch the second half of *The Black and White Media Show* in the same way as the first.
(C) Follow the viewing by asking the group to work out their own rules for combating racism in TV.

Continuing with *The Black & White Media Show — Part I* from last week when the group discussed racist images of black people, ask the group:

1) What do you know about Morocco?
2) What do you think a Moroccan looks like?

** Now show the tape section . . . Souad the Moroccan girl to end of Robinson Crusoe. (Stop before the 13yr old black boy.)

1) What was Robinson Crusoe's attitude towards the black person he discovered on the island?
2) If you were a black person watching this film what would you feel about it?

177

F

**Tape section . . . from 13 yr old black boy after Robinson Crusoe to the opening credits of the *Six O'Clock News*.

Bob Ferguson talks of racist ideas/images being passed on by radio, by television, by newspapers and by schools. How do you think these ideas are passed on in schools? (By teachers, by jokes, by books . . ?)

G

**Tape section . . . from opening of the Six O'Clock News to end of Mark Tully's short thank-you speech after receiving award. Rewind video in order to hear Alan Whicker's introduction and Mark Tully's speech again. Then stop.

What is the major difference in attitude between the two speeches? Consider: Alan Whicker implies that B.B.C. is the only *true* voice of India. What other assumptions follow from this? (For confirmation of Mark Tully's attitude, read out his article on p.225).

Section G concentrates on the Alan Whicker introduction and makes us stop and listen to what is being said. On first hearing it sounds reasonable and innocuous but it needs to be studied more carefully. What is especially worrying about such examples is that the majority of people only experience such programmes *once* and rarely, if ever, have the possible racist implications explained to them.

Section H is a complex part of the programme and we feel that it probably warrants a separate study at a higher level of engagement than we expect from the fifth year students. At this stage we simply draw the students' attention to the two reports as two ways of viewing the same item.

We found the activity suggested to follow the end of the video worked well; we ask each group to present and illustrate their rules in their own way.

H

Tell the group that they are going to see 2 accounts of the same incident.

**Tape section . . . from Mark Tully's Thank You Speech to end of the 2 versions of the same news item.

I

**Tape Section . . . end of the edited version to the end of the programme.

In groups of 3 or 4 work out together what you consider to be the most important rules for a film maker/TV producer/who is concerned to combat racism on television.

Week Three

Aims
1) Deepen understanding of racism in school context.
2) Help encourage ways of combating racism in schools.
Materials
Video-*Prejudice* in *Starting Out* series, Thames TV Jan. 1986.

This thirty minute play centres on a white racist Biology teacher in a Midland Comprehensive School. The most disturbing part of the film is the violent attack made by the teacher on a bright and well-motivated black pupil. The choice facing the pupil is very well portrayed. Should he report the teacher to the Head or keep quiet and think about passing his examinations?

The film ends with a dramatic climax, the boy is prevented from taking a public examination by the racist teacher who is part of the racist system. He runs out of school shouting 'Stuff your school and your education'.

Method
(A) Show video up to point when Biology teacher physically attacks the black pupil. Stop there and ask group to discuss : *why* is the teacher behaving in this manner?
What do they think the boy should do now?
Outline the clear choices that face the boy.
(B) Continue to show the video to the end.
(B) Here are some possible follow-up activities:
a) Depending on the way the group responds to the video you may like to discuss the last image of the black student rejecting school because school has rejected him.
b) Write down (in silence) thoughts and feelings about the video. Limit this response to approximately ten minutes. Ask class to read out what they have written to their friends.
c) Imagine you are the History teacher (the woman) who cares for and believes in the black student; write down *her* thoughts and feelings.
d) Act out a scene in the Head's office the next day. The Biology teacher, the History teacher and the parents of the black student are each interviewed.
e) Outline the racist remarks that were made by the teachers (i.e. 'back to the jungle' — 'mumbo jumbo')
f) Work out, in groups, what rules should be written into a school constitution to combat racism (i.e. rules on language (written and spoken), rules on behaviour by teachers and pupils, wearing of badges, etc.).

Week Four

Aims
1) To show that racist attitudes are often formed and reinforced at home and within the local community.

2) To emphasise that as these pupils grow older they will have to face choices like the central character in the video. Do I do what I think is correct? or Do I follow blindly the views of my home and school friends? (views which are racist and dangerous).

Materials

1) Video — *Taken on trust* in *Starting Out* series, Thames TV Jan. 1986.

Another thirty minute play which is concerned to show that Youth Clubs only succeed if everybody pulls together and develops trust for one another. This film deals with racism as *part of* the main story. In this way the racist issues arise naturally from the situation and seem very convincing. Asian boys and their white friends are beaten up by a white gang; the police arrest and charge only the Asians. They allow the white boys to go home. The parents of a white boy reveal deep seated racist attitudes when he explains to them the behaviour of the police. 'It's not your fight' says his mum.

The young hero endeavours to show them and the rest of the Youth Club that it is *our* fight.

2) Worksheet — Myths About People (1)

3) Worksheet — Myths About People (2)

Method

(A) Use the Myths About People (1) Worksheet first. Ask group to work out in pairs which are true and which are false (2 minutes). Then give out the Myths About People (2) Worksheet. Discuss with group the false assumptions they had about black people. Emphasise that we are all guilty of ignorance and that very little is being done to present a true picture of how we have become a multi-ethnic society. (Stuart Hall's points about 'inferential' racism as 'natural commonsense' could be useful here — see p.56)

(B) Explain that we shall be watching a video about a Youth Club and the way it is run. Ask the group to consider a) the feelings of the British Asian boys, b) the views of the parents of the central male character, especially when they discover one of their sons is a thief.

(C) After watching the video, there are some points which might be useful to discuss.

1) Why have the British Asian boys formed a Defence Committee?

2) What did you think about the attitude of the police?

3) What does the mother mean when she says to her son, 'It's not your fight?'

4) We shall be talking about the National Front and the British Movement in Week 6 and Week 7, but it might be appropriate to ask the group what they know about such racist movements.

MYTHS ABOUT PEOPLE (1)

Much of the prejudice against the West Indian and Asian population of Britain is because people do not know the facts. People also often believe incorrect facts (myths).

See how much you know. Say for each statement whether you think it is true or false:

1) The West Indian/Asian population is many millions of people. *True/false?*

2) Immigration is making Britain overcrowded. *True/false?*

3) Immigrants sponge off the welfare service. *True/false?*

4) West Indian/Asian people get favoured in council housing. *True/false?*

5) West Indian/Asian people have large families. *True/false?*

6) West Indian/Asian people take the jobs of white people. *True/false?*

7) West Indian/Asian people are more likely to commit crimes than white people. *True/false?*

8) West Indian/Asian people should all be sent home. Nobody asked them to come here. *True/false?*

MYTHS ABOUT PEOPLE (2)

Now read the facts:

1) *False.* The West Indian/Asian population is estimated to be 1¾ million, 3.2% of the population.

2) *False.* About 35,000 more people leave Britain every year than come in.

3) *False.* Official studies show that on average an immigrant gets 20% less from social and welfare services than those people born in Britain.

4) *False.* There are only 4% Asian and 20% West Indian families in council housing, compared with 30% of the population as a whole.

5) *False.* The average West Indian/Asian family has 2.9 children and this number is falling.

6) *False.* Unemployment figures are higher for the West Indian/Asian than for the white population. Also many essential services would come to a halt without their West Indian/Asian employees. One in three British doctors was not born in Britain and over 20% of hospital staff and nurses are West Indian/Asian.

7) *False.* On average, the number of crimes committed by West Indian/Asian people is no greater than the number committed by white people.

8) *False.* In 1950 when business was expanding in Britain, after the war, immigrants from the West Indies, India and Pakistan were actively encouraged to come to Britain. They often did the lowest-paid jobs that nobody else wanted. Now 40% of our West Indian/Asian population were born here.

How did you do?
If you had an incorrect answer, where did you get your information from? Of were you just guessing?

Week Five

Aims
1) To focus in on one aspect of Racism in Britain through the eyes of an Asian/British playwright; Farrukh Dhondy.
2) To widen the students' understanding of white racism in Britain by showing them what groups like The National Front and The British Movement stand for. This will involve revealing groups as fascists and therefore connecting up this module of work with the work on politics.
3) To open up the question 'What does it mean to be British?'

Materials
1) Video *Salt on a Snake's Tail* in the *Scene* programme series B.B.C. T.V.

A play about the life and pressures on a Bengali family originally from Bangladesh, now living in the East End of London. It is based on a short story from Farrukh Dhondy's book, *Come to Mecca.* In particular, it is about the family conflicts that result because of the different ways the son and the father respond to the threat and experience of harassment by local racists.

Unit of 2 Programmes: This play and the next week's documentary, *Every Night we Draw the Shutters,* both deal with the subject of racial harrassment of Asians in this country.

Note about the language spoken in the play
Mr. Miah speaks poor English when talking to the market shopkeeper, but fluently for the dialogue with his family. In fact, Mr. Miah like many Bengalis of his generation, who came to Britain in the early 70's, speaks rather poor English, and we must imagine that all the dialogue in the family is in *Bengali.* This is an important point, otherwise it may appear that Mr. Miah is deliberately speaking poor English with the shopkeeper, which is not the case.

Method
(A) Ask the group what they already know about The National Front or The British Movement. Explain that such groups believe in a *'pure'* British race like Hitler believed in a *'pure'* Germanic race. What does being British mean? Split into groups of 3 or 4 and write down all the characteristics of being British. Give possible examples: language? eye colour? Allow 5 minutes and listen to the various responses. Now by listening to each show what a *myth* the whole notion of being 'British' actually is. When we really get to the bottom of it British racism is about hatred of another's colour of skin, it is *not* about protecting the British nation.
(B) Show the video: Before switching on please draw the group's attention to the note about the language spoken in the play — (see the teachers' notes).

Weeks 6 & 7 are concerned with issues about apartheid and sport, and about issues of discrimination in the workplace. As part of this latter theme we use *Racism,* from the BBC series *16 Up.*

This programme begins with the appalling graffiti daubed on garages. It might be worth freezing the frame on it and asking the class to consider what a black person would feel like seeing this in their local community.

The programme neatly splits itself into three sections — Racism in the home; Racism in school; Racism at work.

Each section is illustrated by a short scene which reveals the dangers of stereotyping black people. The section on school opens up the possibility for the group to consider what is racist about their own schooling — books, attitudes, assumptions.

The last point in the video is powerful. Racism is about who controls the power. In Britain the white middle class control the power. Now that at last (1987) we have some black MPs, this may begin to change.

Week 8 we build around viewing extracts from *The Black and White Media Show — Part 2,* as suggested in the producer's commentary notes (see p.214ff). The intervening work makes it possible for the class to pick up the more complex issues implied in Part 2. It is necessary to start with a recap of the end of Part 1.

A Questionnaire for viewing *The Black and White Media Show* — Part One

by Mary-Lynne Durrell

First, the context: The Beaufort Community School is a comprehensive T.V.E.I. school with approximately 1,000 pupils. Media education is taught as part of a Life Skills module to the 4th and 5th year pupils (i.e. aged 15 and 16 years). Life Skills modules comprise 1½ hours once a week for 6 weeks. With such a limited amount of time it was difficult to decide what areas of media education should be taught. I was determined that a technical skills approach should not be allowed to overshadow the theoretical underpinnings which I felt were vital to the course — although I realised that with 24 mixed ability, rather rebellious adolescents, the task would not be easy. I eventually decided to build the course around the theme 'messages of persuasion in the mass media'. Much of the work in the following 3 units is inter-related and therefore cannot be taught in isolation.

(1) **Core Activities/Concepts**
    Practical exercises in image analysis/primitive semiotics/de-constructing images/significance of editing, cropping & framing/newspaper codes/photo journalism and anchorage of text.

(2) **Advertising and Representation**
    Representation of specific groups across the media/stereotyping and the production and marketing of images/representation of issues and ideologies across the media.

(3) **Magazines and Comics**
    A comparative study of different types of magazines or comics. A case study of a magazine — an analysis of its system of messages, its signifying system and its ideology.

Week 1 A general introduction to Media Education. How opinions are formed by methods of persuasion used in the Mass Media including advertising. Class briefly looks at power structures, stereotypes and learns how to de-construct images.

Week 2 Racism in the Mass Media. Class is reminded of power structures and stereotypes before questionnaire is handed out. Class watch *The Black and White Media Show — Part 1* with their questionnaire. A discussion follows the film.

Week 3 Education Officer from C.R.O. invited to discuss prejudice and racism with class.

Week 4 Exercises to look at covert messages in teenage magazines. People not represented there, e.g. ethnic minority groups, hero/heroine with a physical or mental handicap, gays, women/girls showing leadership and courage, men/boys

185

showing compassion, intelligence, creativity and sensitivity. Class asked to plan a photo-story showing such an area of life not usually portrayed.

Week 5 Class shown ways to 'compose' photographs. Refer to Hitchcock's methods for implied messages in angle of shot. Sent out to make photo-stories.

Week 6 Photo-stories assembled, plus text. General discussion of aspects of 6 week course.

The Black and White Media Show — Part 1

For several years I had used the film *It Ain't Half Racist, Mum*, which I considered excellent. I now use *The Black and White Media Show* as an excellent complementary update to this. My 4th year pupils particularly love the extracts from *Grange Hill* and Lenny Henry, whom they seem to have a particular affection for. Unfortunately, my pupils' attention span is rather limited, so I and my colleague, Bert Holland, devised a questionnaire to be used with the film.

Questions 1-9 concern racist jokes and stereotyping attitudes to the Irish as an ethnic minority group. This was a deliberate ploy because we have very few black children in our school and we did not want them to feel embarrassed or isolated. It has been my previous experience that black children who had taken a great interest in media education and spoken fluently and confidently about other aspects of the mass media, became silent and withdrawn when racism was discussed. As the school's deputy head is Irish, we felt that someone in such a strong role in the school could be used to illustrate the ludicrous nature of racist jokes.

Questions 10 onwards are specifically to do with the film.

The following week I invite the Community Relations Education Officer to talk to the pupils about prejudice, racism and anti-racist strategies. The class discussion which follows usually brings in comments about *The Black and White Media Show.* I make a special point of inviting this officer to join us as she is of Caribbean background and I think gives the children an important, positive image and experience of a black woman in a dominant key position. I have also used *The Black and White Media Show* on an F.P.S. course, Media Education in the Classroom, for which I was asked to organise and tutor a general introduction. The C.R.O. Education Officer was also invited so that the teachers (who were all white) had the opportunity to raise issues with her that were pertinent to the film, and to hear directly about her own experience as a black person. Such a black perspective, I think, is essential to such a study.

THE MEDIA SHOW QUESTIONNAIRE

Before the Programme

1) Do you consider yourself to be prejudiced against any 'ethnic minorities' in Britain?　　　　　　　　　　　　　　　　　　　　　YES/NO

2) Have you ever listened to a racist joke?　　　　　　　　　YES/NO

3) What was your response? LAUGHED/NO RESPONSE/FELT ANNOYED

4) Do you think all jokes about the Irish are funny?　　　　　YES/NO

5) Do you believe jokes about the Irish are based on some truth about Irish people?　　　　　　　　　　　　　　　　　　　　　　　　　　YES/NO

Jokes about the Irish portray them by means of a stereotype. Can you think what this stereotype is? Remember, stereotyped groups are stereotyped by other, dominant, groups.

6) Which people see themselves in a position of dominance over the Irish?
FRENCH/SCOTTISH/ENGLISH/BRITISH

7) Do jokes about the Irish encourage you to think of the Irish as inferior to us?　　　　　　　　　　　　　　　　　　　　　　　　　　　　YES/NO

8) Are the Irish inferior to us?　　　　　　　　　　　　　　YES/NO

9) Have you ever told an Irish/racist joke?　　　　　　　　　YES/NO
If your answer is YES go to 10, if NO go to 11.

10) Write down your feelings after you had told the joke.

During the Programme

11) After the opening titles and introduction, if you had the option, would you change channel? (If you want to say that it would all depend on what is on the other channels then your answer is YES.) YES/NO

12) Why do you think people might get upset watching this programme? Because they: ARE SOFT/DON'T WANT TO HEAR THE TRUTH/DON'T WANT TO HEAR A LOT OF LIES

13) Do you agree with the man who says that black people only cause trouble? YES/NO

14) Do you agree that we get a lot of our impressions of people and groups of people from the media? YES/NO

15) Do you agree that the message we get from television when dealing with black people's grievances and protest is that this is 'trouble for whites'? YES/NO

16) Television . . .
'reflects and affects attitudes'
'focusses and reinforces assumptions'
'legitimises (makes OK) and perpetuates (spreads) opinions'
'portrays stereotypes'
'contributes to a culture of racism accepted implicitly (without question) by the TV audience'
What in your own words does all this mean? What do others in the class reckon to these research conclusions?

17) 'Lionel has just sent a message home' (on his drums) jokes the compere. The compere then goes to the white man and asks him whether his joke was 'all right'.
Why was the compere's joke racist?
Why was what the compere did after telling the joke another example of racism?
Write down your answers to these two questions.

18) Do you agree with Lord Scarman when he says that we are all prejudiced? YES/NO

19) '. . . editorial power is almost exclusively in the hands of whites.' Is this a good thing? YES/NO

20) Is the 'joke' 'paid in bananas' shocking? Are you shocked? YES/NO

21) The fact that there are many black politicians in the U.S.A. makes a difference. But why?

22) You have just seen an extract from *'Carrott's Lib'*.
Which bits did you find funny?
Which bits did you not find funny?
Describe the excerpt and say how it represented black people.
Say whether you thought it was fair.

23) Should T.V. deliberately counteract prejudices expressed in drama or documentaries, or should it just 'reflect' prejudices?   YES/NO

24) You have just seen an extract from *Grange Hill*. Describe what you have seen and say what the writer was trying to do about challenging racist attitudes in society. Do you think the BBC was right to show this episode?

25) Do you agree that the word 'black' often has negative associations in the English language, so that we have to be careful not to think that way about people?   YES/NO

26) Write down the points from our discussion of the Bob Hope picture.

27) *Robinson Crusoe*. What images of black people do we get from programmes like this? (Bear in mind that Robinson Crusoe has been popular for over 200 years.)

28) The audience rating for *Robinson Crusoe* was 8.5 million. A programme that tried to counteract these images of black people was *Anglo-Saxon Attitudes*, from which we have seen extracts. The audience rating for this programme was 0.3 million. What do you see as the significance of this?

29) 'Stereotypes can be unlearned' — Bob Ferguson. Given that stereotypes are handed down by society from one generation to another do you agree with this statement?   YES/NO

30) Why would some see the belief expressed by Alan Whicker that the BBC is the only source of impartial information for India as a racist comment? Would you see it as an example of what is meant by 'dominant ideology'?

31) *Newsnight* reports on a document that affirms that anti-black discrimination does exist in Britain today. The programme then goes on to discuss the internal divisions affecting the Asian community, i.e. the arguments about arranged marriages.

Does *Newsnight*, perhaps without realising it, appear to be suggesting that part of the reason for discrimination against Asians in this country is that Asian Britons are divided about arranged marriages?   YES/NO

Two News Reports

32) The first presents the situation as Asians being a problem for the police. What were your impressions when viewing the pictures? With whom did your sympathies lie?

The second version shows the problem as being one for the Asians — the way they are treated by a white dominated management and union.
The first version opens with a seeming riot. The second version places the 'riot scene' midway through its report emphasising that the 'factory gate scuffles' have only taken place after the failure of the union and management to consider the Asians' grievances.
What is the effect of this different angle on the story?

In the second version with whom did your sympathies lie?

Which was the better example of news reporting?

Why?

33) There is an idea that all you need are a few subversives/extremists to stir up black people and they will all follow them into street battles. Do you agree with this view? YES/NO

Why is this idea racist?

34) Should the T.V. media be positively and deliberately anti-racist? YES/NO

35) The media have two responsibilities according to Dr. Parekh:
   i) They must be truthful in representing various communities.
   ii) They must mediate (provide links and understanding) between various communities.
   Does the media do this at the moment? YES/NO

After the Programme

36) Why do you think it is necessary to look at the numbers of people from minority groups working in the media?

37) Would you have chosen to watch this programme at home?   YES/NO

38) Has the programme influenced you and given you a greater understanding of how the media are contributing to racism in society?   YES/NO

39) Do you think that the T.V. media present black people fairly? YES/NO

40) Do you think it matters whether the representation of black people is fair or not? Please write your comments below.

Ways of using
The Black and White Media Shows
in initial and in-service training

Ways of using *The Black and White Media Show* — *Part I*

by John Twitchin

Introduction

It may be hard to believe, but the average child in Britain watches about 30 hours of television a week — as much or more than the time spent in classrooms. According to *Social Trends*, published by the government's Central Statistical Office in Jan. 1988, the average man spends 25 hrs. 35 mins per week watching 'the box', and the average woman 30 hrs. 42 mins. There can be no doubt that television acts as a powerful 'image-maker' of black people, both in Britain and overseas. The Swann Committee Report summarised research about the effects of the media in legitimating and reinforcing prejudiced attitudes in both adults and children, and particularly in perpetuating negative stereotypes of black people. Those findings indicate why it is vital to any effective anti-racist education that teachers should 'deconstruct' these effects of watching television, not just in specific media studies but across the curriculum. In other words, the teaching which helps children see the racist imagery in materials and books *inside* school needs to be extended to the media influences that are so powerfully working on them *outside* school. The *Media Shows* were made to complement the widely used *It ain't half racist, mum* in helping fulfil that need. Their theme is indicated in this extract from a BBC paper to a conference, 'Swann and the Global Dimension'.[1]

All forms of teacher training need to help teachers aiming to provide an anti-racist 'education for all' to show pupils how they might be being victimised by television output. For example, there are grossly stereotyped images of black people in the 'comedy' of Jim Davidson, Bernard Manning and others; there are the recurrent images of black people only in association with 'trouble', unbalanced by positive associations, in News and Current Affairs; there are the omissions by soccer commentators who ignore, rather than condemn, offensive anti-black behaviour by fans; there is omission of languages other than English in most programmes (outside Wales and Scotland that is!) and in the English editions of Radio Times — i.e. an almost complete failure to support images of bilingualism and to reflect the reality of a society in which twelve languages other than English are in daily use by at least 100,000 people each; and perhaps most significantly, given the official facts of discrimination, the failure in News programmes to identify white racism as a causative factor in reporting those events exclusively referred to by the media as 'riots'. On this last point, we see no news programme acknowledging that to a black perspective the 'riots' are 'uprisings' or 'urban rebellions'; we see newsmen using the word 'people' meaning only white people; we recurrently find racial attacks reported in ways which fail to counter any prejudice in the audience that 'trouble' for Asian Britons is somehow their own fault for being here in the first place. All these points of commission or omission — however unintentionally — serve to legitimate images of, and attitudes towards, black people which are inimical to both the letter and the spirit of Swann's 'education for all'. It is these kinds of unconscious cultural racism' by the white dominated media that have to be brought into conscious focus for young people. Indeed, regular class projects in complaining to the media organisations (demanding written replies from the producers in charge!) could be part of such teaching. How else will the media learn — let alone the pupils — given the Black communities' relative exclusion from power, and given the absence of Black consciousness in the decision-making processes of mainstream broadcasting?

We in broadcasting have yet fully to work out, and to implement across all programme output, what *is* responsible programming in and for a multicultural and multiracial society still characterised — as the Swann Report confirms — by continuing pre-judice and discrimination against black people. The facts of what is often termed in the media 'black disadvantage' result from an interaction of institutionally racist discrimination and the anti-black personal prejudices (ranging from gross, conscious and overt to subtle, unwitting and hidden) which serve both to fuel and to rationalise those facts. The question for educators, and for us in the media, is how to work together to break that circle of interaction in the interests of all children. As with most schools and colleges, the BBC is not yet equipped with those black staff in senior roles needed both to fulfil policies of equal opportunity and to bring a black perspective to its decision-making. While these difficulties are being worked upon, teachers — and particularly teacher trainers — need to give priority to ways of drawing the attention of pupils to the nature of the media influences upon them, as a vital part of those overt and hidden curriculum developments implied by the Swann Committee Report.

The *Media Shows* do not offer an analysis of racism in society, nor of the operation of institutional racism in the broadcasting organisations; they are video/teaching aids to recognition of stereotypical imagery and thinking about black people on TV. Part 1 draws particular attention to popular *fictional* output (comedy and drama), while Part 2 concentrates on *factual* output (News and Current Affairs). Part 3 (1989) gives emphasis to the views of black media workers (see ref.[12] on p.213). As Continuing Education Department productions, it is legal to copy them for educational purposes. They are available at most Teachers' Centres; they can also be borrowed from the NUT.[2] This chapter offers some background commentary on Part 1, together with suggested ways of maximising its effect in use with such groups as students, teachers, librarians, journalists and media production staff.

For groups involved with education, a powerful way to start (if it has not been done already) is to use the questions on page 18, followed by a viewing of the 'Gus the Bus', 'Souad from Morocco' and 'Cumbrian Nursery' sequences from the film *Anglo-Saxon Attitudes.* Ask (a) Where did the boys in the bus and Souad's girl school-fellows get their ideas about black British people from? (b) What should their teachers have done to correct and/or prevent such dehumanised misconceptions and ignorance? Such questions will help the group see *why* there is the need, not only in college courses but in both the staffrooms and classrooms of schools, to 'deconstruct' the effects of the media across the curriculum.

In introducing Part 1, for the reasons given on page 18, trainers should work out questions to help the group identify their own views, and some of their own gaps of knowledge, before the viewing. They could include for example:

1) What percentage of the population acknowledge that black Britons experience racial prejudice?
2) How many hours a week does the average child watch TV?
3) What are the known ways that television affects pupils' attitudes?
4) What is a stereotype?
5) What is a stereotyped image?
6) What would be your first words if, after many months alone on a desert island, you unexpectedly met another person?
7) What do you normally say if you can't pronounce someone's foreign name?
8) What bad things can you think of about the Indian subcontinent over the last 10 years?
9) Now, what good things?

Such questions ensure that the group will then actually register and reflect on the content of the film when those points appear. In addition, trainers and group leaders can secure thoughtful concentration by remarking in advance that there are several deliberate mistakes in the film, together with at least five undeliberate mistakes (where the producer has failed to practise what the film is attempting to 'preach') and that you will be checking if everyone has spotted them at the end. Apart from the fact that analysis of what is wrong with a film is often a most effective learning process, it is one of the aims of anti-racist training to encourage white people not to be defensive but to acknowledge, and to learn from, mistakes and criticisms of our part in racism. One of the significances of *The Black and White Media Shows* is that they are not the work of outside pressure groups, nor are they criticising other organisations and institutions for racism: they represent a model for attempting some self-monitoring — they are made in a spirit of self-reflection by the BBC as an institution.

One of the deliberate mistakes, for example, is the preponderance of white speakers (chiefly Lords Swann and Scarman, Gus Horsepool and Bob Ferguson) in Part 1. This is done deliberately because white audiences often find it hard at first to 'hear' black people on the subject of racism. Part 1 presents white people first as a strategic move, dictated by necessity rather than choice, to gain attention to its theme. Black speakers lead the arguments in Part 2. It is part of the problem of racism that many white people assume, when a black person draws attention to the facts of anti-black discrimination, that he or she will be special pleading to some extent. ('Well, they would say that, wouldn't they?') Such white people might be more challenged initially by those same facts being stated by Lord Swann and Lord Scarman, who cannot be assumed to have any motive for exaggerating. (See also pp.69-70, 202, 210) As Akram Khan Cheema says at the start of Part 2: 'It would be a non-starter if this programme had only black people talking, because I don't believe white people would listen — they have never been on the receiving end of racism'.

A worse 'mistake' in the view of some black critics in particular, is that the film is concerned only with 'consciousness raising', and only with the symptoms of what is wrong with the television media, not the causes. It does not confront those responsible for what is shown on television, especially on the question of why there are not more black staff.

This is fair criticism: the logic of Parts 1 and 2 implies that there should be a Part 3, together with other programmes from other departments, which move on from *recognition* of the still all-too-common surface representations which unwittingly serve to perpetuate prejudices about black people (i.e. as both a reflection and as a reinforcement of 'cultural racism') to examine the *determinants* of those representations (i.e. the socio-economic factors and ideological constraints that constitute 'institutional racism' in the broadcasting organisations). Those determinants need to be dealt with in programmes which (1) would document television producers' and managers' reactions to Parts 1 and 2, and examine the policy and training implications which arose from these, (2) would seek to analyse *racism in* the media, as opposed to simply illustrating the stereotypical images and thinking that express *prejudices on* the media, and (3) would monitor the effectiveness of current moves in both BBC and ITV towards greater recruitment of black staff at all levels of decision-making in all departments. Groups might consult their own experience of the nature of institutional pressures in organisations in speculating why such programmes have not been made. However, that Parts 1 and 2 are admittedly incomplete does not mean that they are not useful as introductory stimuli for white people to think about how black people are represented on television. (see note [12] on Part 3, p.213.)

Black people are immediately aware of what is a stereotyped representation of themselves and they may be understandably impatient of Part 1 as to them, a tedious statement of the obvious. Unfortunately, most white people have been so deeply conditioned by a culture which 'naturalises' those stereotypes, that it is a necessary pre-condition for anti-racist action for them to examine just what is the difference between a stereotype and reality. White people, in a 'white dominant' culture, register the 'blackness' of black British people by a wide spectrum of meanings. As black people often say, at least with overt racism they know where they are — but the various levels of unconscious assumptions in 'white liberalism' can leave them bewildered. Parts 1 and 2 are aids to drawing into consciousness those 'naturalised' constructs that condition what 'blackness' means to most white people in Britain.

Suggested discussion points during viewing
PAUSE at the end of Bob Ferguson's first contribution, on his words: '. . . trouble for white people.'

This point of Bob Ferguson's is so fundamental it could be worth checking that it has been understood. In general we act the way we see things, and in particular we treat other people in terms of how we 'see' them. So the question here is, How do most white people *see* the 'blackness' of a black person? For the man at the start of the film, black people 'only make trouble'. He thinks in terms of that negative stereotype when he registers someone as black; as Bob Ferguson remarks, it is part of his 'perceptual set', something which (a) makes him selectively regard black people on television in that light — even when the intention of the programme is otherwise — and something (b) which is further confirmed and reinforced each time a programme expresses, or is premised upon, that view. One purpose of the discussion points suggested in this chapter is to stimulate the viewing group to explore their own 'perceptual set'. (What this means can be made clearer by using a 'freeze frame' of the calendar picture as described on p.209.) For a more theoretical exposition of these processes, see Angela Barry and Gajendra Verma in Section 2, and the references listed on p.213 and on p.235.

Bob Ferguson has mentioned 'trouble' as a very common category in which black people are presented. Angela Barry on pp.85ff traces the history of black representation on television in terms of three 'myths' — 'the trouble-maker' 'the entertainer' and 'the dependant'. In a very similar way, the authors of the chapter on 'Race' in *Learning the Media*[3] see television as portraying black people in terms of four categories: (1) the 'dangerous' (2) the 'exotic' (3) the 'humorous' (4) the 'pitied'. The group may think of more — but all these common stereotypical images serve to perpetuate a premise (5) of black people as inferior to white people and (6) as a minority which can be scapegoated for society's ills. In *Investigating the Media,* Paul Trowler[12] names the stereotypical roles black people are still often seen in, or thought or spoken of, in terms of 'parasites' 'criminals' 'athletes and musicians' (though only of certain sorts) 'Sambo types' (this includes the 'Mammie' figure) 'brute savages' 'pidgin English speakers' 'the white man's burden' — and, far from least, the 'invisibles'. He evidences these from films and the press; they are evidenced also from television in *The Black and White Media Shows,* so it can be helpful to have the following categories (1)-(6) written up on a board throughout the viewings (as a list to which the group can be invited to add and which they will recognise as the films proceed.)

The (1) *'trouble/dangerous'* category is confirmed by several illustrations in Part 1: for example, the newspaper headlines; the Jasper Carrott joke; the Imperial Typewriters Story; and in Part 2 by Juliet Foster's research on 'the mugging label'; the coverage of the so-called 'riots'; the News item on the Southall burial; the Kilburn Times report; the opening of the *Panorama* on Liverpool 8.

As Bob Ferguson says, this projection of the category 'trouble' on to black British people is presupposing 'trouble' or 'danger' *to white people.* How often is white racism featured and discussed on the media as 'trouble' for black people? Should the media do more to help its audience to distinguish people *with* problems from the commonly held prejudiced view of people *as* problems?

In the Deep South in the 18th and 19th centuries, slavery was a 'trouble' to the conscience of the whites and a source of constant fear of violent resistance. One way of coping with this was to construct a whole set of 'safe', 'unthreatening', images of black people, who contentedly 'knew their place' ('Uncle Tom', 'Aunt Jemima', 'Uncle Remus', 'Man Friday', 'the singing minstrel', the 'golliwog' toy), all of which images — and the way of thinking they represent — are actively retained in Britain today. This is how (1) relates to (3).

The (2) *'exotic/primitive'* category is confirmed in Part 1 by Gus Horsepool's account of the working men's club at the start; by Lenny Henry in *O.T.T.;* by Souad Talsi ('Tarzan and the jungle'); and in part 2 by the *Blankety Blank* and the Sport sequences ('a tremendous header — you learned that in the jungle . . .') as well as by the Army calendar. (On (2) and (5) see also p.116.)

The (3) *'humorous/entertaining/simple figure of fun'* category features not only in the 'comedy' sections of Parts 1 and 2 but also in the *Cheap Day* drama extract and the derisive images that accompany Debussy's *Golliwog's Cake Walk* in Part 1.

The (4) *'pitied/dependant/disaster'* category is illustrated by Alan Whicker in Part 1 and discussed by Zeinab Badawi and Mark Tully, as well as in the News from Sri Lanka and from Mozambique, in Part 2.

Direct confirmation of (5), the general premise of *'black people as inferior'*, is given by 13 year old Stephen in Part 1; and of (6), the tendency to *blame the victim* of social injustice, by Sneh Shah in Part 1, and by Russell Proffitt, the boys in the bus, Lord Scarman, and the purple armband experiment in *Anglo-Saxon Attitudes*. Thus all these overlapping categories and their associated images can be shown to be still determining the way parts of the media represent black people. Just how such categories of thinking, by people who wield powers of discretion within institutions, can lead to black people being 'put down' or being patronised, or being disregarded as having 'chips on shoulder', will be clear enough to any study/training group which has used the 'Target Groups' exercise described on p.16. And how such categories lead to indirect discrimination, or are unwittingly assumed in justifying inaction against it, will be clear to groups which use the 'institutional racism' exercises on pp.49ff. (The general observations on stereotypes on p.207 and 218-220 may also be relevant here.)

> Commentary: Television 'both reflects and affects attitudes'; it 'focuses and reinforces assumptions about racial matters'; it 'legitimises and perpetuates negative perceptions of black people;' and 'to the extent it portrays stereotypes, it contributes to a culture of racism accepted implicitly by the TV audience'.

PAUSE. These phrases summarise the research findings on television's effects on prejudiced attitudes which are reported by Dr. Gajendra Verma in Chapter 2, annex A, *The Role of the Media* in the Swann Committee Report. The somewhat abstract verbs merit some group reflection on what they mean, particularly since they are describing precisely the process that teachers need to teach their pupils about. It is significant that the word 'cause' is not among them; the evidence is that television serves to reinforce and legitimise pre-existing prejudiced attitudes (especially through perpetuating stereotypical thinking) rather than to cause them. *The Black and White Media Shows* give a range of examples of television material doing this — mostly unconsciously — at various levels from fairly gross to highly sophisticated. You should refer back to pp.24, to confirm that attitudes *are* formed before school age, such that any failure at primary level to help children 'unlearn' the prejudices and stereotypes they have already begun to pick up from our culture, through parent and peer group talk, simply leaves those prejudices wide open to re-inforcement by the media. (This is, to a large extent, what has happened in the case of the boys in the bus in *Anglo-Saxon Attitudes*.)

Commentary: 91% of people think Britain is a racially prejudiced country. 33% were prepared to state openly that they were personally prejudiced against black people; and perhaps most worrying, as many as 40% thought that the intensity of racial prejudice will worsen during the next few years.

PAUSE. Some white people come to training groups not wanting to accept that there is indeed a lot of prejudice shown against black people in Britain — especially if they do not feel they come across much in their personal experience. But as the social attitudes survey shows, 91% of people can see it perfectly clearly: and to almost half of them it is patently getting worse.

10 years earlier the middle figure was 13%. Which is the more likely, that there are 20% more prejudiced people since 1974, or that it is 20% more socially acceptable in 1984 to admit it? If the latter, then are the media, by 'legitimising' negative and stereotypical references to 'immigrants', 'riots', etc., partly responsible for how that has happened? (Some optimists will claim that the 20% difference means that people are now readier to acknowledge their prejudices, as a basis for anti-racist action. If so, then the figures demonstrating black peoples' social position would be showing some improvements; however, as indicated by the PSI Report and much other evidence (see pp.26-28), they are not.)

Other research on levels of prejudice are summarised by Gajendra Verma on p.123ff; some additional facts from *British Social Attitudes: the 1984 report* (edited by Jowell and Airey of Social and Community Planning Research) are as follows:

(1) While 40% believe racial prejudice will increase, another 33% say it will remain at its present level. It was found that younger people, who are less likely than older people to express prejudice themselves, are particularly pessimistic about the growth of racial prejudice in Britain.

(2) 50% thought that the general population would object to an Asian or Afro-Caribbean boss; 78% thought that most white people would object to a black marriage in their family.

(3) 65% believe black people suffer from job discrimination.

(4) Those wanting less settlement (when questioned about immigration) are decidedly anti-black: 67% are anti-Indians and Pakistanis, 62% are anti-West Indians, but only 42% are anti-EEC immigrants and only 26% anti-immigrants from Australia and New Zealand.

(5) When asked not about immigration in general, but about settlement in Britain by dependents, 53% opted for stricter control and only 8% for less stricter control.

With a differently worded questionnaire, Barry Troyna (*Public Awareness and the Media,* 1981[4]) sampled 535 British white people and found: 38% strongly anti-coloured immigration; 29% moderately anti-coloured immigration; 14% weakly anti-coloured immigration; and 19% favourable to coloured immigrants. *PAUSE* on Lionel Tuitt's words '. . . living in anger?' Here is a good moment to stop and seek a general reaction: 'What do you think of it so far?' If they have failed to notice it, you could point out the deliberate mistake right at the start: How did this film, about the need for images of equality and respect for black people on television, begin? When a white and a black person were shown together, who did the talking? Iconographically, the form, i.e. the image presented of Gus and Lionel, has been out of key with the content of the film. To offer an explanation for how this happened is, of course, to risk being thought to be making an excuse (racism is defined and measured by effects, not motives, however well intentioned). However, the reason is instructive: when the filming began, Lionel — to his own, and to the producer's, surprise — chose to say very little. 'I was a bit taken aback, though pleased, to hear Gus speaking so strongly. I knew the white audience wouldn't take much notice of anything I said about our experiences around the clubs; it was better coming from him.'

This raised a problem in editing the film similar to the point made on page 47 (in relation to Fred Barker). The benefit of Gus' challenge not to switch to another channel, made to the mass of the white audience to whom a programme about racial prejudice is, to say the least, something of a 'difficult sell', had to be balanced against the possible offence, or loss of credibility, in using such a shot. Of course, in an ideal world, with enough money, the interview would have been re-shot. As it is, we have an issue for discussion.

PAUSE on the words 'Why is this?' (before Lord Scarman speaks). Interpolate here (if not done at earlier sessions) the points made on p.26.

PAUSE at the all-black court scene on the words 'how confident would a white person be of receiving justice?'

Ask the group. Most are likely to acknowledge that it would be something of a shock. Some may be honest enough to admit to some anxiety: while in theory they would accept that black judges, magistrates and lawyers trained in the same universities and chambers as white lawyers will of course offer the same qualities of justice, they will in practice hope that such judges or magistates have never been the victims of any prejudice or discrimination such as to leave them with any 'anti-white' bias. Ask the group if they agree that such an anxiety could only be relieved if the magistrate personally decided to give an overt reassurance that his or her experience of racism would not affect the conduct of this case. If so, then ask the group what reassurances do *they* give when a black parent (or client, or library user. . .) comes into their institution and finds that the staff are all, or mostly white? How clear is it to such a parent that the racist assumptions he or she will be familiar with in most other institutional settings will not be a factor here? Will such a verbal reassurance carry much conviction if not supplemented by an acknowledgement that the under-representation of black people on the staff is a matter of embarrassment on which the staff are urgently working, or if there is no whole staff policy of anti-racism?

PAUSE on the words at the end of Michael Grade's first piece 'there's far too much of it about'.

Ask for reactions to Michael Grade. Anti-sexist men, together with many of the women in the group, will have noticed his reference to women as a minority. Although he is patently referring to what women have in common with other groups under-represented in power, it is numerically incorrect. Your group might like to know that Michael Grade received many complaints from women viewers — and that he acknowledged it as a 'slip' he should not have made. *PAUSE* on the caption of *The Fame Game*. One of the difficulties in making a programme on the theme of *The Black and White Media Show* is that television companies can refuse permission for clips to be shown. This caption is an indication that the relevant sequences were not obtainable from Granada Television. (Some viewers may speculate that the reasons were purely technical; some, that Granada had received much protest and did not want further attention drawn to what they had put out; some, that in a competitive TV system Granada should mistrust how a BBC show would contextualise their material . . .)

The effect is to reduce the credibility and impact of Michael Grade's remarks; a caption is no substitute for extracts from the real thing, which would be the only basis for the audience to make their own judgement about his general point, if they had not seen such material when it was broadcast.

A further constraint on any programme concerned with racism is the constant threat of legal action for libel or defamation. Under the present state of the law, it is very difficult to use the term 'racist' without risking legal action. Broadcasting institutions do not, by and large, see themselves as social campaigning organisations. Least of all would they condone seeking to promote changes in the law by breaking it. They therefore have little motive to take risks — though in certain areas of investigative journalism and coverage of consumer affairs they do so on occasion. It is worth discussing whether it is one element of the institutionalised racism which *The Black and White Media Show* is about, but is itself inevitably constrained by, that programme makers have to decide in advance whether they are in a position to risk libel actions and to fight them if they arise. *PAUSE* on Lenny Henry's shouting of the word 'Katanga'. Ask: who remembers *O.T.T.* and that regular character in it? Of those who do, how many made any protest to LWT at the time? If none, then is it any wonder that we still get Jim Davidson and others playing up to similar grossly stereotyped images on television? How will the media learn and change if those who can see how offensive it is do not protest — not simply as individuals, but preferably as a classroom or staffroom joint exercise? As Michael Grade has just said: 'What is even more shocking is that jokes about bananas, etc, go on without any widespread howl of outrage'. Plainly this is not something to leave to black people to do something about: white producers may all too often disregard their objections as representing only a small minority of the audience for a massively popular show. The group might care to reflect on the significance of who it was took the trouble to 'put Lenny right' about what he was doing: a visitor from Ghana. *PAUSE* at the end of Lenny Henry 'this is awful'. This is a good moment for some discussion of questions like Why was *Mind Your Language* so successful? Why did the black comedian in *The Fame Game* win the competition several weeks running with his brand of gags? Why did Lenny Henry become so popular by playing parts like Josh Arlog in *O.T.T.*? What is the significance of his remark 'Now that I've got my own TV show, I can just be more *in control* now'? In discussion of comedy some points may need clarification and emphasis:

(1) Humour is not neutral: when we laugh along at a racist joke we are legitimating our own and other people's prejudices. We are accepting the derogatory stereotypes upon which so much racist humour depends. As well as reinforcing white prejudices by playing on them, such jokes are also offensive to black (or Irish, or Jewish . . .) people in the audience. In making such jokes, the white comedian either does not care about such offence, or is making a patronising assumption that black people will not, or should not, be offended.

(2) It is true that a great deal of humour depends on stereotypes: cabinet ministers and union leaders, for example, are wickedly caricatured and stereotyped on programmes like *Spitting Image*. But of course those people have power — they can laugh it off. Indeed, it is almost a gratifying sign for them of their importance and of their position at the centre of public attention. It is an entirely different matter where the people being stereotyped as subjects of jokes do not have power and are being actively oppressed by application of those negative and derogatory stereotypes.

(3) Stroking white people's old-fashioned prejudices about black people may gain popularity for a comedian in a racist society (indeed, there is apparently nothing white racism likes more than having its prejudices legitimated — especially by a black comedian) but the price is deep offence to black and ethnic minority people, as well as the perpetuation of those prejudices. These negative effects are not lessened when a black (or Irish, or Jewish . . .) comedian makes the jokes.

(4) It is crucial to emphasise that *The Black and White Media Show* does not intend to 'blame' Lenny Henry or any other black comedian. Most comedians make use of dominant and 'socially accepted' comic formulae which include racism (along with sexism). Black comedians are put under intense pressure to go along with the comedy conventions, or to play up to them, to gain career development. As the commentary remarked, it is the routine stereotyping of black people *by white comedians* that puts black comics into this dilemma and which has the effect of legitimising any demeaning and prejudiced stereotypes in the minds of both teachers and pupils as they watch such comedy at home.

HUMOUR

In a classroom/training module specifically examining racist humour, you could also use here the comedy sequence that appears early in Part 2 of *The Black and White Media Show (see p.220)*. This gives further evidence for discussion and makes some of the points above. Such a module could, of course, also build in the analysis of comic material by Brian Thompson (pp.153-161) and the section on 'jokes' in *Reading into racism* by Gillian Klein (see p.162).

PAUSE at the end of Jasper Carrott, on the words 'what is there to worry about?' Ask the group what they think of that joke; what assumptions has it served to reinforce? What is the commentary about to point out about it? (If there is any uncertainty, prompt with a reference back to what was said at the start of the film about black people being thought of, prejudicially, as 'trouble'.) *PAUSE* on 'simply as trouble makers'. This joke has not been included to pillory or attack Jasper Carrott — his is a generally socially responsible show, which rejects a great deal of potentially funny material because it could be racist or sexist in effect. This is an unconscious and subtle example compared with the grossly stereotypical material used by, for example, Bernard Manning or Jim Davidson, and is used to illustrate Michael Grade's admission — that few of us would not identify with — that 'I don't spot them all, because we all have some inner prejudice — and you don't necessarily see the subtlety of some of the things that are done'. The author and producer assumed that the police shots would be seen as *part* of the image of violence, not as *containing* the violence. This again raises the recurrent point that subtle racism in the media is about the *effects* of programmes, not their intentions.

PAUSE on Gus Horsepool's words 'I find those words totally offensive'. Ask for group reactions to Gus Horsepool's remarks. Then ask if anyone is Irish in the room. Do they find anti-Irish jokes 'little'? It is a slip by Gus, for some people, that he should imply that there is a hierarchy of offensiveness. However, his main point is that public use of offensive terms like 'wog' makes them socially acceptable, thus perpetuating the ideas they stand for.

> Angry father of teenage Harry in *The Hard Word:*
> Are you running around calling people Pakis and Niggers ,are you? Will it make you feel tough? I've heard blokes three times your bloody age coming out with filth like that today and I'm damned if I'm going to have it in this house.

PAUSE. 'Filth like that'; how often do the group hear racially prejudiced remarks labelled in such terms on television? Why is it still so unusual to see outrage of this force being shown in response to such comments? It might be very useful immediately to go back and replay the small scene from *The Detective* to see the contrast. Is it any less 'realistic', or indeed 'dramatic', to reflect anti-racist attitudes in drama as well as prejudiced attitudes?

PAUSE at the end of *Grange Hill,* on the words 'some of the pressures on young people in trying to be non-racist'. Teachers should discuss these pressures. *Grange Hill* was based on a great deal of research, in order to reflect realities young audiences would recognise. Where has Gripper got his ideas from? Would the staff be leaving pupils like Stuart and Claire, who try to argue with him, in an unsupported false position if there is no school policy, backed by the whole staff, about what is acceptable talk in the school? What should the staff have done to educate Gripper and his friends about what those ideas represent?

An additional discussion point might be the dilemma for the producers of *Grange Hill,* a drama which included many black children in the cast, and which explicitly condemned racial prejudice and bullying. How far should they have gone in showing that which they wished to condemn? In broadcasting how sure can you be that the bigotry shown will not win its share of imitators — especially if teachers are ignoring this dimension of children's social experience?

PAUSE at the end of *Chinese Detective:* 'I'd like a pint of lager'. An undeliberate mistake in this film can be revealed by asking the group what they think of the introduction to the extract from *The Chinese Detective.* Ask if they have any disabled friends, colleagues or relatives. If so, ask what those disabled people think about the word 'crippled' and what it represents to them. It was an insensitivity, born of ignorance, that led to that term being used to describe the fact that the man in the pub was sitting in a wheelchair, as a result of an accident earlier in the storyline.

DRAMA

In a classroom/training module concerned specifically with questions of drama you could add in here the two extracts from *East Enders* and *Albion Market* included in Part 2, along with the scenes from *Cheap Day,* and (as contrast) from *Eastenders,* which appear later in Part 1, and material from *South of the Border* in Part 3.[12]

PAUSE after *Star Wars* on the words 'portrayed all the while'. To some viewers this point of Gus Horsepool's seems weak. This is because the film has not spelt it out fully enough. It is important to refer back here to the exercise about 'black' and 'white' on p.42, and the observations on p.24.

PAUSE at the end of *Cheap Day* on the words 'but could that be the result?'

This scene is not in the original short story, of which this is a TV dramatisation — it is inserted to add some action and tension. Why is this character chosen?

Note how his lack of good standard English is unconsciously underlined by having the woman immediately saying the 'correct' version in impeccable Home Counties tones.

That stereotypes are different from reality can be further exposed by asking: (a) that actor does not speak or use his eyes like that in real life, so why is he asked to do so in playing this character role (written and directed by white people)? (b) how likely, in fact, is it that a student, going to Cambridge, would not speak English in a more standard way than that? (c) if a student at Cambridge really did speak like that, then how likely is it that such a person would be dressed in such expensive clothes? If there really was someone like that in real life (a Nigerian prince, perhaps?) then how many are there like him living in St. Paul's, Bristol, or Toxteth, or Brixton, or indeed in rural Surrey stockbroker belt? Does this image represent any reality, or is it just a re-presentation of an all-too-familiar, old-fashioned image of black men, stereotypically constructed by (and for) white people?

PAUSE at the end of 'The Golligog's Cake Walk' music from the documentary *Black.*[5] Here is clearly the moment to check whether everybody in the group is aware of what is wrong with golliwogs. At this point you could deploy the material in *I love my golly*[6] and extend the analysis to the large collection of similar imagery of black men and women from the history of American culture given in *The Black Book*.[7] (This could be supplemented from sources listed on p.78.)

STEREOTYPES

An introductory module on stereotyped images could be built around use of (a) 'Gus the Bus' (p.18ff) (b) the imaginary 'hooligans' sequence in Part 2 (p.218ff) (c) Fred Barker (p.46ff) (d) Bob Ferguson's exposition in Part 1 (e) the Juliet Foster and Kilburn Times sequences in Part 2 (p.217ff), together with *As others see us*, by Ann Hurman,[8] and the checklists in Section 3.

PAUSE at the end of Souad the Moroccan girl on the words '. . . old-fashioned films and books.' Here, if not done previously, you would deploy the information associated with Souad in *Anglo-Saxon Attitudes*, which is given on pages 22-23, and in the Chapter on Checklists, pp.162ff.

PAUSE where Man Friday points to Robinson Crusoe and asks 'Day? Day?' Discussion points:

What would the group say to a black man met unexpectedly on a desert island? (Do you speak English? perhaps, or Who are you? What is your name?). Notice that Robinson Crusoe (1) addresses the black man exclusively in English; (2) does not ask him anything, but (3) tells him his name is to be Friday; (4) which is not a proper name for a person, even in English.

If addressed in a totally strange language, would members of the group comprehend, as 'Man Friday' apparently does, that they are being told their name; that it is Friday; and that it is Friday because that is the name of the day of the week on which they have met — as indicated by the calendar notches Robinson Crusoe has recorded on the post? How many would accept being *told* their name — even in their own language?

The black man understands and points in return asking 'Day? Day?' This is the only word he knows of English so far except for Friday. He means, of course, 'What day are you?' i.e. What is your name? (since he does not yet know the word 'name' in English). Is the white man's reply 'Monday', or 'Sunday', as would be expected? It is not. Is the white man's reply (as might equally be expected) 'Robinson Crusoe — pleased to meet you.'? It is not. So what is the second word so-called Man Friday learns? Now play on. ('I am master . . .')

PAUSE at the end of 13-year-old Stephen '. . . going on around you.'

'Everything that's going on around you' includes what the teachers do or do not do in school. It includes the terms, the images and the contexts in which comics, books, films and television show black people and which condition white children's ideas such that Stephen 'feels inferior'. Perhaps the group could reconsider the *Robinson Crusoe* extract here: do they themselves remember those extracts from their own reading? If not, then why not? Perhaps because no teachers contextualised *Robinson Crusoe* as an 18th Century white man's creation that was typical of its times but inapplicable in today's terms? Even if Robinson Crusoe's assumptions of total superiority were thought to be obvious enough, the really insidious effect on white children today is the hidden message that, when a white man meets a black man, the black man automatically 'knows his place' — *he* wholly accepts that he is not only to speak entirely in English but is to act as a slave. Is one result of reading about black people in such terms at an early and impressionable age — and in a classic of literature (the first English novel) — that many white adults, when they meet black people who have self-respect and who treat them as equals, think of such black people as 'aggressive', or as 'chip-on-the-shoulder' types? This question can be picked up and developed further at this point by using the working party sequence from the film *Anglo-Saxon Attitudes* (as detailed on pages 69-70).

PAUSE on the calendar picture, on the words: '. . . in January 1985'.

January 1985

Several useful points of discussion can be made of this calendar, made available free to schools by the Army Careers Service, if the group leader 'freeze frames' it on the screen.

A) Ask the group to imagine they have come into school (or library or college) to find this hanging in the entrance hall or corridor. What would they do? And why?

To those who would ignore it, what hidden curriculum messages are being conveyed to pupils?

To those who would take it down, how would you use it in class as an anti-racist teaching resource — i.e. to communicate what you find unacceptable in it?

To those who cannot decide, do you not need a whole-school policy so that individual teachers are not left isolated and uncertain in such a situation?

B) Ask the group to say what, on first glance, this image meant to them. After some contributions, ask how many saw it as a symbolic image of black resistance to imperialist occupation. If none, or few, did see it that way, then what Bob Ferguson meant by the term 'perceptual set' has just been illustrated. Most people will 'interpret' or 'read' the image like 'Paris in the the Spring': a mere glance is enough to trigger or bring to bear a whole set of associations and assumptions from what we are familiar with as cultural inheritance from the imperialist era — an inheritance which makes white people 'automatically' identify with a 'white' point of view. Ask the group what they think a black African artist today might be intending to represent.

C) Ask the group to invent descriptive captions for the picture; or to imagine what the main protagonists are thinking.

The actual caption under the picture setting out what the picture is recording begins: 'Captain Neville Maskelyne Smythe of The Queens Bays (2nd Dragoon Guards) was at the Battle of Khartoum on 2 September 1898, when an Arab armed with a spear ran amok amongst the camp followers.' Disregarding his own safety, and to prevent casualties, Capt. Smyth galloped forward and shot the Arab, an action for which he was awarded the Victoria Cross. (Thus those who prejudged this picture as *not* intended to symbolise black resistance were actually quite correct. But how many thought it might be an Arab?) The question here is: Why has the Arab run amok? As a collaborator, he might well be having a nervous breakdown or identity crisis — particularly if he has relatives among those attacking or being shot to pieces by the British — but no explanation is offered. This will carry the hidden curriculum message (to any pupil who stops to read the caption under this calendar picture) that he has run amok simply because he is an Arab: or rather, that is the sort of thing you can expect Arabs to do — no explanation is necessary. It is as much by such omission as by commission that racist assumptions are legitimised and reinforced. (Other examples can be found in an essay, *Black Blue Peter* by Bob Ferguson.[9])

At this stage of the film, some members of the group, especially perhaps those with black friends or colleagues, may be thinking (if not saying) that what has been shown and said about stereotypes of black people has for them been very obvious. They already ensure positive images of black people in their school material; they would not have old-fashioned stereotypical images, either of 'golliwogs' or of 'Man Friday' left uncontextualised on the walls. Nevertheless in the light of the evidence from Gus 'the Bus' and from Souad, they will have accepted that it is worth wondering why what is so obvious to themselves is not equally obvious to pupils or colleagues they can think of.

For such viewers this film may now become more personally involving. So far it has featured relatively conscious — because fictitional — and relatively gross prejudiced images. In moving on to how the media organisations feature black people in *factual* programmes, (when they do, that is), the rest of Part 1 and Part 2 are illustrating wholly unconscious assumptions and stereotypical thinking at work — still illustrative of 'cultural racism' but also, to the extent they are simply taken for granted rather than made the basis for in-service sensitivity training, symptomatic of forms of institutional racism in the media. With no direct accountability to black perspectives, white dominated production teams in television will inevitably tend — quite unwittingly — to reflect and to perpetuate rather than to counter, those power relations between white and black people which have obtained since the age of Victorian imperialism.

PAUSE on Bhikhu Parekh's words '. . . It is all a part of respect for persons': a phrase worth reflecting upon. It is what this book is fundamentally all about.

Now is also the moment to seek responses to the Test Match news extract. Most of the mail sent in after the transmission of *The Black and White Media Show* was concerned with this point. Generally, the view was that any credibility the programme had up till then was finally 'blown' by the apparent suggestion that Sue Lawley was in some way contributing to racism by saying she could not pronounce a foreign name. Ask anyone in your group, who feels that way, what Bhikhu Parekh has just said.

This can prove revealing as to whether white people 'hear' black people: it. is likely that many will not have fully taken in what he has said. Their consciousness is still back with Sue Lawley, partly because they have identified so totally with her apparent difficulty with a foreign name: it happens to all of us. Most Asian viewers who were questioned, when Part 1 was in its research phase, about what they had recently seen on BBC and ITV mentioned this incident as particularly distressing to them. It is hard for many white people to understand this: to them it seems like a neurotic over-sensitivity by the Asian Britons. But of course for people of Asian background who are daily experiencing the pain of their 'Asian-ness' being undervalued or disregarded by people and organisations around them, it has a huge symbolic effect when they see a BBC newscaster *apparently* going along with such dismissive attitudes by not feeling it necessary to apologise for not trying to say the name. As a matter of fact, the BBC has a huge pronunciation unit, and presenters — including Sue Lawley — take tremendous care over names. Thus, it does not matter whether Sue Lawley can say the name or not, nor whether she were to get it a bit wrong if she tried: the point is that she says merely 'whose name I can't pronounce,' rather than 'whose name,

I'm afraid, I can't pronounce'. However inoffensive that omission may seem in terms of white perceptions, and in terms of intentions, it struck many Asians as a 'slap in the face', legitimated by all the institutional authority that news presentation stands upon. The point was made quite clearly by Bhikhu Parekh: 'if a newscaster were to give up on a particular name, and not in any way be ashamed of this . . .' but it is remarkable how few white people in the audience take in this comment that he makes, or indeed have the imagination to think of the effect on Asian Britons among the viewers — and with an India/England Test Match a high proportion of them will, of course, have been watching. A possible contrast is with the commentators at Wimbledon who make constant jokes about how to avoid matches in which Czechoslovak players with long names are in action: but they are acknowledging and expressing that it is their fault that they are avoiding names they find difficult — not the players' fault for having them! The group might discuss why Bhikhu Parekh's point is often not taken, and why this sequence produced more passionately angry reactions from white people than any other in the film.

PAUSE on Alan Whicker's words '. . . disaster in Bhopal'. At this point you could ask the group 'So how is he doing so far?' (in terms of the impression being given about what India, Pakistan and Bangladesh are like). What is the hidden curriculum message to pupils about India and Indians? Of course Alan Whicker would quite rightly say that these were indeed the big stories of Mark Tully's career as reporter from India to date. This raises the question *Why* are these the only stories we get from India — what is it that determines that they should be 'good stories' for a British audience, or rather the only 'good stories' from the subcontinent for a British audience? (This point is developed in Part 2 by Mark Tully himself.)

PAUSE on Alan Whicker's words '. . . impartial information about their own country.' Ask the group their reactions to that statement. Does it appear to be unwittingly implying that the Indians cannot be trusted with democracy, even though it is the world's largest democracy, with a totally free press which expresses a far wider range of ideological positions than the press in Britain? A thoughtful group may want to consider the use of the word 'impartial'. To some views it is culturally imperialistic for a Westerner to apply it to an Asian country, especially since it could be held that Alan Whicker is being hypocritical in his use of it: he has himself just used a highly un-'impartial' phrase, namely 'Soviet-occupied Afghanistan'.

PAUSE at the end of Dr. Shah. Sneh Shah's anxiety is about the effects on the audience of the use of the word 'but' in linking from the Survey Report into a special report by Jenny Clayton on arranged marriages in the Asian community.

PAUSE at the end of the original version of the Imperial Typewriters strike report, on the question 'What hidden assumptions lay behind that broadcast presentation?' Ask the group: What is the strike about? What is it that the management have done that has resulted in a walk-out by their work force? Put it to the group that if the reporter's account is, shall we say, somewhat incoherent and leaves uncertainty even when we are watching closely, then will not the general audience, who are not watching carefully, simply be left with impressions given by the pictures? What story are the pictures telling to the casual audience? Then play the second version, which tells the same facts, also within 'normal' journalistic conventions, but with a different emphasis.

PAUSE at the end of the alternative version of the strike report on the words: '. . . only long-standing members to become union reps.' So which is the more responsible journalism? What are the different assumptions brought to how the event is described for viewers in the second version, compared with the first?

NEWS

A module on T.V. News as constructed re-presentation (not just a 'mirror' held up to 'what is happening') and on journalistic assumptions about 'news values', could be built on this strike sequence in Part 1, the news sequences in Part 2, and the discussion of the *T.V. Eye* reporter's comments towards the end of Part 2 (pp.228ff and 232ff)

At the end of the film you could note that the implications of the Imperial Typewriters' sequence and the final points from Bob Ferguson are picked up and further developed in the course of *The Black and White Media Show Part 2*. It might be worthwhile to ask the group what they make of Bhikhu Parekh's final reference to 'the larger historical context of the history of racism', in which journalism and the media generally are operating today. This could require back reference to the material on 'cultural racism' in Section One (pp.37ff), and Section Two, particular attention to Bhikhu Parekh's observations on p.116ff. As Lord Scarman acknowledged, no white people — in the audience as well as those working in the media — can be wholly immune from unconscious prejudices that derive from that cultural residue of history; we are products of a society which used racist ideas to justify colonial domination for hundreds of years, and it requires a readiness to be continuously self-critical if we are to recognise, and to counter, their influence on our thinking and behaviour.

Needless to say, Part 1 has not intended to imply that there are no anti-racist particular programmes on television. Rather, it aims to show how the *cumulative effect* of recurrent 'slips' by other programmes works to undermine the anti-racist efforts of some television producers — especially given the weight of anti-black prejudice in the viewing audience. Equally, Part 1 is only an introductory stimulus to further study and discussion of its theme. In terms of the framework of Section One it attempts to draw attention to the media dimension of 'cultural racism'. It is not intended to be a substitute for, but rather complementary to, other contributions made in terms of other departments, such as the Open Door *It ain't half racist, Mum*[5] the documentary *Black*[5], the Open University Course E354 *Ethnic Minorities and Communities Relations,*[10] the BBC Schools TV programmes *Why Prejudice?*[5] and *Getting to grips with racism* (a 5-part series for lower secondary pupils, first shown in Summer 1988)[12].

If used as part of a structured anti-racism 'course' as suggested in Section One, what is missing in *The Black and White Media Shows* will to some extent become clear in the course of the exercises concerning institutional racism (these follow on from the section on cultural racism, for which the *Shows* provide illustrative evidence). After such exercises, the group will be much better placed to discuss the likely reasons why BBC and ITV have offered so little *analysis* of racism on the television screen. For example: is it impossible to make 'popular' viewing, in terms of interesting visuals, out of the somewhat abstract concepts of institutional racism — in other words, is the 'nature of the medium' against it? Or are there subtle self-censoring mechanisms at work which shy away from questioning where the power is — and racism is about the power that white people exercise in defining national and international society in their own terms and interests? Are there deep vested interests at stake which limit how much white people with power in the media can open-mindedly examine how that power might be shared? And are these the sorts of question we need to ask in relation to our own school/college/union branch/library/service department. . .?

References

1. Report of Conference 'Swann and the Global Dimension', Bristol University, January 1986: available from Youth Education Service, 14 Frederick Place, Bristol BS8 1AS.

2. Like *Anglo-Saxon Attitudes,* the *Black and White Media Shows* can be borrowed from N.U.T., Hamilton House, Mabledon Place, London WC1 9BD; or from John Twitchin, Villiers House, Ealing Broadway, London W5 2PA.

3. *Learning the Media,* Alvarado, Gutch, Wollen; Macmillan 1987.

4. Available from C.R.E., 10-12 Allington Street, London SW15 3EH.

5. Available from Concord Films, 201 Felixstowe Road, Ipswich, Suffolk. For book that accompanies the video, *It Ain't Half Racist, Mum,* ed. Cohen & Gardner: Comedia, 9 Poland Street, London W1V 3DG.

6. Pamphlet available from Central Race Unit, Riverside House, Beresford St., Woolwich, London, S.E.18.

7. *The Black Book,* Harris, Levitt, Smith; Random House, 1974: available from Raddle Bookshop, 70 Berners Street, Leicester.

8. *As others see us* Ann Hurman, Network: Social Studies Series, Edward Arnold.

9. In *Television Mythologies,* ed. Len Masterman; Comedia, 1984.

10. Details from O.U. Educational Enterprises Ltd., 12 Cofferidge Close, Stony Stratford, Milton Keynes, MK11 1BY.

11. *Investigating the media,* Paul Trowler, Unwin Hyman, 1988.

12. Some of the issues raised in *Parts 1 and 2* are developed and supplemented by *The Black and White Media Show — Part 3,* shown on BBC1 in February 1990. For information on when this is to be shown again, see references 42 and 55 on p.79. The BBC's *MOSAIC* project includes transmissions of a 30-minute compilation of *Extracts* from *Parts 1 and 2* for use in teaching/training, together with trainers' notes.

Ways of using *The Black and White Media Show* — *Part 2*

by John Twitchin

Introduction

Part 2 is intended to offer a series of examples of factual material on television to help raise questions of news and current affairs on a study group's discussion agenda.

As with Part 1, there will be various ways of using it, depending on the length of the session(s) and on the degree of familiarity brought by the group to questions of the role of the media and of racism in society. Many 'beginners' say they find Part 2 has a strong cumulative effect which is helpfully provocative to thought; some others, however, will find it insufficient in its level of analysis and may learn most from examining how its mistakes or omissions shed light on the constraints of institutional racism in the media (as a model for reflecting on such constraints on their own professional position).

Groups sophisticated in their study of racism are likely to be more comfortable with Part 2: its subject remains white people's perceptions (both as audience and as editorial decision-makers) but it has more black contributors — especially black women — providing perspective and raising issues, without what appears to some as the 'apologetic' tone that results from the tactical training approach of Part 1 (see p.197).

For many viewers, the observations made in Part 2 may seem obvious enough but it has to be said that within the world of television, they have met with a mixed reception. Some of the programme's presuppositions, for example that racism is appraised by effects not motives (that good intentions are not enough) and some of its questioning of the effects of habitual journalistic assumptions and conventions — about 'balance'; about the emotive effects of television pictures; about the level of rationality of the audience — when dealing with 'race relations', have not found universal favour. While the educational *aims* of Part 2 have been welcomed by most senior television managers, its *method* has been strongly criticised by some. With some groups, it may be important to point out that while *The Black and White Media Show* is about current affairs, it is not itself a current affairs programme; unlike current affairs output made *within the terms* of journalistic conventions, it is a Continuing Education Department programme made to 'raise consciousness' *about the effects of those terms* of journalistic conventions. Some producers and managers feel the programme is not subtle and fair enough in its presentation to win respect for its content; some go further, condemning it as 'a one-sided case for the prosecution only', which reprehensibly fails to declare its 'polemic' intentions. Such debate within broadcasting indicates that Part 2 *on its own* may not be clear enough for some people in its attempts to raise and inform the issue of 'balance' in programmes concerned with 'race relations' and racism. Also it is undoubtedly a weakness that it does not include analysis of the varieties of meaning and usage of the word 'racism' and of the differences between 'prejudice' and 'racism' such that 'racist' can refer to television material that quite unconsciously, against all personal intentions, can give comfort to stereotypical thinking in the audience, simply by omissions, or by unthinkingly following habitual conventions and institutional procedures. The fact that the film has been perceived in some quarters as a 'defamatory attack' (in its method, if not in its aim) rather than as a professionally helpful piece of insight or sensitivity training, may be an indication to any policy makers of how vital it is to help their staff work out what the term 'racist' means — not in terms of morality (since that can usually be taken for granted) but in terms of detailed practical implementation within the different traditions and ways of working of different departments. At any rate, it underlines the need, if at all possible, for any group using Part 2 to explore the 'meanings' exercise set out on pages 29-34, before the viewing, and to do a 'subtly racist broadcasting organisation' exercise as indicated pp.49ff, after the viewing.

Pre-Viewing Questions
For the reasons given before (page 18) the group should note down answers to preliminary questions like these:

1. What stereotypical language or thinking have you noticed on television recently — whether in comedy, or in the news?
2. What do you see as the fundamental causes of the events in Brixton and Toxteth in 1981 and in Autumn 1985?
3. What do senior police see as the main needs to prevent any recurrence of such disturbances?
4. For every white person attacked in 1981, how many (a) British Asians (b) British Afro-Caribbeans, were subjected to personal attacks?
5. What impressions have you derived from the media about what is the cause of poverty in the so-called third world?
6. How much do countries like Ethiopia and Sudan have to pay back to the West in interest and loans for every dollar they receive in aid?
7. What is your definition of a 'riot'?
8. What is your definition of a 'rebellion'?
9. How many languages are spoken in England (apart from English) by over 100,000 people each?

Begin with a recap of the first two minutes of the start of Part 1 up to Bob Ferguson's point '. . . trouble for white people'.
PAUSE after the Scotland Yard officer and Juliet Foster, on the commentary words '. . . before they were given any significant public attention'? Some discussion points:

Black people were well aware of the build up of social pressures in their communities from the mid 70's onwards. If the disturbances of 1981 came as a surprise to most white people, then where were T.V.'s investigative journalists before then? Can BBC and ITV do their job of 'keeping the democracy informed' about major social trends if they do not have black reporters who have the confidence of the black communities? Or is the problem rather that reporters who tried to draw attention to the facts later detailed by Lord Scarman were ignored by white editors who considered such facts neither important or 'interesting' enough for a predominantly white audience? If the group feel that BBC and ITV need more black reporters, for those organisations to be adequately equipped to reflect the social realities of Britain, then how much better are their own staffrooms/organisations equipped for that same purpose?

It may be easy to criticise the BBC and ITV, quite correctly, on this score. At the same time, a survey of 20,000 teachers in eight urban authorities with high 'ethnic' populations showed that only 1 in 50 is black, and 80% of those black techers are on the lowest pay scales, 1 and 2 (*Ethnic Minority School Teachers,* CRE, 1988.) What message does this convey (a) to qualified black teachers (b) to black pupils (c) to white pupils, about the credibility of much that is called 'anti-racist' approaches within the teaching profession, or indeed of the 'equal opportunity' policies of many LEAs and the teacher unions?

'Riots', 'Civil Disturbances' or 'Rebellions'?

The words we use demonstrate our attitudes and assumptions: So ask the group What does the word 'riot' suggest to most casual views? What do the group think of Martin Luther King's remark, in the context of the American civil rights movement of the 60's, that 'a riot is the voice of the unheard'?

Why has the perception of the events as 'rebellions' against white racism not been reflected by the white reporters in television news and current affairs? Has the word 'rebellion' as a descriptive term been avoided by newsmen because it raises an implied question: rebelling against what? How much do the group feel, when black politicians like Jesse Jackson and middle class professional British black people like Joan Hafenrichter and Terry Mortimer call the events rebellion against white racism, that they are likely to be somewhat exaggerating the case? At this point you could remind the group of:

(a) The summary of Lord Scarman's report on *World in Action: 'an attack on racial disadvantage is more urgent than law and order reforms'.*

(b) The Scotland Yard Senior Officer Richard Wells: *'the solution is to find a way in which young black people can find a slice of the profits, and in which they can find a legitimate way to gain access to power'.*

(c) Lord Swann at the beginning of Part 1: *'the reasons they are more deprived than whites have a great deal to do with racial prejudice, and particularly discrimination in the housing and the job markets'.*

(d) Lord Scarman (also at the beginning of Part 1): *'they are suffering from a discrimination which derives partly from a deep unconscious prejudice which we have not yet succeeded in eliminating in ourselves — a psychologically hidden racial prejudice in the so-called 'host' community which we have not yet exposed and killed'.*

Why do those men speak like that? Do you agree with their assessment of the disturbances as symptoms of reaction by powerless black people against white prejudice and discrimination against them? Why do many white people find such a view more convincing when it comes from establishment figures like these three men (who have no direct experience either of street disturbances or of colour discrimination) rather than from black people who have direct experience of the conditions that they are speaking of?

An American analysis of TV journalists' assumptions and practice in covering 'race relations' crises is powerfully presented in a one-hour film: *Race against prime time* — available from Albany Video, Douglas Way, London SE8 4AG

PAUSE on the local newspaper report about the 'love triangle', on the words '. . . and he was quickly in trouble with the police'.

Exercise in the study of stereotypical thinking

We might imagine a pupil, after a day of anti-racist education at school, going home to hear Dad or Mum reading out these extracts from that news story:

A LOVE triangle featuring a Soho pimp, a prostitute and a young West Indian came to an end with the pimp blasted by a sawn-off shotgun on the Mozart Estate in Queens Park.

Passing sentence, Judge Micheal Argyle QC said the case showed the 'sleazy' face of Soho, with gangs fighting each other with guns and knives over drugs and prostitutes.

Judge Argyle told Wilkinson: "People who live in this country, which is still a free country and a marvellous country with very sensible laws, must not be allowed to take the law into their own hands.

At a previous hearing the judge said that the trial had revealed some 'really horrible people".

He added: "The case has every-thing about it that is un-English — drugs, knives, guns and the exploitation of whores. Detectives who investigated this case turned over every stone and found some really horrible people underneath."

The court heard that Wilkinson was adopted as a child by a middle-class white family living in a respectable mainly white area of Leeds. The tall powerfully-built youngster was the only coloured person around and he quickly was in trouble with the police.

He eventually ran away from home and was in trouble again when he settled in London.

Wilkinson, of Claydon House, Heygate Estate, Walworth, was convicted of wounding, possesing cannabis with intent to supply the drug to others and burglary. He was sentenced to a total of seven years youth custody.

A powerful hidden curriculum message has already been given in the first three lines. If this is not obvious to your group, ask them to name the odd one out. Being a pimp or a prostitute are forms of occupation, so why does it not say 'a Soho pimp, prostitute, and a young builder's mate' (for example)? In describing the triangle, the important thing it occurred to the reporter to tell us about A is that he is a pimp; about B that she is a prostitute; and about C that he is a 'West Indian'. Why is this? That unconsciously negative stereotypical thinking is at work here, reinforcing and legitimating any tendency to such thinking in the readers, is confirmed by the rest of the report.

Why does the judge think references to 'this free country' are relevant to a black defendant? What assumptions is the judge making in his remark about what is 'un-English'? What unconscious stereotypical associations lead the reporter to think the next relevant facts to tell us, following the end of that quote, should be about the social background of Wilkinson — the 'West Indian' — rather than the background of, for example, the judge, or of the other members of the triangle? (Wilkinson is not a West Indian at all, of course, but a black British citizen of Caribbean background.) Why do we need to know that he was brought up by a white family? What is the point being made in telling us it was in a 'respectable — mainly white — area in Leeds'? Why is he described as 'the powerfully-built youngster'? What is the assumption indicated by the 'and' in the phrase 'he was the only coloured person around and he was quickly in trouble with the police'? This can be brought out by imagining alternative phrasings, such as 'he was the only coloured person around *but* he was quickly in trouble with the police' or 'he was the only coloured person around and so was an easy target for police harrassment'. (And incidentally is it likely that Wilkinson would describe himself by the term 'coloured'?) This is conventional journalistic writing; unless there is protest from readers, and unless there is teaching to help pupils see its premises, perhaps through a whole class project of letters to the Editor, how will journalists learn to avoid such thinking?

In connection with Juliet Foster's comment on the 'mugging label', the answer to previewing question No.4 is that by Home Office figures for every reported attack on a white person in 1981, there were 50 on people of Asian background, and 36 on people of Afro-Caribbean background.

PAUSE after the beefeater and bowler hat shots, on the commentary words: '. . . feature of programmes which surround the news'.

Like the Fred Barker story (p.46), the question about a foreign TV station referring to white English people only in terms of football hooliganism aims to stimulate reflection about the negative stereotyping of black people in terms of 'trouble'. Refer back here to the relevant material of Part 1 — summarised in the comments on p.198.

Stereotypes
Some further discussion points:

For some people, to the extent that stereotypes act simply as loose generalisations, they may not be in themselves 'bad': all depends on how they are used.

It is when *individuals* are judged or perceived in terms of *group* stereotypes that unfairness or injustice occurs, and all the more so if they are seen only in terms of *negative* stereotypes.

For others, stereotypes are in themselves problematic. As the authors of *Learning the Media*[1] remark:

> A stereotype is often seen to represent the shorthand descriptive form which explains the nature of a prejudice to others. Projected onto particular persons or groups, the stereotype reveals more about the holder's beliefs or personality than the reality described.

The unconscious confirmation of stereotypical imagery and thinking by the media gives institutional legitimation to, and helps perpetuate the effects of, such categories of thought (or, as some describe them, 'cultural constructs'). These serve to rationalise or justify inaction or indifference to the social injustice of racism. As an example, when immigration is a topical political issue, the television news producers will often quite unconsciously select pictures from the news library film of Asians entering through British passport control. This common practice on television is likely to imply, and to confirm, a stereotypical impression that all immigrants to the UK are non-white, which is not true. The fact is that there are many more white immigrants to Britain from Ireland and Southern Europe than there are black immigrants from all the countries of the 'New Commonwealth' put together.

In *Positive Images?* (see p.234) David Buckingham offers another view of stereotyping:

> What does it mean to talk about a 'stereotype'? The original use of the word did not imply a pejorative connotation: stereotypes were originally defined as a means of imposing order on the confusion of experience, a kind of 'short cut'. The danger in the commonsense concept of stereotypes as always inaccurate is that it may prevent us from understanding the *ideological* power of stereotypes. The crucial distinction is not between the stereotype and the reality; rather, it is a question of who controls and defines stereotypes, and whose interests they serve. Stereotypes of oppressed groups clearly serve to conceal the 'real' cause of their subordinate position, and to legitimise that position by blaming it on genetic causes. What is important is the *ideological* function of the stereotype, and what interests it serves, rather than its degree of accuracy to 'reality'.
>
> Thus what one can do is define the power relations involved in the process. It is an inversion, whereby the effect becomes the cause, that is the characteristic *ideological* operation at work in stereotypes of oppressed groups, since it serves to legitimise their oppression; and it is this complex combination of validity and distortion which gives stereotypes their power — if stereotypes bore no resemblance to reality, they would clearly have very little effectiveness. The power of dominant stereotypes lies in the fact that they derive from a consensus — they 'fit' with the dominant ideology and power relations of society. Thus, we may not *notice* 'negative' stereotypes — we may not be aware of them *as stereotypes* — because they fit so neatly with 'commonsense' ideology.

The 'positive image' disturbs these commonsense definitions: we become aware of an ideological *intention* behind the image, and as a result it no longer remains 'merely' an image — it refers to an idea, and thus becomes 'propaganda'. And propaganda, precisely because it is noticeable as such, may be easier to reject than ideology. I would argue that replacing 'negative' with 'positive' is *in itself* unlikely to change attitudes and may even reinforce racism. As with any stereotypes, the questions we need to ask of 'positive images' are concerned with their ideological effect rather than with any degree of adequacy to 'reality'. For whom are these images positive, and whose interests do they serve? Images of black people which show them being assimilated into a white society may be reassuring for liberal white people, but they may also detract from the unique strength and identity of black cultures, and draw attention away from continuing inequality and injustice. To promote 'positive images' while simultaneously ignoring the fact that students are constantly surrounded by negative images and attitudes, is to invite disbelief and resentment.

PAUSE at the TVS clip on the words '. . . I tried to scrub myself white.'

This sequence, from Michael Grade's back reference to *Mind Your Language* up to this point, supplements the 'comedy' section of Part 1:

(a) in showing that little seems to have changed between the showing of Part 1 in August 1985 and the making of Part 2 in late Spring of 1986;

(b) in showing the *Spitting Image* writer who supports Michael Grade's Part 1 observation that just because some derogatory 'jokes' seem funny or amusing to some people does not make them any less offensive (together with the points made on page 203-205);

(c) in confirming that 'jests' like 'Alf Garnett's do affect young black children's self-rejecting behaviour as well as white adults' insensitivity towards it. Here it could be relevant to refer back to comments on the Cumbrian nursery in *Anglo-Saxon Attitudes* (page 24) and to the comments on the word 'black' in connection with 'Gus the Bus' in Part 1, pages 206 and 42.

PAUSE on Terry Mortimer's comment on the budget '. . . all the pictures we see are white.' The point is that the term 'average family' in this context is referring to average earnings, not ethnic background. In this sense, the average family includes black people: but they all too rarely feature in television presentations which are not specifically concerned with 'racial matters'. The result is a hidden curriculum message that 'blackness' equals some form of 'deviance from the norm'.

'People' exercise

You could deploy here Statement 21 of the Assumptions Exercise (pp.58 and 63) to demonstrate how white people in a white dominant society do not see themselves as 'white' people — simply as 'people'. Ask if Statement 21, as a thought or question, is familiar to the group. Ask, What is it really saying? Repeat the statement several times. If someone points out that you are presupposing people's 'blackness', or the obvious thing is to *ask* people if 'black' is acceptable to them, then acknowledge those as good points, but further repeat the statement, until it dawns that its logic shows you to be using 'people' to mean *only* white people. Then use the Comment on p.63. (If it is not obvious even when the logic is staring us in the face, how much less obvious is it when there is no logic making it clear?)

The analogous failure of BBC and ITV output to reflect the living languages of England — other than English — could also be reviewed here, by referring back to the points on pp.44-8; Assumptions 4, 12, 25-6, 30, 36-9 and 54 on pp.57-9; and p.195..

PAUSE on the Ariel photograph with the commentary words '. . . and indeed to white staff?'

This may be another example of how good intentions are not enough. Those responsible for this edition have, after all, commendably chosen to feature as a front page headline story the need to be sensitive to black people's interests and rights to equal opportunities in the BBC. They have chosen to feature, with a specially shot photo, the staff who make the programme *Ebony* . However, it would *appear* to have been assumed not to matter (if noticed at all) that their names are not given, even though the white senior manager is named.

A similar point arises if the group consider how when a picture of Wole Soyinka was featured on television news in October 1986 as the winner of the Nobel Literature prize, it was accompanied by the observation that he was 'the first Black' — indeed the 'first African' — to win such a prize. Since anyone with good sight and hearing can see that he *is* black and can hear that he is African, why does this have to said? And why did *The Times* feature Debbie Thomas, who had won the World Figure Skating Championship, as 'the new black queen', when a photo also accompanied the article? Though maybe newsworthy or interesting to some, could there not be an underlying presumption and message to the effect that 'people different from the majority white culture do not contribute much to this world so when they do they are some sort of freak'? Are the media inferring that accomplishment is something that white people do?

PAUSE at the end of the Sport sequence on Terry Mortimer's words '. . . doesn't worry me'. Sports departments not only feature crowd violence, or 'hooliganism', but also overtly condemn it as anti-social ('look at this . . . absolutely disgraceful'). Indeed, whole programmes have been specifically made on the subject, not only drawing attention to it by showing it on the screen but discussing what to do about it. The question for discussion therefore is, Why is the same not done for anti-social 'monkey chanting'? Do the group feel the broadcasting executives are right to avoid drawing attention to racist behaviour on the terraces? Would condemning it on the air be drawing attention to any more than most soccer fans already know goes on at most matches with black players? If a considerable proportion of the audience knows it happens, and can hear racist chanting going on (and indeed might be joining in at home) what is the effect of never hearing it condemned by the commentators? Are the commentators avoiding condemning it, perhaps because they know a large proportion of their audience share those racist attitudes? What does the group feel is revealed by the pronunciation of 'Zimbabwe' and the turn of phrase 'which we have to say nowadays'? What is the effect of 'you learned that in the jungle'?

Music Fanfare: State Visit by King Juan Carlos

Commentary   In a commentary on a British state occasion, most of us expect a tone of respect for the music played and for the traditional courtesies displayed. How would we feel if a foreign news reporter were to adopt a patronising and denigrating manner like this:
'Today the British had a chance to show how they're not letting their economic problems get them down. The king's visit provided an occasion to indulge in their traditional love of horses and royalty and to enjoy some enthusiastic playing of their brass fog horns. Their royal elite may not have much in the way of continental flair and chic, but they've clearly made an effort to bring a bit of sparkle to the proceedings, particularly their custom of walking backwards in slow motion.'
However, when the news was of a royal visit to a black African country, a real BBC T.V. report included these remarks:

Newsreporter   Inhambane is a seaside town that's picturesque from a distance. Close to, it's as destitute as the rest of Mozambique. They rolled out the brown carpet for Princess Anne. Inhambane doesn't run to a red one, but made up in enthusiasm what it lacked in style . . . Princess Anne is an old hand at African arrivals — part of the art of being a royal is to act precisely as if you were at Gatwick even though the temperature's 95 and the band's playing foghorns. Down the road a nutter was waiting for the Princess, hundreds of nutters in fact, planning a surprise. This is the town's only thriving industry, a cashew nut factory. Outside, they wrapped up a huge chest of cashews as a gift, not perhaps the first time a nut-case has been presented to the Royal Family.

PAUSE at the end of the Mozambique news report, on the words '. . . presented to the Royal Family'.

One can ask of any report: first, What do we need to know here? second, What extra is being given to help excite our interest? and third, How is that 'extra' being done? What assumptions are being made? In the above case, the news is not politically significant — it is a rather minor 'royals' story. So to make it more watchable, the reporter seeks to enliven his account of what is hardly, in news terms, a big event, by giving it a 'light touch'. The question is whether, with the lack of humour in the voice, a patronising effect is created.

In addition to the King of Spain example, a contrast could be made with the dignified, not to say reverent, tone brought regularly to describing the scene of Black Rod in his knee breeches banging with a stick at a door he knows people are already waiting to open. Why can it be assumed acceptable to report another culture's rituals and traditions in a flippant and patronising fashion? Incidentally, an ITV documentary in 1986 on the Commonwealth showed the Queen responding to a film recording of her first Commonwealth tour through Asia, the South Pacific, and Australia and New Zealand. It was noticeable that, unlike many reporters, she took no such patronising attitude towards the local customs: she appreciated and respected them in their own terms.

Zeinab Badawi The colonial relationship — the fact that British whites were masters and the blacks in Africa were colonised people — is still the image which we get in a very subtle way on British television when it's covering news stories in the Third World, as it's called. It tends to focus on what is often called the coup-war-famine syndrome, in other words, Africa won't make the news unless there's a coup or a war or a famine happening there. Now I'm not saying that television shouldn't respond to events like this, but it must put them in context.

Music 'Feed The World'

Zeinab Badawi When we see news reports about the famine in Africa, we have pictures of starving children shown on the television screens, and then when we ask ourselves what can be done about that, all we see mentioned is Aid — Aid on humanitarian grounds.

This exaggerates the importance of Aid given for humanitarian reasons, and I think that why this has happened is because efforts like Band Aid, Live Aid and Sport Aid — laudable as they are — are prone to a great media hype. It obscures the real causes of the famine, which are very complex economic and political ones, all about the relationship between the developed world and Africa. It is always the developed world which is in the powerful position which determines trade, which determines not only what sort of crops should be grown, but what price should be given for crops which they don't even grow themselves.

Bob Geldof Perhaps it looks a bit boring to watch normal farming shots on TV, but to me it's semi-miraculous, when you consider that these people last year were dying in their camps, and now they've got cattle; and I mean it is a tangible result of just a bloody pop concert!

Commentary Bob Geldof himself points to the difficulty for the media in drawing full attention to the long-term reasons for the famines. As if in confirmation of the point, when Band Aid's own film was first shown on television on New Year's Eve, these few minutes of explanation of the deeper causes were cut out:

Extract from In the early 1970's when international credit was easy to obtain and com-
Band Aid film modity prices were high, Africa was encouraged to borrow huge amounts of money and forsake food production for cash crops. Then commodity prices collapsed. Cotton, Sudan's major export crop, fell in value by over 50%. This left sub-Saharan Africa drowning in a sea of debt. For every dollar we send famine-stricken Africa in aid, we demand ten dollars back in debt settlements.

PAUSE at the end of Mark Tully: '. . . could with justification look at'. Zeinab Badawi expands on her filmed contribution on pp.133ff. Her observations, from a Sudanese Muslim woman's viewpoint, about the media's inadequate treatment in broadcast news coverage of the *causes* of famines and poverty, are confirmed by Mark Tully, who has lived in and reported on India for many years, and by the Philo and Lamb analysis, *Television and the Ethiopian famine*.[3] Her point about 'media hype' is confirmed by Bob Geldof himself: ordinary farming shots are 'boring' on TV, he says, though to him these are 'semi-miraculous'. The group might speculate whether these scenes would be on show in a 'one year later' news review of the Band Aid concert if Bob Geldof was not himself doing the talking about them. (Incidentally, the BBC gave financial support to the Band Aid film and the cut on its first showing was made by agreement with the Band Aid committee.)

FAMINES IN 'THIRD WORLD'

A teaching/training module on media coverage could also use here the two-part film *Consuming Hunger*[2] produced by Ilan Ziv for Channel 4 in February 1987; Philo and Lamb's report *Television and the Ethiopian Famine from Buerk to Bandaid*[3]; the group simulation *Deadlines, Media bias about the Third World* from Oxfam.[4] A wider historical context is given in *News out of Africa* by Harrison and Palmer, Hilary Shipman, 1987. Back refer to pp.40, 117-119, 123-139. Video pack *Developing images,* IBT[13], and slides unit *Aspects of Africa* (Manchester DEP, 061-445 2495) are especially useful.

What Zeinab terms 'coup-war-famine syndrome' overlaps with that category of thinking which the authors of *Learning the Media*[1] call 'the pitied':

1985 was the year of representations of famine. Television and the press have intermittently paid attention to the 'needy' of the world, but not on the scale of 1985. Charitable organisations such as Oxfam and Save the Children have also adopted a fairly high media profile in the past in terms of constant advertising campaigns. Nearly all the images of black people — in particular mothers and children — represent them as victims and sufferers. Passively unable to help themselves, the images emotively encourage us to send a donation and to relieve the suffering not of the person in the image (who is quite possibly already dead) but of black people generally.

What these advertisements and news stories never offer is any form of explanation of the causes for this suffering beyond 'natural' disasters such as floods, earthquakes and drought, with occasional references to either incompetent or malevolent domestic rulers. What is never offered is a historical account of how such persons find themselves to be in the plight they are, *nor* of the role a country such as Great Britain has played in creating those situations.

Having plundered, expropriated and enslaved the African continent the 'Western' world now observes the results — famine and devastation — and pities the sufferers. As Anne Simpson elucidates in *Ten 8:*[5] Aid is projected as the humanitarian solution to the sad situation in which the underdeveloped countries are unable to provide for themselves. It is the duty of the humane and privileged white developed world to offer help. And if only there was enough of this help, all would be well. More seeds, more tractors, more experts to 'help them help themselves' would put things straight.

Such idealism is fundamentally flawed because it rests on a potent racist myth: that the crisis of 'Third World' countries are caused by a lack of Western seeds, tractors or experts; and that their poverty is due to their own inadequacies. This projects 'Third World' people as helpless victims and Westerners as saviours, and neatly ignores the fact that Western agents created the basis for under-development in the first place through colonialism, and that they continue to profit from that same underdevelopment today. Aid would be better termed repatriated profit — because the net flow of resources is from the 'Third World' to the West.

The myth also ignores the actions and proposed solutions of 'Third World' people themselves — and the Western-sponsored repression and destabilisation that such efforts often meet. The world is conveniently divided into two, along Brandt's snaking red line, ignoring the real links between elites around the globe and the shared need for change among the poor.

The mutual inter-relationship between the West and the 'Third World' is rarely represented. Instead, the most visible representations of black people (particularly on school notice boards and in assemblies) are those which inform European children of their superiority simply by virtue of their ability to help. And while those helped are to be pitied, the helpers can, of course, only be applauded.

No education should omit the teaching of respect and compassion towards others, but the dangers are that in emphasising the 'positive' aspects of our own children we accentuate the 'negative' aspects of others'. In her *Ten 8* article, Anne Simpson goes on to describe how these media images of the 'Third World' inform the consciousness of 'First World' children, especially through children's television: A group of third form pupils in an ILEA secondary school, when asked about their images of the 'Third World' listed the following: poverty, babies dying, monsoons, war-devastated crops, starvation, disease, drought, refugees, flies, death, Oxfam, dirty water, India, Cambodia, curries, beggars, malnutrition, bald children, large families, insects, stealing, poor clothing, bad teeth, kids with pot bellies, mud huts, injections.

When asked where these images came from the class said that *Blue Peter* had many appeals for blankets and water pumps to help poor people in poor countries: *John Craven's Newsround* often showed pot-bellied children eating rice; TV programmes about wars and refugees provided some more of the images. One girl wrote: 'our images come from progammes like *Blue Peter,* the *News, Village Earth* and special films. In most of these films they show sickening sights of poor people. In *Blue Peter* they ask for donations to help these people. They always have an appeal to send thousands of bags of rice to Cambodia yet again. And wherever Simon, Peter, Sarah or Janet go off to find out more about 'what's going on in Cambodia' they always show screaming pot-bellied kids having injections from white doctors in short sleeved shirts with other kids waiting in queues for the same thing, or screaming babies getting weighed by nurses that look like nuns'.

Many of these images are extremely emotive. Media teaching has to confront these horrific images directly, though, if students are to appreciate the history which generates such suffering. An oblique approach is to compare those forms of coverage of 'Third World' affliction with the media's (rather rare) investigations of racial violence in Great Britain. It will be noted that the category of the 'pitied' extends to Asian families helplessly waiting in their homes to be attacked in London's East End.

Images of Indians

In a *Radio Times* article introducing his 1987 radio series *From Raj to Rajiv,* Mark Tully observed:

We are now living in the clear light of independent India. A huge new middle class has been born, confident, self-assured and demanding. Delhi has become an industrial city and India now ranks as one of the world's largest industrial nations.

Twenty years ago it used to be said that India lived from ship to mouth. The green revolution has put an end to all that. The country is now self-sufficient in grain. There has been a renaissance of traditional Indian culture and a revival of India's pride in its past. Modern education has spread too, with Indian scientists and doctors in demand around the world. Deomocracy has put down deep roots and even the remotest villagers are aware of their rights.

Recently an Indian minister attacked the BBC and me in an after-dinner speech in London: 'While in England recently one could see the general impression that prevails about India. Do you honestly think that it is a fair image of our country?' To that I could only answer no, and accept my share of responsibility.

Many people in Britain are unable to see beyond India's poverty. India itself is showing the world the wonders of its past in spectacular festivals mounted in different countries. Britain, I am glad to say, was the first; the latest is the Soviet Union.

India sees its nuclear power stations, its dams, its growth in gross national product and other economic indicators as its achievements. The Western audience asks one simple question: 'If there has been such remarkable economic progress, why is there still so much poverty?'

We relive the glamour of the British Raj through television spectaculars and conveniently forget the legacy of poverty we bequeathed to India. I came to Delhi because I too wanted to relive my imperial past but I have been seduced by independent India. I have been overwhelmed by its generosity to me, by the fact that I have criticised so much that happens here and yet remain free to say exactly what I like surrounded by Indian friends — including that critical minister — and am even given platforms in India itself to air my views.

That is the great marvel of modern India, its freedom. Freedom is one value we are taught to cherish. I wonder how much we cherish it in others, especially in India. I fear there are many in the West, and particularly in Britain, who still believe that India is not ready for freedom.

India has set itself the task of conquering poverty without destroying the past, of developing its economy without diminishing individual freedom, of encouraging not just one but all the great religions. It has rejected the extremes of communism and capitalism. It has not fallen prey to a military dictator, to a religious bigot, or to a one-party 'democrat'. India is the world's largest demolcracy. That, surely, is why we in Britain should celebrate the 40th anniversary of Indian Independence.

Images of Arabs

The group could consider analogous points in the case of the image of Arabs on British television. In *The Listener* in June 1987, Gerald Butt offered these reflections on his five years as BBC Radio's correspondent in the Middle East — an area whose map is in many ways an arbitrary creation of imperial history:

Many Westerners have two immediate images of the Middle East: a peculiar, alien religion; and violence. Certainly, if you get your information from the headlines, and in particular from the headlines of the popular press, then you're bound to see the region in these terms. Violence is the bread-and-butter diet that news consumers outside the Middle East expect; they've been getting it for decades. Shi'ite extremists in Lebanon kidnap Westerners (including Terry Waite); Shi'ite fanatics blow up American Embassy in Beirut; Muslim fundamentalists assassinate President Sadat; tens of thousands killed in new offensive in Gulf War; and so on. Day after day.

Trying to present a broader picture can have its problems, but it's important for the West in general, and for Europeans in particular (being geographical neighbours of the Arabs) to understand why the Arabs behave in the way they do.

The conflicts in the region make the headlines. The issues — the Gulf War, the Palestinians, Lebanon, and so on — are often mentioned but seldom explained. The crippling of a US warship in the Gulf will bring the international spotlight on to that conflict for a few days; the disappearance of Terry Waite in Lebanon will lead to a brief flurry of wild Fleet Street fantasies about Islamic kangaroo courts, mad mullahs and Shi'ite extremists. And then it's all forgotten again.

The Arabs, from their side, feel bitter at the way they believe they're misunderstood in the West. They believe that the West has chosen to ignore the enormous contribution to science and culture which the Arabs made in centuries gone by, at a time when Europe was sunk in the dark ages. They have a point. The Europeans have, by and large, forgotten that algebra (itself one of the many Arabic words in the English language) was introduced here by the Arabs — along with the concept of zero, to give just two examples.

'We are prisoners' one Arab historian told me, 'of decisions made by foolish politicians in Europe'. Certainly, there is no ignoring the fact that after the First World War Britain and France created artificial boundaries which are at the root of many of today's conflicts. Lebanon has a flag and a nominal government. But Lebanon is not a country in any natural sense. The borders are artificial. First allegiance is not to the nation state, but to 'the tribe', as Professor Kemal Salibi of the American University of Beirut puts it. Tribes happen to be based around religious groupings, so the conflict in Lebanon (a conflict about territory and political strength) is portrayed as one between religious sects. The French colonialists decided that Lebanon should be a state dominated by the Maronite Christian community. These days, the Lebanese Muslims have both the strength in numbers and the self-confidence they lacked in the past. They want a more equitable distribution of power. The Christians feel threatened and cornered. They are determined not to give an inch.

The most dramatic example of the results of outside intervention is the Palestinian problem. To this day, Arabs will not tire of telling you how Britain played the leading part in the creation of the state of Israel. Sixty-eight years have passed since the Balfour Declaration was made, but it's still clear in the minds of even the youngest generation of Arabs.

Useful background on this theme is to be found in *Split Vision — the Portrayal of Arabs in the American Media,* edited by Edmund Ghareeb[6]; and *The Arab image in the US press* by Issam Suleiman Mousa.[7] Alisdair Ross, in *The Story of Mathematics*[8], a children's book, gives an account of how Eastern mathematics became 'assumed' into Western 'knowledge'.

PAUSE at the end of Bob Ferguson on *The Honeyford Affair*, on the words '. . . is one of us'.

A key aim of Part 2 is to expose as naive any assumption or view that racism in or on the media is simply a matter either of individual personalities, or of deliberate intentions. The *Panorama* and *TV Eye* are simply two examples Bob Ferguson has taken to make general points about possible unintended and subtle effects of conventions of presentation used by current affairs programmes. These are not a personal matter — rather they raise questions of the professional traditions of journalism, or of the need for more detailed policy guidelines and staff training. Bob Ferguson's reference to the reporter by name is therefore incidental; his subject is the effects of conventions used in that *Panorama* which are used in many other programmes and by almost all other reporters, and which were normal accepted practice so far as the rest of the *Panorama* staff were concerned who shared editorial responsibility for the programme. He is concerned with the need to consider the ways images are received, not with the motives of any individual programme makers. It might be worth underlining Bob Ferguson's remark that each small aspect he draws attention to might be inconsequential in itself — it is the *cumulative* effect over many programmes of such minor presentational points that he feels unwittingly gives comfort to pre-existing tendencies in the audience to negative stereotypical thinking about black people.

PAUSE on the Social Attitudes Survey, on the words '. . . actually getting worse'. Here the programme is provoking serious consideration of what journalists maintain — sometimes with an almost religious conviction — are 'news values'. The question is being raised whether the sort of reporting exemplified in the *Panorama* story and the *TV Eye: Racial Outlaws* has certain effects, not because of the information and content but because of the conventions used in the ways reporters choose to tell their stories. Is the reporter admitting that some of their choices were made because they thought the public wanted to see the stories presented in these ways? If so, what is implied by the fact that these stories did not offend against the canons of 'news values' as most journalists see them?

A question of balance

The *TV Eye* reporter acknowledges that they had emotive film of the McDonald family — but he says it was 'balanced by interview material from their own researchers and the Chairman of the Local Authority Housing Committee. In terms of points of rational argument, he may be right — but what do the group think about his assumption of the audience's perception of the emotive effects of the film? Can interview material balance emotive material?

More generally, the reporter is voicing a fundamental journalistic argument as justification of the *TV Eye* programme; it was 'balanced'. As Bhikhu Parekh says, however, we do not expect balance in putting their case as between terrorists and their victims; nor are those who favour pornography or child abuse or blasphemy allowed on television in the interest of balance — it would be regarded as giving licence to offensively anti-social behaviour. So why is it thought acceptable to show convicted racists on the screen, as long as they are 'balanced'? Is the assumption that anti-social racist behaviour is somehow a form of party politics? Does not any attempt to give equal prominence to pro — and anti — racist positions or behaviour imply that such racism is at least presentable?

The concept of 'balance', of course, implies some sort of imaginary central fulcrum around which opposing views act. But even in the narrow sense of the laws of physics, at least two factors need to be accounted for in balancing objects: their weight and their distance from the fulcrum. By analogy, in the so-called balanced presentation of opposing social views the question whether each should be equidistant from the supposed point of balance depends on how extreme they are. However, a greater difficulty arises in deciding upon the position of the point of balance. The location of the fulcrum is itself a value judgement, which in turn, may be 'unbalanced'. Indeed, by definition, any value judgement could be said to be unbalanced. In other words the question is not so much of balance, but of where you put the fulcrum.

The *Media Shows* are asking whether programmes about racism *should* be *balanced* in the same way that different party political viewpoints are required to be balanced either within programmes or over groups of programmes. Anti-racism is of course not a party political issue — all the parties in Parliament deplore racism. Given the prejudices held by the audience and the current facts of discrimination is such 'balancing' in fact being collusive to racism in society? In effect as much as in presentation, a programme is surely either racist or anti-racist — not both.

In the context of the *TV Eye* report, the group may wish to discuss how far they think the coverage is implicitly condemning the council's actions — in other words is it suggesting that the council should be finding an easier or 'nicer' way of dealing with racist attacks? Could the programme not have made its theme 'Why was the council not doing far more to apply the law, and far sooner?' When the *TV Eye* commentary says 'Will these moves win hearts and minds in the East End?' is it implying that you should not punish people for breaking the law if it might offend others? Instead of asking 'Is the law the way to deal with the problem of racial harrassment?', should the programme rather have been asking, 'Is the law *enough* in terms of the need to combat the problem of racial harrrassment?'

Given the evidence of the weight of prejudiced attitudes in the audience, and the way that the audience will selectively take comfort from any presentation of racist sentiment on the television (1) can journalists serve the interests of 'truth' if they tell stories in ways that leave undisturbed such misleading pre-existing prejudices in the audience's mind? and (2) can assumptions about 'balance' and 'rationality of the audience' act as fig leaves, or as defensive journalistic myths for unwitting — or unselfcritical — collusion with racism? Bhikhu Parekh's discussion of 'freedom of the press' (pp.121-123) should be referred to here.

Further discussion points could include:

— The reporter sees the white family as 'receiving their just deserts'. How safe is it to assume that the bulk of the audience sees it that way? Can a programme questioning the implementation of the law avoid feeding the prejudices of those in the audience who sympathise with the McDonald's behaviour?

— The *TV Eye* commentary might have asked, 'How is it that the police were comforting proven lawbreakers?' Is this omission significant?

— The objective, to start with, was 'to relay the grim reality of racial harrassment'. Stake-outs were organised to get shots of harrassment to help prove that victims were telling the truth. But *TV Eye* did not get such shots. Is this why

they changed theme? Are the programme's objectives thus being determined (a) by the timing of an eviction and (b) by no film of harrassment?
— If they had got 'action' shots of harrassment they would presumably have been used at the start and end of the film instead of the McDonalds, and so given an entirely different emphasis. This point can be discussed by viewing again the Imperial Typewriters news story, in its two versions, from the last section of Part 1. Current affairs and news are not just a mirror held up to what is happening: we are not getting 'facts' as if there were 'unemotive', 'impartial', 'neutral', facts — we are getting white journalists' and editors' assumptions in the *presentation,* the *selection* and the contextualised *framing* of what they show. Journalists, like academics, 'get the facts they fish for,' and according to the tackle they employ: this will include the interpretative assumptions and criteria for the way shots and material are arranged, or constructed, to carry meaning to the viewer.
— On p.56 there is reference to Stuart Hall's distinction between *inferential* and *overt* racism. The inferential has racist premises, based on *unquestioned assumptions,* and as such tends 'to disappear from view into the taken-for-granted naturalised world of commonsense'. How much of the work of journalists and broadcasters — and of teachers and librarians — is impregnated with this 'racist commonsense'? When current affairs producers/editors decide to examine subjects like the efficacy of equal opportunities policies, or of local education authorities' efforts to tackle racial prejudice among pupils and staff, should their investigations include looking at their own role to ensure they do not (1) bring such objectives into disrepute (and so making such anti-racist action even harder to pursue) (2) help legitimate those 'commonsense' racial prejudices in the first place (3) operate on 'white' journalistic assumptions about what 'the story' is, and how it should be told, by expecting blacǩ contributors unconditionally to participate in programmes made by white teams, from white departments, for a largely white audience?

Can 'race relations', i.e. issues of social relations of black and white people, ever be examined properly by white people alone, without patronising effect? How much can programmes which fail to win the confidence of black people in a community, be rightly criticised as racist? Does justice to black perspectives on television (as in local authorities, schools, libraries, unions) *depend* on new forms of shared power over editorial decision-making?
PAUSE at the end of the *Horizon* sequence, on the words '. . . without that end statement.'
Various discussion points here:

(A) Terry Mortimer and Joan Hafenrichter say that to them, the idea of such an *Horizon* is an exploitation of black people by white programme makers, to provide some vicarious, voyeuristic, interest for whites, in an artificial environment in which black people can 'safely' be insulted. The group may wish to discuss, Why is the programme not a dialogue between four 'racists' and four *white* 'anti-racists'? or Why is the programme not a dialogue between seven white 'anti-racists' and one white 'racist'? Perhaps even more pertinently, Why is the programme not an examination of the white 'racists'' views by a psychiatrist, or perhaps in terms of analysis such as that offered in *The Authoritarian Personality* by Adorno et al?[9]

(B) Some people feel that it is well worthwhile television at least exposing the reality of white prejudiced attitudes as the *Horizon* does: and that this is a value in itself. In the drama *The Hard Word* in Part 1 and in the soap operas which follow as the next sequence of Part 2, racially prejudiced attitudes are expressed, but it is not 'liberally' assumed that the audience will see them as anti-social. They are characterized in terms such as 'filth like that' and 'it's like a cancer'. Since neither the facilitator in the *Horizon*, nor the programme itself (at least in its repeat), took such an overt position on the prejudices of the participants, was the programme in effect legitimising such attitudes to and in the audience? There may be value in 'having the dirt out on the table', but what about the large section of the audience who do not see it as 'dirt'?

(C) Joan Hafenrichter's point is not only that the evil of racism should have been acknowledged and overtly labelled as such from the very beginning of this programme, but that the programme should have gone on to give some clues as to *how* this evil can be positively combated, i.e. not simply watched as drama, as a provocatively set up piece of 'guilt tripping' for 'liberals' in the audience.

(D) Is the title 'Are you a racist?' of the *Horizon* programme obscuring the distinction that has to be made between prejudice and racism? The participants in this programme are racially *prejudiced,* but they are not among those who have the most direct power over the position of black people in our society. *Racism* is a result of the ways white people, including so-called 'white liberals' — people with no conscious personal prejudice — operate our institutions to the disadvantage of black people. Does calling a programme Are you a racist? which is about individual prejudices serve to let such 'white liberals' off the hook of examining their part and responsibility for the racism in society? (See comment on statement 1 in Assumptions exercise, pp.57 and 61.)

(E) The sequence reveals something worth discussing of the internal power structures of television. The producer did not anticipate that the 'racists' would show so little change in their position even after a week of person-to-person contact, mediated by an expert 'facilitator'. The producer was concerned (a) that he should therefore share what lessons he had learned from this experiment in the country house — only thus could it be justified — and (b) that the programme should not risk being thought to be presenting racially prejudiced views as if they were acceptable to him or to the BBC, even if not to the black participants. His superiors, however, holding to concepts of 'balance' and 'fairness to the contributors', and to the views that, as Michael Grade puts it later, 'underlining a message too much can be counterproductive, and patronising to an audience', prevented his doing so.

PAUSE on Bob Ferguson's final words '. . . in favour of Parliamentary democracy'.

Discussion of this point could be informed by reference to extracts from the article *The news project* by Merril Hammer in an article in *Multi-racial Education* (Volume 9, Number 3) in the summer of 1981:

The notion of 'bias' is problematic since it seems to imply a divergence from 'the truth' or 'reality'.[1] Roland Barthes has expressed

'a feeling of impatience at the sight of the "naturalness" with which newspapers, art and common sense constantly dress up a reality which, even though it is the one we live in, is undoubtedly determined by history.'[2]

Things happen — but we make sense of them by organising 'happenings' through language. It is language which imposes order or structure on experience. Since language is cultural, 'reality' is culturally determined. 'Bias' is frequently used to describe a point of view which diverges from a commonly held consensus of what is true (this consensus may well vary from group to group). However, any consensus is also taking a position. It is therefore less confusing to examine *viewpoints* in texts, rather than 'bias'. Given the power and social penetration of the mass media in contemporary society, a close examination of one feature, the production of news, was selected for the project.

In *Policing the Crisis*[3] Stuart Hall et al identify three aspects of the social production of the news: 1 the bureaucratic organisation of the media, 2 the 'professional ideology' of the newsman, and 3 the moment of the construction of the news story. This third aspect

'involves the presentation of the item to its *assumed* audience, in terms which, as far as the presenters of the item can judge, will make it comprehensible to that audience. If the world is not to be represented as a jumble of random and chaotic events, then they must be identified (i.e. named, defined, related to other events known to the audience), and assigned to a social context (i.e. placed within a frame of meanings familiar to that audience). This process — identification and contextualisation — is one of the most important through which events are "made to mean" by the media . . . This process of "making an event intelligible" is a social process — constituted by a number of specific journalistic practices, which embody (often only implicitly) crucial assumptions about what society is and how it works.'(pp.54-55)

The authors go on to identify one of these crucial assumptions as the *consensual* nature of society:

'Because we occupy the same society and belong to roughly the same "culture", it is assumed that there is, basically, only *one* perspective on events . . . This "consensual" viewpoint has important political consequences . . . "Consensual" views of society represent society as if there are no major cultural or economic breaks, no major conflicts of interests between classes and groups . . . this consensus view of society is particularly strong in modern, organised capitalist societies; and the media are among the institutions whose practices are most widely and consistently predicated upon the assumptions of a "national consensus".'(p.55)

While the authors are fully aware that different newspapers address different sections of the readership spectrum, they go on to say:

'. . . this emphasis should not be taken too far. It is not the vast pluralistic range of voices which the media are sometimes held to represent, but a range *within certain ideological limits.'*

One aspect, raised in the first discussion session by my own group of pupils, relates to how news is gathered:

'. . . "news" becomes a simple function of the operation of certain journalistic practices — deadlines, scoops, competition with rival media or channels, etc — without the practitioners becoming aware of the ideological consequences of the practices.'[4]

This is of obvious relevance to how news is structured and presented to its audiences. The further development from this is the question of control of the media and how this affects the point of view being presented:

'. . . every use of the media presupposes manipulation . . . There is no such thing as unmanipulated writing, filming, or broadcasting. The question is therefore not whether the media are manipulated, but who manipulates them.'[5]

This is not to suggest that such manipulation is a conscious act on the part of a devious agent of emission. The task for teachers is to get pupils to recognise that 'news' is both constructed (manufactured) and thus not 'natural' and that it serves to express a diversity of viewpoints, which may be related to class, race, sex etc. In this context, 'bias' is misleading with its overtones of deviation from a recognised truth and its further overtones of conscious manipulation. It is counterproductive to simply denounce the media for conscious bias and manipulation of its audiences. After all, the teacher has a similar relationship to her or his pupils as the media has to its own audience.

James Donald's statement on racism and television is applicable more generally:

'The important thing to stress, though, is that work in this area should not start from vague assertions that television is racist because society is racist, but from precise and detailed questions about where the camera is placed, about how events are sequenced and presented, or about how particular groups are presented in different types of programme. The really important questions about how all these practices come together to produce certain social effects (and why) should really come after students have mastered these critical tools. This at least allows for a progressive development of understanding rather than a propagandist pedagogy.'[6]

Thus, as teachers, it is our responsibility to give our pupils the necessary tools to understand *how* such manipulation functions. For it is only through such understanding that class, racist and sexist (and other) practices can be questioned and challenged.

1. Cf 'Editorial' in *Multiracial Education,* v9 n2 Spring 1981.
2. Roland Barthes *Mythologies,* Paladin 1973 p.11.
3. Stuart Hall et al *Policing the Crisis,* Macmillan 1978. See Chapter 3.
4. Jim Grealy (1979) *op cit* p.56. Footnote 1.
5. Hans Magnus Enzensberger 'Constituents of a theory of the media' (1970) in *Raids and Reconstructions,* Pluto 1976 pp.20-53.
6. James Donald 'Anti-racism in media studies' in *Teaching and Racism: an ALTARF Discussion Document,* p.17.

PAUSE at the end of the film.

Michael Grade acknowledges the need for more black staff in television, at all levels of editorial and managerial responsibility. This is not simply in order to increase employment opportunities for black people, and to fulfil policies of equal opportunities in recruitment and production, but also because 'the more there are, the more sensitive we will all become'. Some critics regard it as a form of exploitation if black staff are seen as the mechanism for making white staff more sensitive in their dealings with, and image-making of, black communities. The group may wish to discuss as an issue how far the presence of more black staff can or should serve as a substitute for in-service training of white staff as to their detailed and practical responsibilities with a general policy of opposition to racism. It is recognised that the 'sensitivity' needed for getting reporting of Parliament (or of economic issues, or of religious affairs) 'right' is not simply 'instinctive' — reporters need specialist expertise, built from a range of contacts and background study before they are entrusted with the task: should not reporting the symptoms of racism in Britain require at least as much expertise? To achieve such 'sensitivity' is it just a question of numbers of black staff, or as much a question of how much their black perspectives are sought and valued by the white staff, such that they are not seen as 'trouble-makers' when they point out to colleagues and seniors the sorts of points of commission or omission indicated in *Parts 1 and 2* of the *Media Show* (An issue in *Part 3* — see p.213.)

Is it a difficulty for the 'percolation' view (that those recruited at lower levels will rise to positions of authority) that organisations tend to institutionalise or 'incorporate' people? Could, or should, the sensitivity Michael Grade wants to see across the board in television be achieved, if not by 'formalised training' about racism, then by workshop approaches within production departments, accompanied by new procedures giving more direct accountability to black *viewers,* not simply to black staff? How have these issues been handled in the discussion group's own training course, LEA, library service, union office, college, service department or school? Have they heard what their black colleagues think about how these issues have been handled?

Groups wanting to move on to questions of institutional racism in broadcasting should note that it is best studied by first tracing the effects and constraints of institutional racism in their own organisations — Section One pp.49-67 and 71-76 indicates one practical framework for starting such a process.

Teachers who want to use the *Media Shows* in class will find some direct practical suggestions by Alec Roberts and Mary-Lynne Durrell in Section 3 and a range of further background information to deploy in the contributions that make up Section 2. For *Guide to Anti-Racist Resources,* Runnymede Trust, see p.78.[9]

They could also seek out three relevant articles in the journal *Multicultural Teaching*[10]:

(1) *'Positive Images?' Some observations* on *Racism in Educational Media* by David Buckingham (Vol.2 no.1, Aut. 1983)
(2) *Asian Women in the Media* by Amina Patel (Vol.1, no.1, Aut. 1982)
(3) *Mixing the Messages . . . Television versus the Teacher* by Mark Puddy (Vol.4, no.1, Aug. 1985)

One way of keeping up-to-date on new resources, books and articles is through the Society for Education in Film and Television (SEFT).[11] A summary but highly practical approach for teachers is outlined in 'Racial Minorities and the Media', Chapter 9 of *Investigating the Media,* by Paul Trowler.[12]

References

1. *Learning the Media,* Alvardo, Gutch, Wollen: Macmillan Education 1987.
2. Channel Four Television Co., 60 Charlotte Street, London W.1.
3. *Television and the Ethiopian Famine,* Philo and Lamb: Report available from Television Trust for the Environment, 46 Charlotte Street, London W1P 1LR.
4. Oxfam Education Department, 274 Banbury Road, Oxford OX2 7DZ.
5. *Charity Begins at Home:* Ten Eight Quarterly Photographic Magazine, No.19, 1985.
6. *Split Vision — the portrayal of Arabs in the American Media,* ed. Edmund Ghareeb: American-Arab Affairs Council, 1730 M Street N.W., Suite 411, Washington D.C. 20036.
7. *The Arab Image in the U.S. Press,* Issam Suleiman Mousa: Peter Lang, New York, 1984.
8. *The Story of Mathematics,* Alistair Ross, A and C Black, 1985.
9. *The Authoritarian Personality,* T.W. Adorno et al, Harper Row, 1950.
10. *Multicultural Teaching,* Journal from Trentham Books, 151 Etruria Rd., Stoke-on-Trent, Staffs, ST1 5NS.
11. SEFT, 29 Old Compton St., London W1V 5PL.
12. *Investigating the Media,* Paul R. Trowler, Unwin Hyman, 1988.
13. International Broadcasting Trust, 2 Ferdinand Place, London NW1 8EE (01-482 2847).

Next steps of study

Groups already familiar with the 'conceptual weapons' of current media/cultural studies will already have begun to discuss the *Media Shows* in terms of hidden agendas of what they both do and do not say. Such groups will have speculated on questions like: Why they were made? Why shown at the times they were? How much effect would they have on different 'target' audiences within the mass viewership? What sub-text is indicated by the viewing figures for the extracts in Part 1? How significant is the concept of 'dominant ideology' as an element of 'institutional racism' in broadcasting, as this affects (a) all programmes aimed at mass audiences, (b) all programmes aimed at minority audiences, (c) *The Black and White Media Shows* specifically (i) as general broadcasts or (ii) in 'secondary use' as training visual aids for use in professional groups? Can programmes be decodified (as much for their omissions as for their overt content and presentation) only in interactive usage such as indicated in this book?

Teachers/trainers new to the study of television, who wish to develop their understanding of the issues raised or implied by the *Media Shows,* could read:

The books *Learning the Media,* and *Investigating the Media,* as above.

Multiracial Education (NAME journal) Special Double Issue, Race and the Media, Vol.9, No.2, Spring 1981: Includes (a) article by Bob Ferguson: *Race and the Media — Some Problems in Teaching* together with (b) a critique of: *Racism and the Mass Media,* Hartmann and Husband: Davis Poynter, 1974.

White Media in Black Britain, ed. Charles Husband: Arrow, 1975.

Reading Television, Fiske and Hartley: Methuen, 1978.

Policing the Crisis, Stuart Hall et al.: Macmillan 1978.

Racism and Reaction, Stuart Hall in *Five Views of Multiracial Britain:* C.R.E. (10-12 Allington Street, London S.W.1.) 1978.

Bending Reality: Pluto Press, 1986.

It ain't half racist, Mum ed. Cohen and Gardner: Comedia, 1982.

Media, Knowledge and Power, ed. Boyd-Barrett and Braham: Croom Helm, 1987.

Language, Image, Media, ed. Davis and Walton: Basil Blackwell, 1983.

Index

240